Ancient Historians

Ancient Historians

A Student Handbook

Susan Sorek

continuum

Continuum International Publishing Group

The Tower Building	80 Maiden Lane
11 York Road	Suite 704
London SE1 7NX	New York, NY 10038

www.continuumbooks.com

First published 2012

British Library Cataloguing-in-Publication Data
A catalogue record for this book is available from the British Library.

ISBN: HB: 978-1-4411-3756-2
        PB: 978-1-4411-7991-3

Library of Congress Cataloging-in-Publication Data
A catalog record for this book is available from the Library of Congress.

Typeset by Fakenham Prepress Solutions, Fakenham, Norfolk NR21 8NN
Printed and bound in India

Contents

Preface   viii
Timelines – Greek History and Roman History   xi

Introduction   1

1 Greece Third–Fifth Centuries BCE   10

2 Herodotus   21

3 Thucydides   29

4 Xenophon   37

5 Diodorus Siculus   45

6 Other Early Greek Historians: Hecataeus of Abdera,
   Hellanicus of Lesbos, Ctesias of Cnidus, Ephorus
   of Syme, Theopompus of Chios, Ptolemy I Soter,
   Hieronymus of Cardia, Timeaus, Apollodorus,
   Posidonius   50

7 The Rise of Rome   57

8 Roman Historiography   63

9 Quintus Ennius   67

10 Cato the Elder   70

11 Polybius   76

12 From Republic to Empire   84

13 Gaius Julius Caesar   91

14 Sallust   98

15 Livy   105

16 Augustus   113

17 Josephus   117

18 Tacitus   125

19 Dio Cassius   133

20 Arrian   139

21 Men of Letters: Cicero and Pliny the Younger   144

22 The Biographers: Plutarch and Suetonius   159

23 The Later Roman Empire   174

24 Ammianus Marcellinus   178

25 Tertullian   184

26 Eusebius   186

27 Other Roman and Early Christian works: Gnaeus
   Naevius, Quintus Fabius Pictor, Cornelius Nepos,
   Quintus Curtius Rufus, Velleius Paterculus, Nicolaus

of Damascus, Alexander Polyhistor, Pliny the Elder,
Appian, Herodian, Historia Augusta, Marcus Terentius
Varro, Gaius Asinius Pollio, Dio Chrysostom, Marcus
Junianus Justinus, Sextus Julius Africanus, Theodoret,
Zosimus, Sozomen   190

28 Alexander the Great: A Case Study   214

29 Concluding Remarks   222

Bibliography   226
Index   235

Preface

This work is designed to introduce students to ancient historical source material. It originally appeared in a shorter version in 2004, and was successful as a guide for students tackling the difficult subject of how to deal with this source material. While teaching a Study Skills module for undergraduates in Classics and Ancient History, I found that one of the most frequently asked questions was 'how do we handle "gobbets"?' These 'gobbets' comprise a passage taken in isolation from the text of an ancient historian which the student has to comment on. Not only do they turn up in coursework but also in examinations, and often pose something of dilemma. What should we say about the passage? How reliable is the source? What do we need to say about the author?

The reason for writing this book on ancient historians is to help unravel some of the mystery in dealing with ancient source material. Each section contains relevant information about the author, their agenda for writing, the period they write about, and the respective merits, or lack of them as the case may, and their value to modern historical research. The main chapters concern those ancient historians who are encountered most often during the period of an undergraduate's study. Also included are chapters containing information about some of the lesser known ancient historians, some of whose works have been lost or survive only in fragmented form. The final chapter deals with the subject of Alexander the Great and examines the various sources available for this most famous of all historical figures of the ancient world. These writers are by no means all of the ancient historians, nor those who have contributed most to the sum of our knowledge of the ancient world, but they are perhaps the most informative, or the best stylists, or even potentially the most controversial.

This version of the work has been updated and incorporates additional material such as timelines to the various historical periods as well as including other sources of historical evidence to complement the work of the ancient historians in question. Greek historiography began with the Persian and Peloponnesian wars, the two most dramatic events in Greek history. The Roman period saw a continuation of the historiographical tradition, but had its own very distinctive character. The Roman period covers a vast time span, so it has been necessary to condense the information given in this work. However, students may pursue the history in more depth at their leisure and further reading can be found in the bibliography.

No work is the sole accomplishment of one individual. Ideas are often generated and formulated through a variety of individual conversations and discussions, some of which are forgotten over time. However, I would like to acknowledge the contribution made to the production of this work by the following individuals and hope that I will be forgiven if I have, inadvertently, left anyone out.

First I must thank Michael Greenwood of Continuum for commissioning the work. I would also like to thank Dr David Noy for reading drafts of the chapters and making many valuable and constructive comments, and the first-year undergraduates of the Classics Department, Trinity St David's University Lampeter (2004) for being my initial 'guinea pigs' and trying out some of the chapters in the Study Skills module. Likewise the 'A' level students of Buckinghamshire County Council evening class in Classical Civilization – all their comments were most appreciated. A debt of gratitude must go to family and friends who have supported this enterprise, and to Judith Loades of Davenant Press who commissioned the original version in 2004. Last but not least is my indebtedness to Margaret Aldridge BA, a former Classics student, with whom I spent many hours discussing the difficulties in understanding the use of ancient source material, and who, as a consequence of these discussions, encouraged me to write this book.

Susan Sorek,

Lampeter (2011)

Timeline of Greek History 750–31 BCE

750–700   Invention of Greek alphabet. Homeric poems written down

730   First Messenian War. Sparta invades Messenia: Syracuse founded

640   Second Messenian War

630   Sappho born in Lesbos. End of Second Messenian War

594   Solon replaces Draconian law in Athens, lays foundation for democracy

569   Pythagorus born in Samos (569–475)

546   Pisistratos becomes tyrant of Athens

527   Pisistratos dies, his sons become tyrants of Athens

510   Alcmaeonid family and Spartans free Athens from tyranny. Introduction of democracy in Athens

508   Kleisthenes begins reforming Athenian laws establishes democratic constitution

499   Ionian revolt

494   Ionian revolt defeated by Persians

497   Persian wars begin

490   Battle of Marathon. Athenians defeat Darius and Persian army

483   Silver mines discovered near Athens. Athens begins building naval fleet

482   Aristides ostracized

480   Xerxes marches on Greece. Battle of Thermopylae. Persians burn Acropolis. Athens and allies defeat Persian fleet at Battle of Salamis

479   Battle of Plataea. Greeks defeat Persian army

465	Earthquake in Lakonia. Helot revolt against Sparta in Messenia
460	Pericles leads Athens into its Golden Era
458	Aeschylus produces the Oresteia trilogy of plays
454	Delian League treasury moved from Delos to Athens
449	Acropolis and other major building projects begin in Athens. Parthenon (449–432)
446	Thirty Year Peace treaty signed between Athens and Sparta
431	Peloponnesian War
430	Plague in Athens
429	Death of Pericles
421	Peace of Nicias
420	Construction of Temple of Athene Nike
418	Athens resumes hostilities with Sparta. Spartans defeat Athenians at Mantinea
416	Athens razes Melos
415	Athenian expedition to Syracuse. Alciabades defects to Sparta
413	Syracuse defeats Athens
404	Athens surrenders to Sparta. Thirty tyrants rule Athens
403	Democracy restored in Athens
399	Trial and execution of Socrates
380	Plato establishes Athens academy
371	Sparta defeated in Leuctra
362	Thebes defeats Sparta at Mantinea
359	Philip II becomes king of Macedonia
338	Macedonian army defeats Athens and its allies at Chaeronea. League of Corinth founded
336	Philip II assassinated. Alexander the Great becomes king
335	Aristotle founds the Lyceum in Athens
334	Alexander defeats Persian army at Granicus River near Anatolia
333	Alexander defeats Persians at Issus
332	Tyre capitulates to Alexander

331	Alexander invades Egypt. City of Alexandria founded. Alexander defeats Persians at Gaugamela
329	Alexander's army reaches Bactria (Afghanistan)
327	Alexander marries Roxanne (princess of Bactria)
326	Alexander reaches India
323	Death of Alexander the Great
300	Ptolemy I founds museum in Alexandria
284	Achaean League founded
279	Invasion of Greece by Gauls
238	Gauls defeated by king Attalus I
214	First Macedonian War. Rome defeats Philip V of Macedon
200	Second Macedonian War
172	Third Macedonian War. Lucius Aemeilius Paulus of Rome defeats Perseus of Macedon at Pynda. Macedonia divided into four republics
146	Roman invasion of Greece. Mummius Achaicus sacks Corinth and ends Achaean League. Rome rules Greece from this time on
86	Rome led by Sulla sack Athens
31	Battle of Actium Octavian defeats Mark Antony and Cleopatra

Timeline of Roman History
753 BCE – 565 CE

BCE

753 Rome is founded by Romulus

616 Tarquinius I becomes an Etruscan king of Rome

509 Last king of Rome expelled, Rome becomes a republic

450 The Twelve Tables of Roman law re-enacted

387 The Gauls/Celts sack Rome

343 Rome fights the Samnites

326 Circus Maximus built, second Samnite War begins

321 Rome defeats Samnites at Battle of Caudine Forks

298 Third Samnite War

295 Rome defeats Samnites at Sentinum Defeats Gauls in northern Italy

264 Rome and Carthage engage in the First Punic War

225 Gauls invade Rome (Gauls defeated 222)

218 Hannibal invades Italy

202 Scipio defeats Hannibal: Rome annexes Spain

171 Third Macedonian War begins when Perseus attacks Rome

167 End of Third Macedonian War, Macedonia divided into four republics

151 Roman troops massacre Celts in Spain

149 Rome attacks Carthage: Rome conquers Greece after Battle of Corinth

146 Rome destroys Carthage: Macedonia becomes a Roman province

139 Slave revolt in Sicily (First Servile War)

135 Second slave revolt in Sicily
133 Tiberius Gracchus enacts law to redistribute land
123 Gaius Gracchus enacts populist laws
121 Gaius Gracchus commits suicide
111 Rome declares war on Numidia
106 Marius defeats Jugurtha, king of Numidia
101 Marius defeats Cimbri at Vercelli
95 Rome expels all non-citizens
90 Central and Southern Italians start the Social Wars over citizenship rights
88 Sulla marches on Rome and seizes power from Marius
80 Sulla retires from public life
74 Cicero enters senate
73 Spartacus leads the slave revolt (Third Servile War)
71 Crassus puts down slave revolt, 6,000 slaves crucified
70 Crassus and Pompey elected consuls
68 Julius Caesar is appointed to Spain
67 Pompey launches campaign against pirates of Cilicia; senate gives him dictatorial powers
64 Syria becomes a Roman province under Pompey
63 Cicero thwarts Conspiracy of Catiline: Pompey captures Jerusalem, Palestine becomes a Roman province
60 Crassus, Pompey and Caesar form the 'First Triumvirate'
59 Caesar elected consul
57 Caesar conquers Gaul
55 Caesar fights German tribes and crosses the Rhine
53 Crassus killed in the Battle of Carrhae by Parthians
51 Caesar crushes Vercingetorix in Gaul
49 Caesar crosses Rubicon and marches on Rome
48 Caesar defeats Pompey at Pharsalus and becomes sole dictator
47 Caesar invades Egypt, places Cleopatra VII on throne
44 Caesar murdered in senate
43 Triumvirate of Mark Antony, Marcus Aemilius Lepidus and Octavian, Caesar's nephew and heir

36   Octavian defeats Sextus Pompey and is made tribune for life
32   Antony divorces his wife (Octavian's sister) and marries Cleopatra
31   Octavian defeats Antony at Battle of Actium
30   Antony and Cleopatra commit suicide, Egypt annexed as Roman province
27   Octavian appoints himself Augustus
20   Treaty between Rome and Parthia
18   Augustus enacts Julian law of chastity and repressing adultery
13   Augustus expands borders to region of Danube

CE

14   Augustus dies, and his adopted heir, Tiberius becomes emperor, Sejanus appointed chief of Praetorian Guard
23   Sejanus left to run empire while Tiberius retires to Capri, Reign of Terror begins
26   Sejanus plots to murder Tiberius, Sejanus executed
37   Tiberius dies, Caligula becomes emperor
41   Caligula assassinated, Praetorian Guard appoint Claudius emperor
43   Claudius invades Britain
48   Claudius marries his niece Agrippina
54   Claudius murdered by Agrippina, Nero becomes emperor
62   Nero marries Poppaea, reign of terror begins
64   Great Fire of Rome
68   Gaul and Spain rebel, Nero commits suicide
69   Year of Three Emperors: Galba, Otho and Vitellius
70   Vitellius and his followers defeated by Vespasian, who becomes new emperor; Vespasian's son Titus sacks Jerusalem and destroys the temple
77   Rome conquers Wales
79   Vespasian dies, Titus becomes emperor; Pompeii destroyed by eruption of Vesuvius

81   Titus dies succeeded by his brother Domitian
96   Domitian is assassinated monarchical system abolished, senate appoint Nerva emperor
98   Nerva dies, his nominated successor Trajan is emperor
106 Trajan conquers Dacia
116 Trajan conquers Mesopotamia
117 Trajan dies, succeeded by Hadrian
122 Hadrian's wall built
132 Bar Kokba rebellion in Judaea
138 Hadrian dies, Antonius Pius succeeds
161 Antonius Pius dies, Marcus Aurelius succeeds, he co-rules with Lucius Verus
162 British Celts revolt, Parthia declares war on Rome
167 Roman empire attacked by barbarians
175 Aurelius defeats the German barbarians
178 Aurelius and his son Commodus fight the Third Marcommanic war against the Germans
180 Aurelius dies, succeeded by his son Commodus
182 Reign of terror established by Commodus
192 Commodus killed by Praetorian Guard
193 Septimius Severus seizes power, turns Rome into a military dictatorship
202 Severus expands Roman frontier of African Rome
203 Christians massacred at Carthage
211 Severus dies in Britain, succeded by sons Caracalla and Geta Severus last emperor to die of natural causes until 284
212 Caracalla murders Geta
215 Caracalla massacres inhabitants of Alexandria
216 Battle of Cannae
217 Caracalla begins campaign against Parthians, murdered by his soldiers
219 Elagabalus emperor
222 Elagabalus murdered by Praetorian Guard, Alexander Severus his cousin emperor

235 Alexander is assassinated by soldiers loyal to Julius Maximinus

238 Maximinus assassinated; Praetorian Guard appoint 10-year old Gordian III

244 Gordian III assassinated by his soldiers

249 Emperor Philip the Arab killed in battle

250 Emperor Decius orders first empire wide persecution of Christians

251 Decius killed by Goths

253 Both emperors Gallus and Aemilianus killed by their soldiers, succeeded by Valerian who appoints his son Gallienus as co-emperor in west

256 Persians defeat the Romans

258 Valerian persecutes Christians, Postumus declares independence of Gaul

268 Gallienus assassinated by his officers

269 Goths raid Greek cities defeated by the emperor Claudius II

270 Claudius dies of plague, army selects Aurelian as new emperor

271 Aurelian defeats the invading Germans

273 Aurelian destroys Palmyra

274 Defeats Gauls

275 Aurelian killed by his officers, succeeded by Tacitus, who dies within a month

276 Probus restores peace by expelling last barbarians on Roman soil

282 Probus assassinated by his soldiers

284 Diocletian, son of a Dalmatian slave, becomes emperor

285 Diocletian reunites empire, ends 50-year civil war

286 Diocletian appoints Maximian to rule the West

293 Diocletian introduces tetrarchy under which each emperor chooses his successor ahead of time, Diocletian chooses Galerius; Maximian chooses Constantius Chlorus

303 Diocletian and Maximian order general persecution of Christians

305 Diocletian and Maximian abdicate in favour of Galerius and Constantius, civil war breaks out
306 Constantius dies appoints his son Constantine, while Praetorian Guard appoint Maxentius
311 Galerius dies, leaving Constantine and Maxentius to fight over Western throne
312 Constantine defeats Maxentius at the Battle of Milvian Bridge; becomes emperor of West; disbands Praetorian Guard
313 Constantine's ally Licinius becomes co-emperor in East, Constantine ends persecution of Christians (Edict of Milan)
314 Constantine defeats Licinius Licinius keeps Africa and Asia
323 Constantine defeats Licinius and becomes sole emperor
324 Constantine I founds new city of Constantinople
330 Constantine moves the capital of Roman Empire to Constantinople
337 Constantine dies and his sons split the empire
360 Pagan general Julian the Apostate declared emperor by his German troops
363 Julian dies in battle; Valentinian emperor
364 Valentinian declares Valens emperor in East
376 Valens allows Visigoths to settle in Roman Empire
378 Visigoths defeat Roman army at Hadrianopolis
380 Theodosius I proclaims Christianity as the sole religion of Roman Empire
395 Theodosius divides empire into two with Milan and Constantinople as their capitals
402 Western empire moves its capital to Ravenna
406 Barbarians invade France from the north
410 Visigoths sack Rome; Roman withdrawal from Britain
425 Theodosius II installs Valentinian III as emperor of West
450 Theodosius II dies, succeeded by Marcian
452 The Huns invade Italy
455 Vandals sack Rome
476 Western Roman Empire terminated

493 Ostrogoths conquer Italy
527 Justinian becomes emperor and decides to reconquer Italy:
      Byzantium enforces anti-Jewish laws and Jews all but
      disappear from Eastern Empire
533 Justinian's code of law, Corpus Juri Civilis, is published
534 Justinian's general Belisarius destroys Arian kingdom of the
      Vandals, reconquers Spain and N. Africa
536 Belisarius reconquers Rome
540 Belisarius takes Ravenna from Ostrogoths, reconquers Italy
542 Plague decimates the Empire
546 Visigothic rebels sack Rome
551 Imperial troops reconquer Rome
552 End of Ostrogothic resistance in Italy
554 Rome reduced to a camp of about 30,000 inhabitants
565 Justinian dies

Introduction

Every generation must rewrite history in its own way.

(Raditsa, L. Gallatin Review, XII, 1, 1992–3, 19)

The most obvious reason for studying the writings of the ancient Greek and Roman historians is because we have inherited the very fabric of our present existence from their culture and society. A variety of methods have brought their world into ours: political, social, artistic and literary developments still play a part in the development of our own time and culture and will continue to influence events in the future. We are still progressing along the road of history; therefore knowledge of what has gone before can be a useful tool to understanding the history of humankind, what it is capable of achieving and what it is capable of destroying. There are still many lessons to be learned.

The ancient historians were remarkable writers. They may not always be objective or accurate, sometimes they can be frustratingly misleading when fact and fiction become merged. Their criteria were different from that of a modern historian; in its infancy historical writing was very close to other genres of literary works. Historiography in antiquity dealt mainly with important and noteworthy events, or those that were considered to be so. The intended readership was most often people who belonged to the elite class and the works would primarily be aimed at them.

We need to remember also that rhetoric played an important role in ancient historiography. In its original Greek form it was a systematic study of public speaking (oratory). It became the most popular form of advanced education, and so exercised a great influence over historiography. In the Roman period rhetoric reached dizzy heights, and the power of rhetoric in great affairs became much more pronounced. By the Imperial period rhetoric pervaded the whole of Roman culture and Roman historians used it as a mechanism to discredit or praise their subjects. Historiography became essentially rhetorical and was intended to entertain.

Thucydides was a rhetorical historian; Xenophon, although trained in the art, was largely free of rhetoric in his writings. It was Cicero who tried to distinguish between rhetoric and history in a similar way to how he tried to distinguish between poetry and history. He makes the orator Marcus Antonius say,

> Do you see how great a responsibility the orator has in historical writing? I think that for fluency and diversity of diction it comes first. Yet nowhere do I find this art supplied with any independent directions from the rhetoricians.
>
> (Cicero, *On the Orator* II, 15:62)

Ancient philosophy and history were often linked because they were the two main types of literature in artistic prose. However, most Greek philosophers were indifferent to history as a discipline, whereas historians often paid homage to philosophy. Plutarch sometimes attempted philosophical discussion and could perhaps be described as a Platonist.

There was a wide range of source material for the ancient historian to draw upon, although this was not the case for the early Greek historians and they often had to rely upon other people's memories of past events. The use made of these sources by ancient historians varies considerably. In some cases sources were not cited, and there was a tendency to amalgamate various sources into an adapted account, a practice that would be frowned upon today.

Herodotus lived at a time when there was little factual information written down about the Persian wars and so he had to rely on oral evidence. Thucydides was often sceptical about the quality of the source material he had at his disposal. When we come to the later historians we find that Sallust hired secretaries to do his research and Livy copied everything he found without checking any of it, a practice that was also followed by Plutarch.

At the other end of the spectrum, Tacitus conducted very little research, he quoted the sources that were available to him but not systematically, and he constantly reorganized material and offered alternative explanations which were little more than innuendo. So, bearing all these things in mind how do modern historians begin to unravel the 'truth' in the ancient writings?

WHAT WAS HISTORY?

> History enhanceth noble men, and depresseth wicked men and fools.
>
> (Ranuphus Higden Polychronicon, fourteenth century)

History and poetry were first linked in the eighth century BCE, when Homer, in his epic poem the *Iliad*, recounted the history of the Trojan war, a war that had taken place hundreds of years before. Homer based his work on the early oral traditions and made no claims of historical accuracy. However, because he left this record of earlier times he was later recognized as an important historical source. As there was no alternative version the early historians, in particular Thucydides, writing in the fifth century BCE for his introductory material on pre-historic Greece, used Homer as a historical source. Thucydides did, however, express his doubts on the reliability of the material and clearly made the distinction between poetry and history. He realized that Homer may have made inaccuracies because as a poet his priorities would have been vastly different from those of a historian.

It was Aristotle (384–22 BCE) who made the definitive distinction between the two roles. Although he better known as a philosopher he was also influential in the realms of literature. He suggested that poetry and history are clearly distinguished by one thing: 'that the one [history] relates *what has been*, the other [poetry] *what might be*'. He also claims that 'poetry is chiefly conversant about *general* truth, history about *particular*'. This point has serious implications for their relative status, since because of its more general nature, poetry is to be accounted 'a more philosophical and more excellent thing' (*Poetics* II vi).

Therefore Aristotle's definition of history is concerned with particulars rather than generalities, implying that it is a simple record of past events, giving the historian a mechanical task that requires just a gathering of empirical information. Elsewhere Aristotle says that those who try to investigate the causes and try to formulate some general principles about them are superior to those who just accept the outward appearance of an event as it is literally given. But for Aristotle, poetry is the superior art because it concerns itself with universal truths, unlike history which is concerned only with particular events. Poetry concerns itself with general human traits and conditions, whereas history concerns the particular, as he said in the *Poetics* 'what Alcibiades did, or what happened to him is particular truth.'

This distinction between history and poetry became even more sharply defined in later centuries. Francis Bacon, although something of an intellectual revolutionary, nevertheless discussed the issue of history and poetry in much the same way confirming the old Aristotelian distinctions:

> Because true history propounded the successes and issues of actions not so agreeable to the merits of virtue and vice, therefore feigns them more just in retribution, and more according to revealed providence.
>
> (*The Advancement of Learning* 1605 I liv.2)

History's recording of past events is seen as a virtue, but one that lacks any poetic or imaginative input. This Baconian view of history was long-lasting; the historian was like a scientist and should investigate data with 'an observant but empty mind'. The long continuation of this tradition lasted into the twentieth century, epitomized by J. B. Bury's contention in 1908 that:

It is … of supreme moment that the history which is taught should be true; and that can only be attained only through discovery, collection, classification and interpretation of facts.

It was Bury's assumption that the historian's goal was to achieve straight forward non-judgemental descriptions of 'the truth' about the past.

WHY IS IT IMPORTANT TO STUDY HISTORY?

The first answer that springs to mind is because it entertains. If we think back to the origins of historical writing, that is poetry, and consider the Trojan wars, Homer was merely repeating what had been handed down over generations. The stories of the war were interesting and entertaining and this was no doubt the motivation for repeating the account. These stories often provided a means of escape from contemporary troubles and this fact was recognized by the Roman historian Livy (59 BCE – 17 CE). Unhappy about the moral decline of his own time he wanted to encourage a return to what he saw as earlier Republican virtues. His writing helped him to *withdraw my eyes from beholding the raging wickedness of the times* (*Roman History*, Preface). Both for the writer and the reader the writing of history can provide a shelter from current problems. In modern times we can see this idea as a tangible fact. From the many films, books, television programmes and a flourishing heritage industry, we see that people find some kind of solace in the past.

However, there are many who would not see the study of history in this light-or at least not own up to it. History also supplies a moral teaching. Herodotus, for all his entertaining story telling can be seen to have had a moral purpose. In his Introduction Herodotus hopes that his work will cause the great deeds of the Greeks in their battles with the might of the Persian Empire to be remembered. Clearly Herodotus sets the moral framework by which the Greeks triumphed over their enemies and so good triumphed over evil. The Persian king, Xerxes displays *hubris* (pride) the greatest of all sins. This is inevitably followed by the *nemesis* (retribution) of defeat and so some moral order is achieved.

Thucydides, on the other hand, deliberately distances himself from anything that could be likened to entertainment. He believed his work would be of lasting value because it contained a moral lesson that is universally applicable. He sees a moral order of which mankind should be aware and so to organize their lives with this in mind. The Athenians had ignored these lessons to their cost. They, like the Persians before them, had become imperialistic and had treated their enemies badly, exemplified in the account of the Melian debate. The Melians were the inhabitants of a small island who wanted to remain neutral. Athens wanted them to join their side. The moral arguments of the Melians were pushed to one side, and Athens rode roughshod over them. The *hubris* of the Athenians was followed by the *nemesis* of defeat in Sicily and their ultimate defeat by the Spartans. As Southgate says:

> So Thucydides' particular history of the Peloponnesian war unfolds like a tragic drama, intended to teach its audience some general truth about the human situation.
>
> (Southgate, B., *History: What and Why?* 1996 31)

In most historical writing some kind of moral is present, either to try to make sense of the past or to give the past some meaning. Usually moral teaching seeks to provide good examples from the past for emulation in the present and the future. Often this moral order can be seen in biographies. This genre originated in the first century CE with Plutarch's *Lives*, a series of books about the lives of famous Greeks and Romans. The works:

> Teach us how great vices, accompanied with great abilities, may tend to the ruin of the state ... how Ambition attended

magnanimity, how Avarice directed by political sagacity, how Envy and Revenge armed with personal valour and popular support, will destroy the most sacred establishments, and break through every barrier of human repose and safety.

(Plutarch, *Lives* trans J. Langhorne)

No doubt Plutarch had this moral idea as an agenda for he clearly distinguished the difference in purpose between the writing of biography and that of history.

The search for truth is another motivating factor behind the writing of history. The historian often takes the stance that they wish to correct what they perceive as other people's misconceptions. A very good example from the ancient world is the Jewish writer Flavius Josephus, who chronicled the first century CE confrontation between the Jews and Rome. He stated that it was his mission to set the record straight about what happened to his people. He says that the accounts of others 'contain sometimes accusations and sometime encomiums, but nowhere the accurate truth of the facts' (*The Jewish War* Preface).

Despite Josephus' good intentions to tell the truth, he was aware that his position, by birth a Hebrew and a priest, who had fought against the Romans, could on occasion become a stumbling block, for it is not an easy task to keep personal bias from creeping into the account. The Twentieth century has also seen people desirous to tell the truth about their experiences; for example the writer Primo-Levi who was determined to survive the death camp of Auschwitz to tell the world of the atrocities that the Jewish people suffered.

However, in the search for the 'truth' it is almost inevitable that people will want to justify what they have done in the past. This is something that we see all too often in modern times. Ancient historians are especially guilty of this crime. Xenophon's *Anabasis* was full of self-defence and self-praise in order to justify what he did. Even Thucydides is not as objective as we would like to believe, for his ill will toward Athens, from where he had been banished, comes across in his account of the treatment of the island of Melos, referred to previously. When we come to the Latin writers, personal motives become very apparent. A good example is Julius Caesar's *Commentaries* which, although providing useful information, are extremely subjective works of self-glorification and propaganda. His aim was to revenge personal insults, and so we read of him taking the credit for the successes of his subordinates. Sallust and Tacitus also have very personal motives.

But ancient and modern historiography are two different things as Woodman says:

> Our primary response to the texts of the ancient historians should be literary rather than *historical* since the nature of the texts themselves is literary. Only when literary analysis has been carried out can we begin to use these texts as evidence for history.
>
> (Woodman, A.J., *University of Leeds Journal* 1983: 120)

Ancient history was understood not as history as we would understand it, but as literature. There can be no doubt that this does handicap the ancients work in the sense of historical content. The ancient historian's job was to entertain his readers and the modern historian can read them simply because of the influential literature that they wrote.

The study of history is a fascinating subject; we can be constantly surprised by events whether in the past or in our own time. The sense of empowerment is heightened by a realization that the direction of history, both as past narratives, and as future events, can actually be changed. The ancient Greeks used the word *tyche*, which is often translated as chance, but the concept of *tyche* was that it was related not only to what one was allotted, by destiny or the gods, but also what one attained for oneself through individual effort. The ambiguity of the word suggests that what befalls human beings is not necessarily outside their power to change. A historical awareness that past events may have turned out differently prompts the notion that there are therefore possibilities that present and future events can be directed. As Southgate says: 'it becomes evident that history could have been different, and that things could have been and could be other than what they are' (Southgate 1996: 54). It is therefore, I believe, for this reason alone that history (the study of human endeavour) has much to offer: 'history can liberate us from our present constraints, for clearly it can demonstrate how we might affect its future course' (Southgate 1996: 55).

Chapter One

Greece Third – Fifth Centuries BCE

The Classical period also known as the Golden Age of Greece saw the rise of two city states, Athens and Sparta, and these two rival states bought the ancient world to its height in art, culture and historiography. Nevertheless it was the same two states whose thirst for power and territory brought about the Peloponnesian wars which lasted 30 years and left both Athens and Sparta shadows of their former glorious selves.

THE PERSIAN WARS (499 – 493 BCE)

The Persian wars were a defining moment in Greek history. The Athenians, who came to dominate Greece both culturally and politically during the fifth and part of the fourth century BCE, regarded the wars as their greatest achievement. The wars started inauspiciously when in 546 BCE the Persians conquered the Greek city state of Lydia (Asia Minor), all the states subject to the Lydians now came under the close control of the Persians, and they appointed individuals to rule the states as tyrants. They also enforced citizens to serve in the Persian army and pay heavy taxes.

Aristagoras, the tyrant of Miletus began a democratic rebellion in 499 BCE and went to the Greek mainland for support. First he approached Sparta but they rejected his idea, so he turned to the Athenians who promised him 20 ships. In 498 BCE the Athenians conquered Sardis the capital of Lydia and the Greek cities now joined in the revolt. However, the Athenians lost interest in the revolt and left Asia Minor and by 495 BCE the Persians, under their king Darius I (521–486 BCE), restored control over the rebellious Greek cities.

The Persian king decided that Athens should be punished for the role it had played in the revolt and destruction of Sardis. So, in 490 BCE the Persians launched an expedition against Athens, only to be met on the field of battle by Miltiades, one of their former soldiers who had defected to Athens after angering the Persian king. The two armies met at Marathon (490 BCE), and this is perhaps the most important battle in all Greek history, for had the Athenians lost. all Greece would have come under Persian control, and Western civilization, as we know it, would not have existed. The success of the Athenians gave them the grandiose notion that they were the centre of Greek culture and power and acted as a spur for much of their cultural achievements.

The Persians, however, still controlled almost the entire ancient world – Asia Minor, Lydia, Judah, Mesopotamia and Egypt – so in their eyes Marathon was seemingly of little significance in the scheme of things. It was not until the reign of Darius' son, Xerxes (486–465 BCE) that the Athenians once more came to the attention of the Persians. In 481 BCE Xerxes gathered together an army of approximately 50,000 men and a navy of 600 ships determined that the whole of Greece would be conquered. However, the Athenians were not unprepared, for the politician Themistocles had been convinced that the Persians would return at some point to exact revenge. He managed to convince the Athenians of the Persian intent. He proposed that they used the new found wealth from the gold mines at Laurion to prepare for war. So while Persia delayed through the 480s, Athens began building its own war fleet and by 481 BCE Athens had a navy of 200 ships. The first sea battle with the Persian fleet took place at Artemisium but the outcome was inconclusive. On land the Greeks were undecided on the best way to fight the Persians. Their first defence at Tempe was abandoned and the plan was to fall back as far as the Peloponnese and make their stand there. The Spartan king Leonidas was dispatched with 300 men to delay the Persians at the narrow pass at Thermopylae, where they held out for three days before finally being betrayed and slaughtered. The epitaph of the heroic Spartans was written by the poet Simonides and carved into the stone walls of the pass:

> Tell them in Lacedaemon passerby, that here obedient to their words we lie.

Now unimpeded, the Persian army continued its march toward Athens. The Greek fleet was sent to lure the Persian fleet into the straits between Attica and the island of Salamis, where their smaller and more manoeuvrable ships had an advantage. This was a brilliant strategy and resulted in the loss of 200 Persian vessels. The Persian army now retreated north to sit it out through the winter with the idea of returning the following summer to sack Athens. The Greeks now numbered 100,000 men and were led by the Spartan general Pausanias, reinforced by other Greek city states that now had faith a Greek victory was possible. They defeated the Persians at Plataea while the Greek navy destroyed the Persian fleet at Mykale off the coast of Asia Minor. The Persian Wars were finally over.

In 478 BCE the Delian League was formed by Athens and its allies on the island of Delos, the island sacred to Apollo. Members were required to swear an oath, (some were actually forced to join by threats); they then began to clear the land of the last remaining Persians and free the seas of piracy. Athens, however, soon began to dominate the other city states, and proceeded to set about conquering all Greece with exception of Sparta and its allies. This period was referred to by the historian Thucydides as the *Pentecontaetia* when Athens increasingly became recognized as an Athenian Empire. Under the brilliant statesman Pericles, the increase in Athenian power meant that some of the formerly independent allies were reduced to the status of tribute paying subjects, and this tribute was used to support a powerful fleet, and after the middle of the century, to fund massive building works in Athens.

Naturally this caused a great deal of friction between Athens and the Peloponnesian states, especially with Sparta. Sparta attempted without success to prevent the reconstruction of the Athenian walls, without which Athens was completely undefended against land attack, and more importantly subject to Spartan control. In 465 BCE conflict erupted again when a helot revolt broke out in Sparta. The Spartans summoned the help of their allies including Athens who sent a force of 4,000 hoplites. However, upon their arrival they were dismissed by Sparta while the other allies were allowed to remain. Athens was greatly offended by this but it is possible that Sparta was afraid that the Athenian contingent would join forces with the helots, such was the mistrust of Athenian motives. The helots were finally forced to surrender and allowed to leave the country; Athens settled them in the strategic city of Naupactus on the Corinthian gulf.

THE FIRST PELOPONNESIAN WAR

In 459 BCE war broke out between Megara and Corinth both allies of Sparta, and Athens took advantage of the situation by concluding an alliance with Megara, which then gave the Athenians a foothold on the Corinthian isthmus. This incident started a 15-year conflict (known as the First Peloponnesian War) which saw Athens intermittently at war with Sparta, Corinth, Aegina and other states. During this time Athens controlled not only Megara but also Boeotia; however, at the end in face of a massive Spartan invasion of Attica, the Athenians ceded the lands they had won on the Greek mainland. Athens and Sparta agreed to recognize each other's right to control their respective alliance systems and the war was officially ended by the Thirty Years Peace which was signed in the winter of 446/5 BCE.

However, the peace was soon to be put under strain when Athens' powerful ally Samos rebelled from its alliance with Athens in 440 BCE. The rebels gained the support of a Persian satrap, and Athens faced the possibility of revolts throughout the empire. The Spartans called a congress of their allies to discuss the possibility of war with Athens; Corinth, the most powerful of Sparta's allies was opposed to war and so the congress voted against such action. Shortly afterwards the Athenians crushed the revolt and peace was maintained.

There were several other sources of provocation to the Peace. The first involved Athens and Corinth. After suffering a defeat by their colony of Corcyra, Corinth began to build an allied naval force. Corcyra immediately sought an alliance with Athens, which after debate and input from both Corcyra and Corinth, decided to swear a defensive alliance with Corcyra. Athenian ships played a decisive role at the Battle of Sybota, preventing the Corinthian fleet from capturing Corcyra. The Athenians were not allowed to directly attack Corinth in order to uphold the Thirty Years Peace but the presence of their warships was enough to dissuade Corinth from exploiting their victory.

Following this incident Athens instructed Potidaea, a tributary ally of Athens but a colony of Corinth, to tear down its walls, send hostages to Athens and dismiss Corinthian magistrates from office. The Corinthians were enraged by this and encouraged Potidaea to revolt, while at the same time was unofficially bringing armed men into the city to help defend it. This was a direct violation of the Thirty Years Peace which had expressly stipulated that the Delian League and the Peloponnesian League would respect each other's autonomy.

A further problem occurred when Athens issued a decree, known as the Megarian decree, imposing trade sanctions on Megarian citizens. This factor is ignored by Thucydides in his account of the war, but many modern historians believe it was a major contribution to bringing about the war. In 432 BCE Sparta summoned members of the Peloponnesian League to make their complaints to the Spartan assembly. The Athenians warned them of the dangers of opposing a nation that had had many military successes, notably the defeat of the Persians. Undeterred by this the Spartans voted to declare that the Athenians had broken the Peace, which meant a declaration of war.

THE 'ARCHIDAMIAN WAR'

The Spartan strategy, under its king Arcidamus II (after whom the first war is known), was to invade the land surrounding Athens. However, Athens was able to maintain access to the sea so did not suffer unduly. The Spartans occupied Attica for only three weeks at a time, because soldiers were expected to return home to participate in the harvest and the helots (slaves) needed to be kept under control and so could not be left unsupervised. The Athenian strategy was initially guided by Pericles who advised the Athenians to rely upon their fleet. The fleet went on the offensive winning a victory at Naupactus. In 430 BCE an outbreak of plague hit Athens and ravaged the densely packed city; in the long run it was a significant cause of its final defeat. The plague killed over 30,000 citizens, sailors and soldiers and even Pericles succumbed to the illness. Obviously this reduced the manpower of Athens and foreign mercenaries refused to join the plague-ridden city. Even Spartan troops refused to risk contact with the city, so the invasion was abandoned.

Following the death of Pericles the Athenians adopted a more aggressive policy under their new general Demosthenes and managed to achieve some success with their naval raids on the Peloponnese. The Athenians also began fortifying posts around the Peloponnese, one of which was on the tiny island of Sphacteria, where the course of the first war changed in Athens' favour. Demosthenes outmanoeuvred the Spartans in the Battle of Pylos in 425 BCE and trapped a group of Spartan soldiers on Sphacteria. Demosthenes was unable to finish off the Spartans and it was left to the inexperienced Cleon to complete the victory by capturing between 300–400 Spartan hoplites giving the Athenians a bargaining chip.

The Spartan general Brasidas retaliated by marching to Amphipolis, which controlled several silver mines that supplied the Athenian war fund. Thucydides was dispatched with a force but he arrived too late. Thucydides was exiled for this, and his conversations with both sides of the war inspired his later writing. Both Brasidas and Cleon were killed, and eventually both sides signed a truce – the Peace of Nicias – which lasted for approximately six years. There was constant skirmishing during this time and with the help of the Athenians the Argives forged a coalition of democratic states within the Peloponnese. Spartan attempts to break the coalition failed and the Athenians under the leadership of Alcibiades moved on Tegea, near Sparta.

The Battle of Matinea was the largest land battle fought within Greece during the Peloponnesian war. The Spartan forces were greatly outnumbered and the allied forces gained considerable success but failed to capitalize on them, which allowed the Spartan elite forces to defeat them. The Spartans achieved complete victory, and with the defeat of the coalition Sparta pulled back from the brink of disaster and retained complete hegemony throughout the Peloponnese.

The seventeenth year of the war saw Athens come to the aid of one of their distant allies in Sicily who was under attack from Syracuse. The Athenians had visions of conquering all Sicily and so acquiring a huge amount of resources. Alcibiades was accused of desecrating statues (the *hermai*) and charged with religious crimes. Alcibiades asked to be brought to trial before the expedition was sent, but he was allowed to go; however, as soon as he reached Sicily he was recalled to stand trial. Fearing he would be found guilty he defected to Sparta where he informed the Spartans of the Athenian plans.

The Athenian force consisted of over 100 ships and 5,000 infantry. Cavalry was limited to 30 horses which proved no match for the elite Syracusan cavalry. Nicias was in charge of the Athenian forces and his procrastination gave Syracuse the opportunity to call on Sparta for aid. Sparta sent their general Gylippus to Sicily with reinforcements; he took command and in a series of battles defeated the Athenian forces. Nicias and Demosthenes marched their remaining forces inland in search of friendly allies, but the Syracusan cavalry tracked them down and mercilessly slaughtered or enslaved all that remained of the mighty Athenian fleet.

THE SECOND PELOPONNESIAN WAR

The Spartans were now ready to deal with the Athenians on their own soil. Alcibiades fortified Decelea near Athens and prevented them for making use of their land. The fortification of Decelea also meant that all supplies were now only available by sea which meant increased expense for the Athenians. Perhaps more devastating was the disruption of the nearby silver mines when as many as 20,000 Athenian slaves were freed by the Spartan hoplites.

Following the defeat of the Athenians in Sicily it was believed that the end of the Athenian Empire was at hand. Her treasury was almost empty, her docks depleted, and her young men either dead or imprisoned. Sparta encouraged the revolt of Athens' other allies while the Syracusans sent their fleet to the Peloponnesians, and the Persians decided to support the Spartans with money and ships. Revolt and factional strife also threatened in Athens. However, the Athenians managed to survive. At the start of the war Athens had put some money aside and also 100 ships that were to be used as a last resort. These ships were released and served as the core of the Athenian fleet for the rest of the war.

An oligarchical revolution occurred in Athens in which a group of 400 seized power. In 411 BCE an Athenian fleet which refused to accept a possible peace with Sparta attacked the Spartans at the Battle of the Syme. The fleet appointed Alcibiades as commander and continued the war in Athens' name. Within two years their opposition led to a reinstatement of a democratic government in Athens.

Although condemned as a traitor Alcibiades led his fleet in a series of attacks against the Spartans and at the Battle of Cyzicus in 410 BCE the Athenians obliterated the Spartan fleet. Between 410 and 406 BCE Athens won a string of victories and eventually recovered large portions of its empire. The faction triumphed in Athens and Alcibiades exiled himself from the city.

The new Spartan general Lysander was not a member of the Spartan royal family but was formidable in naval strategy; he was also a cunning diplomat who had cultivated good relationships with the Persian prince Cyrus, the son of Darius II. Seizing an opportunity, the Spartan fleet sailed to the Hellespont, the source of Athenian grain: threatened with starvation the Athenian fleet had no option but to follow. In 405 BCE at the Battle of Aegospotami, Lysander destroyed 168 ships and captured 3,000–4,000 sailors. Only 12 Athenian ships escaped and several of these sailed to Cyprus, carrying the *strategos* (general) Conon, who was anxious not to face the judgement of the Assembly.

With the threat of starvation and disease Athens surrendered in 404 BCE, followed soon after by the surrender of its allies. The surrender stripped Athens of its walls, fleet and all overseas possessions. Corinth and Thebes demanded that Athens should be destroyed and all its citizens enslaved. However, the Spartans decided against this and took Athens into their own system. Athens was to have the same friends and enemies as Sparta (Xenophon, *Hellenica* 2.2.20, 404).

For a short time afterwards Athens was ruled by the Thirty Tyrants and democracy was suspended. The oligarchs were finally overthrown and a democracy was restored by Thrasybulus in 403 BCE. Although the power of Athens was broken it made something of a recovery as a result of the Corinthian war and continued to play an active role in Greek politics, Sparta was later humbled by Thebes at the Battle of Leuctra in 371 BCE but it was brought to an end a few decades later when Philip II of Macedon conquered all Greece.

When the Persian wars were finally over and with the threat from the east gone Athens began a 50-year period under the direction of the brilliant statesman Pericles. It was during this period that the Parthenon was built on the Acropolis and the city became the artistic, cultural, intellectual and commercial centre of the Hellenic world.

This period was known as the Golden Age and many of the great philosophers, historians and playwrights lived during this time. Among the dwellers of Athens was Socrates whose philosophy, although he left no writing of his own, was handed down to his pupil Plato whose works have survived. Plato's pupil Aristotle went on to become the tutor of Alexander the Great. The sculptor Praxitelis was the most famous artist of the time, although few of his original works remain. Other well-known inhabitants of Athens were the great dramatists Aeschylus, Aristophanes, Euripides, Menander and Sophocles who all performed their works at the theatre of Dionysius at the foot of the Acropolis. Their comedies and tragedies tell us a great deal about ancient life as well as supplying historical and psychological insights into the period.

GREEK HISTORIOGRAPHY

The first semi-historical work was that of the poet Homer who lived between the twelfth and tenth centuries BCE. His epic poems the *Iliad* and the *Odyssey* were committed to writing circa eighth century BCE, and this work created, in some respects, an ethnic identity for the early Greeks. Although not a history as such the work has proved useful for our knowledge of the period concerned and many archaeological discoveries have proved the validity of some of the details of the poem.

The historical period of Ancient Greece is unique as the first period in the ancient world that was directly attested to in historiography. Earlier ancient history or proto-history is attested to by more circumstantial evidence, such as annals, king lists and epigraphy. Herodotus from Halicarnassus moved to Athens and became known as the 'father of history' because of his writings on the Persian wars. Written between 450s and 420s BCE the scope of his work extends into roughly a century in the past and discusses sixth century BCE people such a Darius I of Persia, Cambyses II and Psamtik III. However, his work which was detailed contained a mixture of fact, fiction and even mythology. Nevertheless his work became eponymous of the entire field.

The generation that followed Herodotus witnessed a spate of local histories of the individual city states, written by the first local historians who used as their sources the local archives of the city and sanctuary. Dionysius of Halicarnassus says that these historians were the forerunners of Thucydides. Two early figures stand out: Hippias of Elis, who produced the lists of winners in the Olympic Games which provided the basic chronological framework for as long as the pagan classical tradition survived; and Hellanicus of Lesbos, who compiled more than two dozen histories from civic records, all of them now lost.

Thucydides, who came a few decades after Herodotus, had more of a journalistic style collecting information and writing history from his own viewpoint. His primary subject was the Peloponnesian wars, which he believed was the greatest of all wars. His aim was to provide future generations with an analysis of war, its causes and progressions but not necessarily how to prevent it.

These two major historiographers were succeeded by other writers such as Xenophon, who introduced biographical elements into his work. The proverbial Philippic attacks made by Demosthenes (384 BCE – 322 BCE) on Philip II of Macedon marked the height of political agitation. The history of Alexander's campaigns by Ptolemy I may represent the first historical work composed by a ruler. The Chaldean priest Berrosus (third century BCE) composed a Greek language *History of Babylonia* for the Seleucid king Antiochus I combining Hellenistic methods of historiography and Mesopotamian accounts to produce a unique composition.

The earliest known systematic historical thought in the Western world was born in ancient Greece, a development that would become important throughout the whole of the Mediterranean. It is these early historians that contributed greatly to the development of historical methodology.

Chapter Two

Herodotus (c.480 BCE – c.425 BCE)

> To preserve the memory of the past by putting on record the aston-
> ishing achievements of both our own and of other peoples; and
> more particularly, to show how they came into conflict.
>
> *(Histories* Book I)

Herodotus was born in Halicarnassus (modern Bodrum) in south-
west Turkey, (Asia Minor as it was known then) around 480
BCE. He has become known as the 'Father of History', although
in antiquity he was also referred to as the 'Father of Lies'.
Nevertheless he was born during the time of the Persian wars,
and was witness to the great age of Pericles, and saw the start of
the Peloponnesian wars with Sparta.

In his great work *The Histories* he describes the expansion of the
Persian Empire under its kings, Cyrus the Great, Cambyses and
Darius I, culminating in Xerxes I's expedition against the Greeks
in 480 BCE. However, ancient references to him, notably by the
other great historian of the ancient world Thucydides, endowed
him with the less flattering title of 'liar', primarily because some
of his stories were literally beyond belief. The most elaborate tale
is *Rhampsinitus and the Thieves* (Book II:121) which stretched the
credulity of his successors and insulted them by the fact that they
should have been expected to consider this as historical material.
Modern historians have agreed in part with this assessment, for
in the modern sense of the word 'historian' Herodotus left much
to be desired.

Nevertheless, the modern reader can be grateful to Herodotus
for preserving this glimpse into the past by recounting the stories
that were circulating at the time and so giving us an idea of how

the ancients related to the world in which they lived. The main focus that Herodotus provides for the modern reader, however, is a general historical picture of the Greek world from the mid sixth century BCE onwards. His life work, for that is what it was, takes the form of an inquiry or research, which is the original meaning of the Greek word *historia*. What is significant is that his work which culminates in the great Persian invasion of Greece in 480 BCE marks an axial point in the history of Western civilization.

When Herodotus was born his homeland was subject to Persian rule. The mere fact that he could write means that he must have come from a fairly privileged background, possibly a member of the old aristocracy. Other than that we know tantalizingly little about the man. Growing up in the shadow of the great Persian Empire may have allowed him a unique insight into both sides of the conflict between the Greeks and Persians. It may also have helped facilitate his travels within the Empire, first to Egypt, then Tyre and Babylon. He also tells us that he visited the Crimea and North Africa but Herodotus' travels were not confined to these far-off realms alone. He also visited many Greek cities, including Athens, where he played an active part in the intellectual life of the city.

From these travels Herodotus collected a vast array of information and wanted to include everything in his work. The *Histories* were probably designed originally to be read aloud but are now, in modern translations, divided into two principal parts. The first deals with the long-standing strife between east and west, the origin and extent of the Persian Empire, and the historical background of the Greek lands, with special reference to Athens and Sparta. The second part, which is the longer, focuses on the Persian wars, the invasion by Darius I in 490 BCE and ten years later the expedition to Greece led by Xerxes I, and includes accounts of the battles of Thermopylae, Salamis, Artemisium and finally Plataea in 479 BCE. For Herodotus these events were the most significant happenings in world history and he wished to portray them within a wider framework, so that 'the doings of men may not be forgotten.'

Ancient society was more oral than it is today for written material was sparse and inadequate. Therefore it is not surprising that Herodotus collected nearly all of his material orally; from men who had served in the war, from Athenian and Spartan family traditions, from priests at Delphi and Egypt. Clearly he also had Persian sources one such person was possibly Zopyrus, the son of the marshal Megabyzus, who deserted to Athens, (mentioned at the end of Book III). He did not always believe what he was told. For example what Darius' queen told to him in bed, as reported in Book III (134), can really only be conjecture. But he would offer alternatives without giving his own opinion, suspending his own beliefs but at the same time feeling no obligation to report the truth. He says:

> I am not obliged to believe it all alike, a remark that which must be understood to apply to my whole history. For I am reporting.

Following in the Homeric tradition he employed speeches to liven up his narrative and to formulate his judgements but he never implied that they were accurate accounts of what may or may not have been said. For example the debate on constitutions ascribed to seven Persians is definitely a work of fiction, but it was employed by Herodotus to stress the main themes of the book. Another example can be found in the meeting between Solon of Athens and King Croesus of Lydia which probably never took place but provided a backdrop for other moralising themes (1: 9–34).

Interestingly, perhaps surprisingly to modern historians, among other sources that he may have used, especially concerning the kingdom of Lydia, is drama. The story of Atys and the boar (1:34), with the vegetation god of Asia Minor made into a son of the famous king Croesus, conforms to the type of an Attic drama, culminating in the Messenger's Speech and Funeral Procession. For Herodotus, stories are only right or wrong and drama was no less acceptable as a source than poetry.

He did occasionally overstress the importance of great men and laid far more emphasis than was necessary on the Homeric theme of the valour of individuals who he saw as playing a far more significant role in historical events than was the case. This preoccupation with the great and mighty sometimes led him into accounts of doubtful reliability. However, the main purpose of composing a history was to attract an audience and in order to do that you had to tell a good story. In fact the distinction in ancient times between storytelling and history was often blurred.

The influence of Homer upon ancient writers is particularly true in Herodotus' case. Although he criticized old Greek themes and tried to separate the ages of myth and history, nevertheless he saw the Persian wars as a direct descendent of the Trojan wars. His dialogues, speeches and digressions are wholly Homeric as are his stress on divine intervention, heroic leaders and catalogues of armies; there is hardly any reference to strategy. In his description of the Battle of Thermopylae he relates how the Persians and the Spartans fought over the body of Leonidas, echoing the scene in Homer's *Iliad* where Greeks and Trojans fight over the body of Patroclus. In a true hoplite battle, such as that of Thermopylae, this would have been impossible. For this reason he has been given another nickname, the 'Homer of the Persian Wars' (Shotwell 1922).

Another important aspect that he borrowed from Homer was the so-called circular composition. However, Herodotus constantly interrupts his narrative to digress. Other writers had attempted this in the past, e.g. Hecataeus of Miletus had written a detailed geographical work with history thrown in, but Herodotus wanted to better him. Herodotus' plan was to recount his story of two generations, encompassing four Persian kings, taking in the history of other peoples as they came into the story. As he says in Book IV (30), 'digressions are part of my plan.' Nevertheless, some of the digressions are enormous, especially Book II, which contains the geography, social anthropology and history of Egypt, conveniently situated between the Persian king,

Cambyses' decision to conquer the country and the inevitable conquest itself. These digressions can be counted among the most entertaining parts of the *Histories*. For example he tells about an interview he had with an employee of an Egyptian mummy factory (Book II), a hilarious tale about Indian gold mining (Book III) and lots of other fascinating incidents. On the other hand these digressions merely set the scene for he never loses sight of the main theme of his work.

Also in keeping with Homeric tradition we find in the *Histories* a lack of personal bias on the part of Herodotus. Just as Homer treated Greeks and Trojans with equal respect, so Herodotus portrays the Greeks and Persians, showing sympathy and understanding for both sides This is unique, for comparisons with other ancient texts from oriental monarchies of the time show that they go to great lengths to relate the wickedness of their enemies, whether or not their wickedness was justifiable.

As with many ancient historians religion and portents played a significant part in the shaping of historical events, so we should not be surprised to find that Herodotus saw the hand of the gods always at work in the affairs of men. These gods jealously and fatefully punished ambition or impiety and pulled down the mighty in order to preserve a balance. Although Herodotus was strongly influenced by the new Ionian enlightenment, he did believe in divine intervention and causation, and this, according to him, was exemplified in the Persian wars. His scepticism is only partially revealed in his work and some scholars believe that this was due to his fear of being accused of blasphemy. What does become clear is that even if he found divine power incomprehensible he believed in its intervention. He also believed in oracles even though he often distrusted them (8:77). To him, as well as to other ancients the divine nature of dreams played an important role in foretelling future events. For Herodotus there was an inescapable fate despite mankind's best efforts to avert it.

Time after time throughout the *Histories* we see this theme of scepticism emerging; the gods, according to Herodotus, tempt mortals to act beyond the limits of their greatness and bring about their own destruction. But Herodotus was not alone in this kind of thinking. That overconfidence (Greek *hybris*) evoked retribution was a pious and traditional explanation for the downfall of kings and the disasters that inevitably followed. Even the gods themselves were subject to this law, not even human piety could prevent human beings from misery. One case in particular is shown by the story of Croesus. Croesus was a devout king of Lydia who sent wonderful gifts to Apollo and his oracle in Delphi. However, Croesus was badly defeated by the Persians and when he inquired why the god had been so unappreciative, the god replied that not even he, Apollo, could escape destiny, even he, a god, was not able to divert the course of fate.

Herodotus sees this as one cause of the wars that followed. Because Croesus became over-confident he had attacked Persia who in turn defeated Croesus. After a generation or two the Greeks rose in rebellion, helped by Athens. The Persians retaliated and attacked the Athenians, who defeated them at the Battle of Marathon. The Persians swore vengeance but Xerxes' expedition in 480 BCE was a disaster, and now it was the Greeks' turn to attack. It seems unfeasible to modern historians that all historical events are subject to this 'action-reaction' theory. Herodotus was probably the first writer ever to question this theory and come up with an abstract answer to why people fought a war: imperialism. Herodotus offers his more sophisticated interpretation of events, indicated by the compositional principle of the *Histories*: the Persians subjugated the Lydians, but they also subjugated the Egyptians, Indians, Scythians, Libyans etc., so it follows that the Greeks will also have to fight the ever expanding Persian Empire.

If Herodotus showed any bias at all it is with respect to his treatment of the cities that had been patriotic during the war with Persia. Athens was his particular favourite, for this city had admitted him and repaid his efforts with all manner of rewards. He grossly exaggerated the deeds of the Athenian victors of the Persian wars, for it was arguably just as much due to the efforts of the Spartans. It is no great surprise to know that his informants were predominantly Athenians, and this could account for his presentation of the stories. Plutarch, in his work *On the Meanness of Herodotus*, commented on his bias toward Athens as well as highlighting his mistreatment of Corinth's admiral Adamantes (Book VII). Corinth was proud of its admiral, and he was described on his epitaph as 'he who by his counsels saved all Greece'. But throughout Herodotus' story of the naval campaign he is depicted as a corrupt coward.

The accounts of the Persian wars need to be read with a critical eye especially regarding the sources he used. Herodotus believes that he knows what was said in the councils of war but we have to remember that his information was based on oral 'sagas' from men who had served in ranks some 30 years earlier and who would have been included in the councils. The Battle of Plataea (Book IX) is one such occasion when Herodotus preserves all the old animosities against Athens' and Sparta's allies (who later nearly all became Athens' enemies). In particular his reporting of the allies' actions at the Temple of Hera, where he states that the Corinthians missed the battle, seemingly on purpose. He also says that the cenotaphs erected to their dead were nothing but a sham. These incidents show that Herodotus could be severely misled by his sources, but to his credit he did visit the battlefield and identify the landmarks; it would appear to be a case of naivety rather than malice, for had he been more aware of military tactics he may have questioned his sources' reliability.

Herodotus left behind a great legacy. Not only did he relate the historical events of his own era, but also provided an ethnographic description of all the peoples that the Persians had conquered. His pages are occupied with gossip, legends and fairy tales that expand his narrative. His unqualified statements and bizarre accounts make Herodotus a *mythologos*, a teller or weaver of tales. According to the historian Edward Gibbon he 'sometimes writes for children and sometimes for philosophers; the anecdotes he relates often appeal to both.' This all combined to create a new literary genre: history. He combined empirical research with epic and set it all in prose, a combination that was to prove revolutionary and set the scene for all those who would follow him in the search for understanding and truth about the human condition.

Chapter Three

Thucydides (c.460 BCE – c.400 BCE)

Thucydides the Athenian wrote the history of the war fought between Athens and Sparta, beginning the account at the very outbreak of the war, in the belief that it was going to be a great war and more worth writing about than any of those that had taken place in the past.

(Book I)

The power that Athens had acquired in the fifth century BCE with the expansion of her empire aroused fears not only among the Spartans but other mainland states, especially Corinth, who saw their trade interests threatened. The Greek world effectively became split in two, Athens and her empire on one side, Sparta and her allies on the other. Eventually in 431 BCE war ensued, provoked by certain incidents in Corcyra and Potidaea (Book I). This intermittent war between Athens and Sparta known as the Peloponnesian War, lasted almost 30 years until 404 BCE, when Athens was finally defeated.

Thucydides was living in Athens when the war began; his father was an Athenian citizen, although the family originated from Thrace where they owned property, notably gold mines. Coming from an aristocratic background he was expected to defend his country in time of war. In 424 BCE Thucydides was elected one of the ten Athenian generals for the year and given the command of the fleet in the northern Aegean. However, he failed to prevent the Spartan general Brasidas from capturing the key Macedonian city of Amphipolis, so was subsequently recalled to stand trial in Athens. He was found guilty and condemned to 20 years exile. During this period of exile he lived at his Thracian property and

from this base he travelled widely. He visited the countries of the
Peloponnesian allies, only returning to Athens after the war had
ended in the defeat of the city in 404 BCE. The great plague that
claimed much of Athens' population also claimed Thucydides
as one of its victims but fortunately he managed to recover.
However, he died not long afterwards in Thrace; the precise date
is unknown.

Thucydides sought in his great life's work to tell the truth,
and he made every effort to establish a distinction between the
immediate causes of the war and the more remote fundamental
causes. He was above all analytical, deducing general truths and
rationales from contemporary actions and events, very much in
keeping with the modern notion of what an 'historian' should aim
to do. He had spent his long exile from Athens collecting evidence
and interviewing participants in the various campaigns of the
war. So his methodology is one of informed enquiry, research and
evaluation. He tells us that on principle he never wrote down the
first story he heard nor was he influenced by his own impres-
sions; he checked everything in order to be objective (Book I:22).
Basically he saw that human nature was the prime causal factor
in historical events. Unlike Herodotus, he did not ascribe these
events to the machinations of the gods or Fate. For example, the
accidental fire that was a prelude to the Athenians' capture of
Sphacteria (Book IV:30) or the plague (Book II:47–54) are both
methodically recorded by Thucydides without any attempt to
evaluate the causes. He said:

> … as for the gods, it seemed to be the same thing whether one
> worshipped them or not, when one saw the good and the bad
> dying indiscriminately.

Thucydides stresses the inadequacies of his predecessors,
especially with regard to their uncritical evaluation of the past.
Although he never mentions Herodotus by name it is clear that
he had read *The Histories* for he notes inaccuracies in the accounts.

In Book I he makes reference to two errors concerning Sparta that occur in Herodotus' work in Books VII (57) and IX (53) and also corrects his geography. However, this is far from being a malicious attack, for in general Thucydides presents himself as Herodotus' critic and rival but also primarily as his successor. He did not feel that there was any need to repeat what Herodotus had already said about past events. He merely filled in the gap between the end of Herodotus' account and the beginning of his own. To this end he writes a brief digression (Book I:89–118) in which he highlights some important events that occurred between 479 BCE and 435 BCE. This digression is now referred to in literature as the *Pentecontaetia* (Fifty Year Period).

He also tells us that he will not be as entertaining as some previous historians, presumably referring to Herodotus, and to a lesser degree, Homer, but in order to compensate for the lack of entertainment he will attempt to offer a rational analysis of why things happen. He sees the recurrence of events that happened in the past, happen in his time and promise to happen once again in the future, because human nature is unchanging.

However, what becomes clear throughout his work is that Thucydides had understood what Herodotus had attempted to do: to analyse events by a careful study of the political and moral issues without reference to myth or philosophy in order to explain what had transpired. The main difference between the two historians was that Thucydides was writing about contemporary events in which he had played a small part, while Herodotus had dealt with past events.

Although Thucydides may have dismissed the past as being too far removed to be substantiated, he was not averse to using it occasionally to provide a rationale for the importance of his own work. In the *Peloponnesian War* he makes a number of forays into the past history of Greece. These were designed to give credence to his idea that the Peloponnesian War was the most momentous event of all time. To this end he used Herodotus and Homer as his sources, and combined the results of their work with his own intellectual perspective of the world in which he lived. The result proved to be a brilliant theory of the continuity and development of Hellenic power and greatness. He maintained that it had been achieved through the systematic development of trade, the accumulation of resources and a stable community organization; this was then followed by empire-building which culminated in the greatest power struggle of all time, the Peloponnesian war.

Given the nature of his intellectual brilliance, it is not surprising therefore to find that Thucydides was the first surviving writer ever to comment upon the problem of utilizing speeches in historical accounts. Indeed he went out of his way to distinguish the reporting of speeches from the reporting of actions (Book I:22). However, this did not prevent him from using them, 40 in total, scattered throughout his work, which he had either heard himself or had reported to him by persons who had been present at the time. By his own admission, when he could not remember accurately what had been said he invented what he thought should have been said, given the circumstances. But in fairness to Thucydides, when he had any clue to the tenor of the speech he drew on that rather than merely inventing his own version.

One example is the speech given by the great Athenian statesman Pericles. The speech known as the 'Funeral Oration' was supposedly delivered during the first year of the war (Book II:34–6). A later Greek historian, Dionysius of Halicarnassus (first century BCE), questioned the validity of this speech and wondered why Thucydides had included it at all as, according to him, the occasion was neither a glorious nor a significant one. Dionysius concluded that Thucydides had just wanted to include a Periclean speech in his work whatever its relative value. Indeed he must have repeatedly heard Pericles speak when he was in Athens, during the period that he considered to be its finest hour, and wished to convey this to his readers. One the other hand it should be noted that Dionysius preferred Herodotus as a historian for precisely the opposite reason that modern historians prefer Thucydides' passion for accuracy rather than storytelling. The speech by Pericles was written down some 30 years after its supposed delivery so it is extremely unlikely that it is at all accurate, and it reflects a retrospective view of Athens' greatness and possibilities before the war had begun, written in the light of the city's unnecessary defeat. It was a nostalgic trip down memory lane for Thucydides, designed to refute the anti-Periclean opinions that had been circulating.

The same is true for the Mytilenian debate on the reconsideration of the decision to put all Mytilenian males to death (Book III: 36). Thucydides tells us that there was a sudden change of heart concerning this issue and that a second assembly was summoned at which various points of view were given. Thucydides concentrates on two, one by Cleon and one by an unknown person named Diodotus. Thucydides presents these speeches free from any emotive element, something that would have been extremely unusual in Athenian speeches, especially ones concerning such delicate issues as a general massacre of an entire male population. If, as seems unlikely, Thucydides had reported exactly what had been debated then the lack of emotion would be unprecedented in the ancient world.

Another similar type of omission appears in Book I concerning the Spartan embassy which was sent to Athens in 431 BCE to issue them with an ultimatum. In the assembly opinions were given both for and against war with Sparta, yet Thucydides presents none of the arguments from the anti-war campaigners.

It seems probable that Thucydides utilized speeches to give some psychological insight into the motivations behind the actions that took place; but they also provided a mouthpiece for his own or contemporary views. To the ancient Greek reader a political history would have seemed very strange without first person speeches. Thucydides utilizes them in the best possible way to aid dramatic action to express ideas that were current at the time. The later Greek and Roman historians Polybius, Sallust and Tacitus all follow Thucydides' example in this respect.

However, he was not always as objective as he would have us believe and there are many examples of this to be found in his work. For instance, Thucydides was probably drawing on his own personal experiences as a commander when he imagined the thoughts of Nicias (Book V). More significantly he shows an obvious dislike for the statesman Cleon, seemingly for personal reasons. (Cleon is said to have been the prime mover in Thucydides' condemnation and subsequent exile.) The fact that he is seen to show ill will towards Athens is apparent in his treatment of the Melian affair which some scholars regard as being unfairly handled by him. In this account he gives Athens the justification to attack the small island of Melos in 416 BCE by having Athens declare that those who are powerful need have no regard for justice, human rights or the gods. This is a stark contrast to the high moralistic tone of the Funeral Oration. Thucydides then follows this with an account of Athens' attempt to conquer the large and far more resilient island of Sicily, which proved a disastrous mission which in Thucydides' view heralded the end for Athens. Clearly Thucydides saw the degeneration in Athens from the highly principled period of its greatness under Pericles to a city where its leaders lacked any moral sensibilities and because of this Athens was defeated.

By far the most emotive account in the whole of his work is that of the great plague to which he himself had fallen victim (Book II). He laid out the horrifying details in what later historians have called a 'tragic history' to show the moral and social breakdown that such an event entailed.

> For the catastrophe was so overwhelming that men, not knowing what would happen next to them, become indifferent to every rule of religion and law.

For Thucydides such moral issues were an essential part of politics, just as important in determining events as battles and political assemblies.

Despite the greatness of the work and its value to ancient historians, for there is no other surviving complete account of the Peloponnesian War, the work lacks one vital element. Fifth-century Athens was one of the most significant periods in European history. The expansion and consolidation of the empire was completed and Athenian genius was flourishing. Yet we read nothing about the magnificent building works of Pericles. Thucydides alludes to the newly built Parthenon only to say that it contained the treasury, and other references to new buildings are simply to show how these building had depleted the 'war fund'. And we have no information on the great writers of the time, Aeschylus, Sophocles, Euripides or Aristophanes, the architect Ictinus and the great sculptor, responsible for the friezes on the Parthenon formerly known as the 'Elgin Marbles', Pheidias; no mention either of the philosophers Anaxagoras and Socrates or the physician Hippocrates. Sadly, there are no digressions on men of letters, or art, like those we would have found in Herodotus. On all these matters Thucydides remained tantalizingly silent.

The *Peloponnesian War* is divided into eight books which may well have been the way that the author arranged them originally. The first book after a brief introduction sets out the causes of the war. The following four books cover the first nine years, two years to each book. The fifth book contains the tenth year followed by the interval of 'insecure peace'. The Sicilian expedition is the topic of the sixth and seventh books The eighth book opens with the last chapter of the war known as the 'Decelean' or 'Ionian war' and breaks off abruptly in mid sentence, in the year 411 BCE. The reason for this may be that Thucydides died suddenly, and there is a preponderance of testimonies to suggest that he met a violent end at his home on Thrace. It has also been suggested that his daughter saved his unfinished work and placed it in the hands of an editor. His remains were brought to Athens and laid in the vault of Cimon's family, to whom he may have been related; the later historian Plutarch (46–120 CE) claims to have witnessed his resting place.

It could be said that Thucydides was the cleverest and most intellectual of all the ancient historians. Although his style often appears difficult for modern readers to find enjoyable, his work *The History of the Peloponnesian War*, as Bury says marks 'the longest and most decisive step that has ever been taken by a single man towards making history what it is today' (Bury, *Ancient Greek Historians* 1958 147). Thucydides saw the war between Athens and Sparta in much the same way that Herodotus had viewed the Persian wars, as the most significant event in the whole of world history. Indeed, from the modern perspective we can appreciate that the war heralded the breakdown of the city state and civilization that had been the principal characteristic of ancient Greece, and therefore it is relevant today in providing a key element for any evaluation of subsequent historical events.

Chapter Four

Xenophon (c.435 BCE – 354 BCE)

> To what god shall I pray and sacrifice in order that I may best and most honourably go on the journey I have in mind, and return home safe and successful?
>
> (Xenophon's question to Apollo at Delphi, *Anabasis* Book III, Chapter 1)

Xenophon was born into a leading Athenian family of the Equestrian order (knights) around 435 BCE during the same era as Thucydides. He, like Thucydides, served in the campaigns during the Peloponnesian War, and early in his life he came under the influence of the philosopher Socrates. After the war, in 403 BCE with the restoration of democracy in Athens, Xenophon moved away from his home. The Equestrian order's devotion to democracy had always been suspect and Xenophon no doubt felt that there would be little opportunity for him to advance his career.

He was persuaded by a friend, Proxenus, to join the cause of Cyrus the younger who had rebelled against his brother King Artaxerxes II of Persia; this was a campaign that held the promise of riches and honour. So, at the instigation of Socrates he went to consult the oracle at Delphi; after a favourable response he then proceeded to the army's rendezvous at Sardis. When Cyrus was defeated and killed at Cunaxa (near Babylon), the army was given the chance to return to their homeland. Xenophon led the evacuation of what had been Cyrus' Greek force, comprising 10,000 men, to Trapezus (north-eastern Turkey) from where they returned home. He wrote a detailed account of this expedition, the *Anabasis* (Up Country March or Persian Expedition).

On their return Xenophon and his men placed themselves at the disposal of the Thracian King Seuthes and, afterwards, the

Spartan commanders Thibron and Dercylidas who were also fighting against the Persians. Meanwhile back in Athens, his mentor, Socrates, had been executed and because Xenophon was one of his sympathizers he was condemned to banishment by the Athenians and his estate and property were confiscated. In 396 BCE he joined forces with Agesilaus I, King of Sparta, against the Persian satrap Pharnabazus and during these campaigns he was at one point allied with Sparta against his own countrymen. Unable to return to Athens he lived in Sparta where the rulers gave him property at Scillus, about two miles from Olympia, and this is where he spent the next 20 years indulging his passion for sport and literature.

The *Anabasis* was composed at Scillus between 379 and 371 BCE. As Thucydides had done, and Julius Caesar would later do in his work, *The Gallic Wars*, Xenophon tells his story in the third person. His style is straightforward and there is a light-hearted aspect to the work which enlists the sympathies of the reader. His descriptions of places and the distances covered are minute and painstaking and generally accurate. However, on almost every page the contrast between Greek and barbarian is sharply drawn. He saw the Greek world as compact, united by the seafaring tradition of trade and colonization and although it encompassed many diverse elements had in essence a common bond. On the other hand the barbarian world was diverse, disunited and savage.

Xenophon lived during a time when the idealized notion of a united Greek crusade against the might of the Persian Empire was popular. The chief spokesman of this Pan-Hellenic crusade was a man called Isocrates (*Panegyric*). He endeavoured to demonstrate that Persia was weak and no match for Greek valour. This was a creed shared by Xenophon and Agesilaus, his hero, and this doctrine is exemplified in the speech made by Xenophon to the assembly of Greek soldiers on an October morning in 401 BCE. (Book III.2:24.).

On the death of Cyrus in the autumn of 401 BCE, 10,000 Greek soldiers were faced with the prospect of submitting to the King of Persia or marching home. They found themselves in the heart of the Persian Empire with half of their leaders arrested and surrounded by the Persian army. Naturally they chose to return home and the *Anabasis* is Xenophon's account of how he took charge of this expedition, not because he held any superior rank but because he was a man of reason. For the Greek 'political animal' reason surpassed hierarchy. Their journey led them over mountains and across rivers, through an appalling winter, constantly facing hostile barbarian tribes, arriving, with some loss of life, at the Hellespont in the summer of 400 BCE.

For the modern historian this account offers not only a unique glimpse into the barbarian world, especially the tribes that inhabited the shores of the Black Sea and Thrace, but also affords a better picture of the Greek colonies, which can be found especially in the fifth and sixth books. We read with some amusement how Xenophon planned to found a city which would trade in cereals and slaves with Greece (Book V, chapter 6). The only other requirement for such a 'utopia', according to Xenophon, was a supply of women, and they could easily be snatched from the tribes, just as the founders of Miletus had taken the Carian women. Only in the *Anabasis* can we glimpse such insights into the Greek mind and their view of the worth of the 'barbarian'.

However, we can also glean some insight into the mentality of the ordinary Greek soldier. It would appear that piety was a significant motivating factor in their everyday existence. For instance when Xenophon was addressing the assembly the day after the arrest of the generals, someone sneezed and the soldiers fell to their knees and offered up prayers to the god that had given them this sign. Similarly, in Book VI Xenophon sought a sign from heaven in the entrails of animals so that he might lead out the army to get supplies. For days he sacrificed without receiving any sign whatsoever and the Greeks were going hungry. Rather than complain or mutiny, the army accepted their fate and believed implicitly that they must await a favourable sign from the gods.

From Book III onwards Xenophon's name occurs over 200 times; his work is full of self-defence and self-praise. He delivers about 20 speeches and makes the point repeatedly that he considers himself to be the saviour of the 10,000. We need only compare his treatment of the speeches made by Chirisophus and Cleanor in the second chapter of Book III which occupy a page, with his own which occupies five pages, to see how biased he could be. His speeches are often witty, dramatic and well argued, but sadly mainly fictitious. It must be taken into account that Xenophon's writings give him the opportunity to ram home his personal, controversial standpoints in the face of his critics and enemies, prompting the reader to question the reliability of his accounts.

Xenophon wrote many other books one of the most important was the *Hellenica*, a history of Greece from 411 BCE. The *Hellenica* has been characterized by Tuplin (*The Failings of Empire: A Reading of Xenophon Hellenica* 1993), as a compromise between historiography and pamphleteering. It was written in Corinth after 362 BCE and is the only contemporary account of the period 411–362 BCE surviving. The work consists of two parts which were intended to form a continuation of Thucydides' work to bring Greek history down to the fall of 'The Thirty'. The Thirty were a 30-man committee that ruled in Athens as dictatorial puppets for the Spartans immediately after the surrender of Athens in the Peloponnesian war. They ruled in a reign of terror for almost a year (404–403 BCE). Indeed Xenophon may well have been one of the knights who had initially supported the Thirty.

Books III–IV deal with the period 410–362 BCE and give the history of the Spartan and Theban hegemonies up to the death of the Theban leader, Epaminondas. This work in particular shows the political biases of Xenophon. He was a partisan of the reactionary movement that triumphed after the defeat of Athens; Sparta is his ideal and Agesilaus his hero. However, the *Hellenica* ignores vital historical developments and contains many omissions and inaccuracies. He was poorly informed about

Athens from which he had become estranged and inaccurate when it came to details about events such as the formation of the Second Athenian Confederacy. He hated Thebes and had nothing to say about the foundation by the Thebans of the Arcadian city of Megalopolis (370–362 BCE) which was often hard pressed by Sparta. Indeed not long afterwards Plato (*Republic* 3:21) coined the term 'noble lies', indicating that some falsehoods were necessary for patriotic purposes. Although the majority of omissions can be put down to political bias on Xenophon's part, some events can be attributed to a lapse of memory, for this work was composed long after the events described and relies heavily on his own reminiscences rather than research.

Chapter 5 examines the diplomatic activities of 372/1 BCE and 370/69 BCE, and then he turns his attention to the tyrants Jason and Euphron. The Jason story illustrates the perils attendant on any search for power, which can only breed disaster and the Euphron episode teaches the same lesson. Chapter 6 discusses Sparta and its military expeditions which according to Xenophon are only successful when Agesilaus is in command; no other leader seems to be at all meritorious. Chapter 7 deals with Athens and Thebes more briefly, especially Athens. We learn for him that the Theban hegemony was bound to fail due to Gods opposition, and that Athens' new empire was a sham.

There were also several lesser works: a biography of *Agesilaus* the Spartan king. Other works comprise the *Cyropaedia* (Education of Cyrus), *Constitution of the Lacedaemonians* (Spartans), and several essays, *On Hunting*, *On Horsemanship*, *Hipparchias* (Dealing with Cavalry), and *Oeconomicus*, expounding his views on domestic and national management, *Poroi* (On Ways and Means or On Revenues).

The *Cyropaedia*, according to Xenophon, is a political and philosophical treatise describing the boyhood and training of Cyrus, however, it is mostly an account of the beginnings of the Persian Empire and its founder Cyrus the Great. It could be viewed as the world's first historical novel. It appears to be based on Xenophon's own ideas derived from the teachings of Socrates and Spartan institutions and it has been said that it was written in opposition to Plato's *Republic*. Spartan life embodied all the virtues that appealed to Xenophon and these he saw embodied in the person of Cyrus. Likewise the other work connected with Sparta, the *Aegislaus*, is a eulogy to the Spartan king of that name, who according to Xenophon had two special qualities. First he was a rigid disciplinarian and second he was particularly attentive to religious observances, which in essence gives us a picture of his virtues rather than an in-depth portrayal of the man himself. Unlike Thucydides', who provided no biographical accounts, Xenophon can be viewed as a pioneer in this field. Although he was capable of distinguishing between history and eulogy, his study of Cyrus and his hero-worshipping of Aegislaus make his descriptions of individuals a little over-idealized.

But Xenophon was also a believer in divine providence and this compelled him to see, in the final fall of Sparta to the Thebans under Epaminondas in 371 BCE, the punishment inflicted by heaven on the treacherous policy that had prompted the seizure by Sparta of the Cadmea and the raid of Sphodrias. The 'King's Peace' of 386 BC had finally unmasked the Spartans. Far from seeking to liberate the Greek cities of Asia Minor from Persian rule they had merely been seeking to retain power in Greece. Although Xenophon makes many omissions in these accounts, as a witness to events he is well informed and attempts to be honest.

The *Memorabilia* (Recollections of Socrates) takes up four books and was written in defence of his mentor who was charged with impiety and corrupting the youth of Athens. This is by no means a great work and does not really do justice to Socrates, who is better served in the works of Plato. Nevertheless it does no doubt reflect the life and style of conversation of the philosopher. Xenophon does not delve into his abstruse metaphysical observations for he much preferred the moral and practical side of Socrates' teachings.

Xenophon left behind many minor works that give insight into the home life of the Greeks. The *Oeconomicus* is sometimes regarded as a continuation of the *Memorabilia* and deals with the management of the home and farm. It presents an amusing yet some may say unpleasant picture of the Athenian wife and her domestic duties. There are practical remarks on matrimony and the duties of husbands and wives. It is presented in the form of a dialogue between Socrates and Ischomachus and was later trans-lated into Latin by Cicero (106–43 BC). The *Symposium* (Banquet) is another edition to the *Memorabilia*. Once again it is presented in the form of a dialogue where Socrates is the leading figure. The occasion is a lively dinner party where the wine is flowing, music playing and a dancing girl from Syracuse amuses the guests with mimicking the feats of a professional conjuror. Socrates discourses on a variety of subjects and ends up with a philosophical disqui-sition on the superiority of heavenly love to sensual earthly love.

But it is in the essays on horsemanship and hunting that Xenophon really comes into his own, for these were matters on which he was something of an expert. In the *Hipparchicus* (Horsemanship) he gives hints on how to choose a horse, how it should be groomed, ridden and managed. This is followed up by an explanation of the duties of a cavalry officer, which is inform-ative to modern readers, for it shows the limitations in the art of warfare during this period. His also goes to great lengths to stress the importance of the moral qualities that a cavalry officer should possess, as well as having a high regard for religious duties. The *Cynegeticus* (On Hunting) deals mainly with hare hunting, although he does mention boars as well. He describes how the hounds should be bred and trained, and he even suggests suitable names for them. The enthusiasm with which he writes displays his avid love of sports; he even goes as far as to suggest that those nations whose upper classes enjoy such pursuits will be the most successful in war.

There are further two essays that have been attributed to Xenophon, *Revenues of Athens*, written in 355 BCE, in which he offers suggestions for making Athens less dependent on the tributes received from her allies. He extols Athens to exert more influence on the maintenance of peace throughout the Greek world. He sees the Temple at Delphi acting as an independent centre, supplying a divine sanction for all efforts at diplomacy to settle issues. The second essay is political, *On the Constitution of Sparta*, which is highly biased in favour of Sparta. In Sparta Xenophon saw the best conceivable mixture of monarchy and aristocracy. His dislike of democracy in Athens induced his lack of patriotism, so much so that he had fought on the side of Sparta against his own country. There is a further work, On the *Polity of Athens*, which has been attributed to Xenophon but is probably an anonymous work written about 415 BCE.

The catastrophic defeat of Sparta at Leuctra changed Xenophon's life; when Scillus was seized he was ejected from his estate and went to Corinth where he lived out the rest of his days, and it was here that he wrote much of the *Hellenica* and *Anabasis*. Although he may have been more of storyteller than historian, his works received much acclamation in antiquity prompting later historians to continue to improve on the traditional methods pioneered by him.

Chapter Five

Diodorus Siculus (c.60 – 30 BCE)

> … for many errors have been committed through ignorance of the
> sites, not only by the common run of historians but even by some
> of the highest reputation.
>
> (*World History* I, 4.1)

Diodorus was born in Agyrium in Sicily in the first century BCE.
There are several clues in his works that establish the possible
dates of his birth and death. For example he mentions that in his
days the Macedonians were still rulers in Egypt, which suggests
that he published his work shortly before Octavian's defeat of
Antony and Cleopatra in 30 BCE. It is interesting to note that one of
only two Greek inscriptions found from this town marks the final
resting place of a 'Diodorus, the son of Apollonius'. According to
Cicero, Agyrium was an impoverished town and it is clear that
Diodorus understood some Latin. He travelled in Asia and Europe
and visited Rome and Egypt, but he gives no indication that he
visited the important cities like Athens, Miletus or Ephesus.

On the other hand he must have been a rich man, because he
mentions no literary patron and could obviously afford to spend
30 years collecting material for his immense 40-volume work
entitled *Bibliotheke Historike* (Library of History). This covered the
period from the creation to the Gallic wars of Julius Caesar. The
work was written between 60–30 BCE and was possibly the first
attempt at writing a world history:

> And so we, appreciating that an undertaking of this nature, while
> most useful, would yet require much labour and time, have

been engaged upon it for thirty years, and with much hardship and many dangers we have visited a large portion of both Asia and Europe that we might see with our own eyes all the most important regions and as many others as possible ...

(World History I, 4.1)

The *Library of History* included Roman affairs, though often only in summary fashion. This task that Diodorus had set himself was indeed immense. In the decade between 70 and 60 BCE the entire Mediterranean had been brought under the control of Rome by Pompey the Great. Roman supremacy extended to the 'bounds of the inhabited world' (1.4.3). Diodorus believed that all of mankind was coming to form a 'common' civilization, and so he could speak of a common life in the sense that the whole Mediterranean world was now interested in the same things and that what benefited one nation benefited all. In preparation for his work Diodorus states that with much hardship and many dangers he visited all the most important regions of Europe and Asia. However, there is no real evidence in his work to suggest that he went anywhere other than Egypt (1.4.1). He claims to have visited Mesopotamia although he places Nineveh on the Euphrates and if he went to Athens he did not even consider the Acropolis beautiful enough to deserve mention.

According to Grant (101), Diodorus has some interesting observations to make on the subject of speeches. He strongly opposes the use of frequent speeches inserted into the narrative.

One might justly censure those who in their histories insert overlong orations or employ frequent speeches. For not only do they rend asunder the continuity of the narrative by the ill-timed insertion of speeches, but they also interrupt the interest of those who are eagerly pressing on toward a full knowledge of events.

Yet surely there is an opportunity for those who wish to display rhetorical prowess to compose by themselves public discourses and speeches for ambassadors, likewise orations of praise and blame and the like.

(World History XX, 1, 2)

Besides a chronological table which provided a list of consuls, Diodorus probably used as his chief source for Rome one of the early annalists Fabius Pictor (fourth century BCE), and so perhaps used a better tradition than Livy or Dionysius of Halicarnassus, who used the first century annalists (that is presenting all the world events in one given year) as their sources. While Diodorus may not be classified among the abler historians of the ancient world there is no reason to doubt that he used the best sources and reproduced them faithfully.

The first five books are extant, the next five are lost; the next ten are complete and cover the period 479–301 BCE; of the remainder only fragments survive. The contents of the books are as follows: Book I, the myths, kings and customs of Egypt; Book II, the history of Assyria, description of India, Scythia, Arabia and the islands of the Ocean; Book III, Ethiopia, the Amazons of Africa, the inhabitants of Atlantis and the origins of the first gods; Book IV, the principal Greek gods, the Argonauts, Theseus, the Seven against Thebes; Book V, the islands and peoples of the west, Rhodes and Crete; Book VI–X fragments from the Trojan War to 480 BCE. Books XI–XXX cover the years 480–60 BCE.

The work itself is fairly undistinguished and unoriginal, even somewhat superficial. Diodorus' method made it almost impossible for him to write an accurate history or a readable story. When he approached the period that allowed him to give precise dates, he became an annalist. For incidents that covered a period of years he either had to break off the story or crowd several years' events into one. He also tried to synchronize the Roman consular year, which commenced on first January with the Athenian archon year which commenced about the middle of July. Even Diodorus recognized the shortcomings of this arrangement (20.43.7).

Diodorus uses second-hand material and he is not afraid to admit to this; he supplies evidence from other writers whose works have since been lost and it is mainly for this reason that Diodorus' work is of value today. He was able to comment correctly that some histories were 'appendages to oratory' but agreed that it was perfectly acceptable for writers to show rhetorical prowess 'since history needs to be adorned with variety.' (*World History* XX, 1, 2).

Although Diodorus announced twice that he wanted to continue his *History* until the moment that Caesar conquered Britain, it seems that the end was in fact the year 59 BCE. This was the year that witnessed Caesar's consulship, the ratification of Pompey's oriental acts, the conclusion of the First Triumvirate, and the beginning of Caesar's Gallic War and rise to power.

Many modern scholars (Schwarz, Mommsen et al.) have criticized Diodorus as an uncritical maker of excerpts and a poor historian. However, Diodorus is only as good as his sources and he does not pretend to offer any more than a collection of summaries. Although he lacks the speeches that make other ancient historians interesting, he writes in a clear unaffected style. In his Introduction he sets out his agenda:

> It is fitting that all men should ever accord great gratitude to those writers who have composed universal histories, since they have aspired to help by their individual labours human society as a whole; for by offering a schooling, which entails no danger, in what is advantageous they prove their readers, through such a presentation of events, with a most excellent kind of experience. For although the learning which is acquired by experience in each separate case, with all the attendant toils and dangers, does indeed enable a man to discern in each instance where utility lies — and this is the reason why the most widely experienced of our heroes suffered great misfortunes ... yet the

understanding of the failures and successes of other men, which is acquired by the study of history, affords a schooling that is free from actual experience of ills.

(World History, Introduction)

For the student of ancient history he is a very important source. The books 11–20 are the only surviving continuous account of the Greek 'Classical' age. It would also be impossible to write a history of Sicily without Diodorus, and for the period 480–31 BCE (the *Pentecontaetia*) and the age of the Diadochi he is our main source. His description of Alexander's last weeks in Babylon is high quality material, and finally his list of Roman magistrates is the best one available.

Chapter Six

Other Early Greek Historians

This chapter will deal with those early Greek historians who wrote about Greek history some of whose works have been lost or only survive in fragments. Those historians who wrote about Roman history are included in the section on Rome.

HECATAEUS OF ABDERA (SIXTH CENTURY BCE)

Hecataeus of Abdera lived in the sixth century BCE and was one of the earliest Ionian logographers (pioneer of history writing). Prose literature began here; the new idea was that simple speech, as the Greeks called prose, could be literature. He wrote a guide or journey round the world entitled *Periegesis*. More than 300 fragments of this work survive, although scholars have doubted the authenticity of some of them.

Hecataeus also illustrated a map and wrote a mythographic work known as the *Genealogies* or *Heroology*. Herodotus used him as a source for his *Histories* although he was often uncomplimentary about him and Polybius sneered at him for telling good stories. Nevertheless, his work on Persia provided the impetus for further historical works. He is famous for having said: 'I write what I believe to be the truth, for the Greeks have many stories, which it seems to me, are absurd.'

HELLANICUS OF LESBOS (FOURTH CENTURY BCE)

Hellanicus was a contemporary of Herodotus, but again very little survives of his works, and what does remain is in fragment form. He wrote mythographic works, studies of regional history and chronological surveys (at least 28 of them) based on archival research that related to local events. Among them were the first history of Athens and many fragments of this work survive. This work coupled with the discovery of a papyrus in Egypt of Aristotle's lost work *On the Constitution of Athens* enables the historian to reconstruct the development of one city in antiquity with some accuracy.

On the negative side Thucydides mentioned that his genealogies were full of inconsistencies and that his claim of chronological accuracy was not true. Also Cicero said that his style was lacking in distinction (*On the Orator* 12:5).

CTESIAS OF CNIDUS (FOURTH CENTURY BCE)

Ctesias of Cnidus flourished in the late fourth century BCE. He was the court doctor to Artaxerxes II of Persia. He had been present at the Battle of Cunaxa, along with the historian Xenophon, although on the opposite side. Ctesias wrote an enormously popular, if fanciful work, in Ionic Greek, on the history of Persia which gave inside information and a view of Persia 'breathing seraglio and eunuch perfumes, mixed with the foul stench of blood' (Meyer in *OCD* 198). Sadly the work is lost but was probably the first historical novel.

Ctesias also wrote a pioneering work on India and a geographical treatise. He questioned the accuracy of Herodotus' works on Persia, yet he himself was far from accurate and would invent documents to suit his own agenda.

EPHORUS OF CYME (FOURTH CENTURY BCE)

Another fourth century BCE historian whose works are no longer extant. Ephorus of Cyme wrote a universal history (*Historia*) of Greece in 30 books, which sought to replace all his rivals by beginning with the return of the sons of Heracles and ending in 341 BCE. He is interesting because he tried to delimit the sphere of history from that of myth. He justified his approach in a series of prefaces to individual sections of his works which asserted the unity of history.

He was a pupil of Isocrates (436–338 BCE) and herein lay the danger of sacrificing history for rhetoric. There were other distractions in his work for he often used poetry as evidence for history, but had little judgement in exploiting it and he tried to disguise his dependence on earlier historians by 'modernizing' facts and figures, and where necessary inventing circumstantial detail.

We know about his work mainly because of Diodorus Siculus, whose books 11–16 follow him quite closely. Polybius disliked his style especially when dealing with accounts of battles, and Strabo the Greek geographer (60 BCE – 20 CE), although he used him extensively, complained of his inaccuracies. Momigliano says of him:

> Ephorus' ambition was to produce, not antiquarian details, but a full account of past political and military events for the whole of Greece. A history of this scope has to define its own limits in relation to the mythical age, and was bound to involve an account of foreign nations (or 'barbarians') in their political conflicts and cultural contrasts with the Greeks ... [But] Ephorus was rather the founder of national history, and already displayed ... patriotic prejudice ... In Ephorus universality existed only in the form of excursuses subordinated to Greek history.
>
> (in Finley, *Legacy of Greece* 1981 167)

THEOPOMPUS OF CHIOS (b. 378 BCE)

Another pupil of Isocrates was Theopompus of Chios (b.378 BCE). He wrote many works among which fragments of his *Hellenica* and *Philippica* survive. The *Hellenica* is mainly a continuation of Thucydides and the *Philippica*, a history of the life of Philip of Macedon. These works exposed the corruption and deviousness of Athenian politicians at all periods and the drunken barbarity of the new Macedonian ruler of Greece.

Theopompus foresaw the need to write a new type of history, one that exposed the pretensions of the great and powerful. Polybius attacked him for his belief in miracles, although Dionysius of Halicarnassus wrote favourably about him. He was famous for the severity of his judgements and was quite willing to shock his readers in order to force home moral lessons.

PTOLEMY I SOTER (*c*.367 – *c*.282 BCE)

Ptolemy was a Macedonian general who served under Alexander the Great, and who later became ruler of Egypt, founding the Ptolemaic kingdom and dynasty. In 305/4 BCE he took the title of Pharaoh. Ptolemy served with Alexander from his first campaigns and played a principal role in the later campaigns in Afghanistan and India. He founded the Great Library of Alexandria and he wrote a history of Alexander's campaigns that has not survived. It was considered in antiquity to be an objective work, distinguished by its straightforward honesty. However, Ptolemy may have exaggerated his own role in affairs. Although lost it is a principal source for the surviving account of Arrian of Nicomedia.

HIERONYMUS OF CARDIA (*c*.354 BCE)

Hieronymus was a Greek general and historian from Cardia in Thrace and was a contemporary of Alexander the Great. After Alexander's death he followed his friend and fellow-countryman Eumenes. He was wounded and taken prisoner by Antigonus who later pardoned him and made him superintendent of the asphalt beds in the Dead Sea. Antigonus' son Demetrius made him polemarch of Thespiae. He died at the age of 104.

He wrote a history of the Diadochi and their descendents from the time of the death of Alexander to the war with Phyrrus (323–272 BCE). This work is one of the chief sources of both Diodorus Siculus and Plutarch.

He made use of official papers and was careful in his investigation of facts. His simple style was not popular among his contemporaries but modern historians believe that it was very good. In the last part of his work he attempted to acquaint the Greeks with the character and early history of the Romans. None of his work survived antiquity.

TIMAEUS (c.345 – c.250 BCE)

Timaeus was born at Tauromenium in Sicily but migrated to Athens where he became a pupil of Isocrates the rhetoritician. While in Athens he wrote his *Histories* comprising of roughly 40 books containing the history of Greece from its earliest days up to the First Punic War. The history dealt with the history of Italy and Sicily in early times, Sicily alone, and Sicily and Greece together.

Timeaus gave priority to chronology, and introduced a system of reckoning by Olympiads. In order to plot his chronology he used the names of Archons of Athens, names of Ephors of Sparta, names of winners of stadia races, etc. This system was later utilized by Greek historians. There are only few pieces of this work that remain, which include some fragments of the thirty-eighth book (the life of Agathocles) and a reworking of the last part of the Histories, *On Pyrrhus*, dealing with the life of this king of Epirus until 264 BCE. There is also a possible history of the cities and kings of Syria, and the remaining fragment comprises a chrono-logical sketch ('The Victors at Olympia' which perhaps formed the appendix to the lager work). His work was utilized by many ancient historians and other writers in antiquity. However he was highly criticized by some ancient historians, especially Polybius.

The most serious charge against him was that he distorted the truth when influenced by personal considerations, therefore he was unfair to Dionysius I of Syracuse and Agathocles but heaped great praise on his favourite Timoleon.

Polybius has to admit that Timaeus was thorough in his research and consulted all the available authorities and records, and his attitude to myths, which he claims to have preserved in a simple form, was preferable to the rationalistic approach which had been the favoured genre. Both Dionysius of Halicarnassus and the Pseudo Longinus characterized him as a model of frigidity, although the latter admits that in all other respects he was a competent writer.

Cicero gives a more favourable opinion and was an avid reader of Timaeus' works. He commends his 'copiousness of matter and variety of expression.' Timeaus was also one of the chief authorities used by Gnaeus Pompeius Trogus, Diodorus Siculus, and Plutarch in his life of Timoleon.

APOLLODORUS (*c.*180 – *c.*120 BCE)

Apollodorus was a Greek scholar and grammarian who was a pupil of Diogenes of Babylon, Panatius the Stoic and the grammarian Aristarchus of Samothrace. He left Alexandria around 146 BCE and eventually settled in Athens. His works included the *Chronicle*, a Greek history in verse from the fall of Troy (twelfth century BCE) to roughly 143 BCE, although it was later extended to around 109 BCE and based on the works of Erasosthenes of Cyrene. Its dates are reckoned by references to the archons that held office in Athens for a year at a time.

On the Gods is a detailed history of Greek religion, a 12-book essay on Homer's catalogue of ships, dealing with Homeric geography and how it had changed. The geographer Strabo was heavily reliant on this work for his own *Geographica*. Apollodorus produced many other works which have not survived.

The encyclopedia of Greek mythology called *Bibliotheca* was traditionally thought to have been written by him, but as it cites authors who lived much later it cannot be his. Today the author of the *Bibliotheca* is known as Pseudo-Apollodorus.

POSIDONIUS (135–50 BCE)

Posidonius was a Greek Stoic philosopher, scientist and polymath, born in Apamea in Syria and nicknamed 'the Athlete'. He studied at Athens as a pupil of Panatius and spent many years on scientific travel and research in Europe and Africa. He finally settled on the island of Rhodes where he became an active citizen. In 86 BCE he was sent on an envoy to Rome, to appease Marius, whom he intensely disliked.

He settled in Rome where he became a friend of Cicero and other notable figures of the day. He wrote on a wide variety of subjects including geography, geology, astronomy, meteorology, history and philosophy, although only fragments of his works survive which makes a reconstruction impossible. Of his history the OCD says:

> In his Histories, which were biased in favour of the nobilities, and consequently strongly opposed to the Gracchi and the equestrian party, let alone the 'independent' Greeks, and their supporter Mithridates VI [of Pontus], Posidonius aimed at showing that the Roman empire, embracing as it did all the peoples of the world, embodied the commonwealth of mankind and reflected the commonwealth of God ...

> Thus politics and ethics are one ... His travels and observations enabled him [to make scientific discoveries] ... He showed also a lively interest in poetry, rhetoric, lexicography, geometry etc. ... In the history of ancient thought he can be compared to no one but Aristotle.

> (*Oxford Classical Dictionary* 867)

Posidonius attempted to show that a universal 'sympathy' connected everything in the world and to demonstrate this by uniting history with philosophy. He was aware of the social unrest of the period between 145–63 BCE, and emphasized both the degeneration of the Hellenistic monarchies and the rapacity of the Roman capitalist.

Chapter Seven

The Rise of Rome (502 – 63 BCE)

The Roman Republic was the period of ancient Roman civilization characterized by a republican form of government. It began with the overthrow of the monarchy c.509 BCE and for 482 years until its subversion through a series of civil wars into the Principate form of government and the Imperial period.

The Roman Republic was governed by a complex constitution which centred on the principles of a separation of powers. This was brought about by the struggle between the aristocracy (*patricians*) and the Romans who were not from aristocratic families (*plebeians*). In the early period of the Republic the aristocracy were in control; however, over time the laws that allowed these individuals to control the government were repealed. This resulted in the emergence of a new aristocracy which depended on the structure of society rather than the law to maintain its dominance.

THE PATRICIAN ERA (509–367 BCE)

Before the revolution that overthrew the last king of Rome, Tarquin, a king could be elected by the senators for a life term. Now two consuls were elected annually: each consul would provide a check to his colleague, and their limited term of office would leave them open to prosecution if they misused their powers. However, these consular powers, when exercised jointly, were no different from those of the system of kingship. Therefore in the immediate aftermath of the revolution the senate and the assemblies were as powerless as they had been under the monarchy.

In 494 BCE Rome was at war with two of its neighbouring cities. The plebeian soldiers refused to march against the enemy and instead seceded the Aventine hill. The plebeians demanded the right to elect their own officials and on the agreement of the patricians the soldiers went into battle. The plebeians called these new officials 'plebeian tribunes'. The tribunes would have two assistants called *aediles*. In 367 BCE a law was passed which required the election of at least one *aedile* per year.

In 443 BCE the censorship was created and in 366 BCE the *curule aedileship*, as well as the *praetorship* was created. Shortly after the founding of the Republic the Comitia Centuriata (Assembly of the Centuries) became the principal legislative assembly. In this assembly, magistrates were elected and laws were passed. During the fourth century BCE a series of reforms was passed, with the result that any law passed by the Plebeian Council would have the full force of law. This gave the tribunes (who presided over the Plebeian Council) a more prominent role as previously they only had the power of veto.

CONFLICT OF THE ORDERS (367–287 BCE)

After the consulship had been opened to the plebeians, they were able to hold both the dictatorship and the censorship. In 337 BCE the first plebeian praetor was elected. In 342 BCE two significant laws were passed, one of these made it illegal to hold more than one office at a time; the other required an interval of ten years to pass before any magistrate could seek re-election to any office.

During this time the senate and the tribunes grew close; the senate realized the need to use plebeian officials in order to accomplish their aims. To win the tribunes over the senate gave them more power, and consequently the tribunes had an obligation to the senate. This resulted in plebeian senators securing the *tribunate* for family members, and in time the *tribunate* became a stepping stone to higher offices.

In the middle of the fourth century BCE, the Plebeian Council enacted the 'Ovinian Law' whereby power was given to the censors to appoint new senators (this had previously only been done by consuls). The law also required the censor to appoint any newly elected magistrate to the senate. Despite all the new won power it still remained difficult for any plebeian to enter the senate unless he was from a well-known political family, as a new patrician/plebeian aristocracy started to emerge. The old nobility existed through force of law, because only patricians were allowed to stand for any high office.

By 287 BCE the economic situation of the average plebeian had worsened due mainly to indebtedness. Although the plebeians demanded relief the senators refused to help. The result was the final plebeian secession to the Janiculum Hill. In order to put an end to this a dictator was elected, and he passed a law the 'Hortensian' Law which ended the requirement that the patrician senators must agree before any bill could be considered by the Plebeian Council. The significance of this was that it robbed the patricians of their final weapon over the plebeians. And control of the state now fell on to the shoulders of the plebeian nobility.

No further important political changes occurred during the years 287–133 BCE. The important laws of this era were still enacted by the senate and the plebeian did not bother to use their new powers. This era was dominated by questions of foreign and military policy and so the senate was in control. The final decades of this era saw a worsening of the economic conditions for many plebeians, with many farmers becoming bankrupt. The long military campaigns had forced men to leave their farms to fight which meant that their property became almost derelict. The landed aristocracy took advantage and bought up derelict farms at discounted prices. The result was that many unemployed people flooded to Rome and so into the ranks of the legislative assembly. A culture of dependency was emerging that would look to any populist leader for relief.

FROM THE GRACCHI TO CAESAR (133–49 BCE)

Tiberius Gracchus was elected tribune in 133 BCE. He attempted to enact a law that would have limited the amount of land any one individual could own; this naturally upset the aristocrats who stood to lose considerable sums of money. The law was submitted to the Plebeian Council but was vetoed by a tribune named Marcus Octavius. Tiberius then used the Council to impeach Octavius. Tiberius' law was enacted but he was murdered when he stood for re-election to the tribunate.

Tiberius' brother Gaius was elected tribune in 123 BCE. His ultimate ambition was to weaken the senate and strengthen democratic forces. The senate would eliminate political rivals either by establishing special judicial commissions or by passing a *senatus consultum ultimum* (ultimate decree of the senate). Both these tactics would allow the senate to bypass the ordinary due process rights that all citizens had. Gaius outlawed the judicial commissions, and declared the *senatus consultum ultimum* to be unconstitutional. Gaius then proposed a law which would grant citizenship rights to Rome's Italian allies. He won many enemies in Rome through his actions and when he stood for election to a third term in 121 BCE he was defeated and murdered. Nevertheless, the powers of the senate were now significantly weaker.

In 118 BCE King Micipsa of Numidia (modern Algeria and Tunisia) died and was survived by his two sons Adherbal and Hiempsal, and an illegitimate son Jugurtha. The kingdom was divided between the three sons, but Jugurtha killed Hiempsal and drove Adherbal out of Numidia. Adherbal fled to Rome where Rome intervened and organized a division of the country between the two brothers. However, Jugurtha was not satisfied and renewed his offensive, leading to a long and inconclusive war with Rome. He had bribed several Roman commanders and tribunes both before and during the war. Gaius Marius, a legate from an unknown provincial family returned from the war and was elected consul in 107 BCE. He invaded Numidia and brought the war to a swift conclusion, capturing Jugurtha in the process. The incompetence of the senate was in stark contrast to the brilliance of Marius and the *populares* party took advantage by allying itself with Marius.

In 88 BCE a Roman army was sent to deal with King Mithridates of Pontus and was defeated. One of Marius' old *quaestors*, Lucius Cornelius Sulla, who had been elected consul for the year, was sent to take command of the war with Mithridates. Marius (a member of the *populares* party) had a tribune revoke Sulla's command and Sulla (a member of the aristocratic *optimates* party) was so provoked by this action that he brought his army back to Italy and marched on Rome. Sulla passed a law that permanently weakened the tribunate, before he returned to the war with Mithridates. While he was gone the *populares* under Marius and Lucius Cornelius Cinna took control of the city. With Sulla out of the way the *populares* party flouted convention by re-electing Marius several times without observing the ten year interval between offices. They also transgressed the established oligarchy by advancing unelected individuals to magisterial office, and submitting magisterial edicts for popular legislation.

Sulla made peace with Mithridates and in 83 BCE returned to Rome, overturned the resistance and captured the city. A bloodbath ensued and Sulla and his supporters slaughtered most of the supporters of Marius. He then sought to strengthen the aristocracy and the senate. He made himself dictator and passed a series of constitutional reforms. He then resigned the dictatorship and served one last term of office as consul. He died in 78 BCE.

POMPEY, CRASSUS AND THE CONSPIRACY OF CATILINE

Gnaeus Pompeius Magnus (Pompey the Great was sent by the senate in 77 BCE to put down an uprising in Spain, retuning in 71 BCE as victor. At about the same time another of Sulla's former lieutenants, Marcus Licinius Crassus had just put down the gladiator/slave rebellion led by Spartacus. When both returned from their respective missions they found the *populares* party fiercely attacking Sulla's constitution. They made an agreement with the *populares* that if they were both elected consul in 70 BCE they would dismantle most of the more obnoxious elements of Sulla's constitution. They were duly elected and quickly set about dismantling Sulla's constitution. Around 66 BCE a movement started with the intention of using constitutional means to address the plight of the various classes. The movement met with failure and several of the leaders decided to resort to more drastic measure to affect their aims. The movement coalesced under the aristocrat Lucius Sergius Catiline. The movement began in the rural town of Faesulae, which was a hotbed of agrarian discontent. The plan was for the dissidents to march on Rome where they would be aided by an uprising in the city. After assassinating the consuls and the majority of the senators, Catiline would be free to implement his reforms. The year 63 BCE was the year the uprising began, and the consul for the year was Marcus Tullius Cicero.

Cicero had managed to intercept letters that Catiline had sent, and the conspiracy was put down, with most of the prominent conspirators being put to death by authorization of the senate. Cicero then sent an army which tore Catiline's forces to pieces. The *populares* party was now discredited and the senate regained some of its former strength. However, the days of the Republic were numbered. The middle years of the first century BCE were marked by rivalries between gangs who supported rival politicians. Two men were to come head to head in civil war they were Pompey the Great and Julius Caesar. For much of this period we can follow the daily course of events from the surviving letters of the contemporary politician, Cicero.

Chapter Eight

Roman Historiography

The Greeks had been writing history for three centuries before the first Roman attempted to write historical prose. Early Roman history had been kept alive by oral tradition from the funerary speeches which were committed to memory; they were called *Eulogia* although by their very nature the eulogia would be biased, they supplied information for later writers of Roman history. However, Roman historiographical forms are very different to Greek ones and deal solely with Roman concerns. Unlike their Greek counterpart, Roman historiography did not 'begin' with an oral historical tradition. The style of Roman history was based on the way that the Annals of the Pontifex Maximus (*Annales Maximi*) were recorded. The Annals include a variety of information including, religious documents, names of consuls, and various disasters throughout history. A part of the Annals are the White Tablets (*Tabulae Albatae*), which consist of information on the origin of the Republic.

The most famous originator of Roman history was Quintus Fabius Pictor also known as the 'Founder of Historiography'. There was no historiography before the Second Punic War in Rome but afterwards there was a need to counter the anti Roman writings of Timaeus. Therefore in defence of the Roman state Pictor took up the challenge and wrote in Greek, using the Olympiad dating system and a Hellenistic style. Pictor's style of writing, defending the Roman state and its actions with heavy use of propaganda, eventually became a defining characteristic of Roman historiography.

Pictor is known for the establishment of the *ab urbe condita* tradition, which is writing concerning the history from the founding of the city. Inspired by this new literary form after Pictor many other authors followed his lead. Among them were Lucius Cincius Alimentus, Gaius Acilius, Aulus Postumius, Albinus and Cato the Elder, who was the first to write a history in Latin. Cato's work *Origines* was written to teach Romans what it meant be Roman. He wrote *ab urbe condita* and the early history is filled with legend illustrating Roman virtues. The work spoke of how not only Rome but other Italian cities were venerable and that the Romans were superior to the Greeks. Other examples that can be cited are Livy's *ab urbe condita* which spends a great deal of time on the early history of Rome and the founding of the city, while in Sallust's work the founding of the city and early history of Rome is almost reduced to a single sentence. Therefore the *ab urbe condita* is variable yet at the same time continues to influence Roman histories.

Historiography became very popular among the upper class Roman citizens, and soon became a respectable way to spend one's retirement years. Almost as soon as historiography started it split into two traditions; the annalistic tradition and the monographic tradition.

ANNALISTIC TRADITION

These authors wrote histories year by year from the beginning which was most often from the founding of Rome up to the time that they were writing. Some authors of this style included Gnaeus Gellius, Lucius Calpurnius Piso Frugi, Publius Mucius Scaevola, Sempronius Asellio and Quintus Claudius Quadriarius.

The term 'Gracchan Annalist' seems to refer to the writers of history in annalistic form who began writing after the time of the Gracchi. Compared to other forms of annalistic tradition these seem more fictionalized as Roman historians used their histories to illustrate points about their own time, and were not necessarily used to point out facts. Gracchan Annalists produced insights into their own time frame, if not necessarily on the time they were writing about. Sallust and Tacitus are examples of Gracchan Annalists.

In contrast 'Sullan Annalists' politicized their past they were partisans of the Sullan faction who carried on the conflict between Marius and Sulla throughout their histories, often rewriting them to suit their own agenda.

THE MONOGRAPHIC TRADITION

Monographs have more in common with the type of history that the modern reader is familiar with. They are usually on a single topic, but more importantly do not tell history from the beginning and are not necessarily annalistic. A monograph could be written on any single subject or event. For example Pliny the Elder published a monograph on the use of throwing a spear by cavalry. They were among the most common form of historical works found in Roman writings. An important sub-category that emerged from the monographic tradition was the biography. Some monographic authors include Gaius Gracchus who wrote a biography of his brother Tiberius, Gaius Fannius, Lucius Coelius Antipater and Sallust.

Roman historiography is also known for its subversive styles of writing. Information in the ancient histories is often communicated by suggestion or innuendo because their attitudes would not be well received. Tacitus opposed the emperors and believed they were one of the reasons for the decline of Rome, even writing disparagingly of Augustus, the most beloved of all the emperors. Naturally he would have to hide these opinions because they would not have been well received by his contemporaries.

In Roman historiography *commentarii* is a simple account of events, very often not intended to be published. It was not considered to be traditional history because it lacked speeches and literary flourishes. These *commentarii* were only turned into historical material much later. Many scholars believe that Caesar's account of the Gallic Wars (*Commentarii rerum Gestarum* (Commentaries on Things Done) was called a *commentarii* for reasons of propaganda but that it was actually a history, because it was so well written and fitted the formula for historiographical work.

Roman historians wrote to convince their audiences. There is often an element of propaganda, and this is basically the function of Roman historiography. Roman historians often had personal and political issues, so they were far from detached observers. Their accounts were written with specific moral or political agendas.

Historians also wrote pragmatic histories in order to benefit future statesmen. The philosophy of pragmatic history treats historical events with special reference to causes, conditions and results. Conflict between the facts and the interpretation of those facts indicate a good historian. Polybius who wrote in Greek was the first pragmatic historian. Tacitus was also a pragmatic historian; his works have literary merit and contain interpretations of facts and events. He was not purely objective; rather his judgements served a moral function.

The historiography that we identify as Roman, coming from such writers as Caesar, Sallust, Livy, Tacitus and other minor historians, owes a great deal to their early roots and Greek predecessors. However, the Roman form differed greatly from the Greek, the Roman form included various attitudes and concerns that were strictly Roman. As the recording of Roman history began to evolve and take shape, many characteristics came to define what we now call Roman historiography. These are most notably the strong defence of, and allegiance to, the Roman state and its variety of moral ideals.

Chapter Nine

Qunitus Ennius (239–169 BCE)

Ennius was born in Calabria and was probably of Greek extraction. He is said to have served in the wars and returned from Sardinia to Rome in 204 or 203 BCE with M. Porcius Cato (Cato the Elder); and here he gave lectures on poetry. He also taught Greek and gained the friendship of Scipio Africanus the Elder. He accompanied M. Fulvius Nobilior on his Aetolian campaign in 189 BCE and wrote in praise of his patron's achievements. One of the benefits of such patronage and links with important individuals was that in 184 BCE he was conferred with the rank of Roman citizen.

Ennius composed tragedies, comedies, satires and a number of minor works in addition to his epic *Annals* and was a far more versatile writer than either Plautus or Terence. The *Annals* is perhaps his most important contribution to Latin literature and covers the history of Rome from Aeneas' flight from Troy down to Ennius' own time. The 18 volumes of this history were written during the last 15 years of his life. Only 600 lines now survive and most of them are single lines and not all of them are complete. This is such a small amount from a work that probably consisted of 20,000 lines or more. Many of the surviving lines have only survived because they were quoted by later authors, often to illustrate a linguistic point, or as an Ennian reminiscence in the works of the first-century poet, Virgil.

We cannot always be sure of their context, and so only the barest outline remains in order to reconstruct the sequence of events of the book of *Annals*: what does survive, however, indicates that the loss of this work could be the greatest loss to classical studies.

Ennius' most important contribution was the hexameter, the traditional metre of Greek epic. He was not the first to write an epic in Latin, this had been done by Livius Andronicus who had written a translation of the *Odyssey*, and Naevius had written an epic about the First Punic War toward the end of the third century BCE. However, these two works had been written in the Saturnian metre, which was rather ungainly. Ennius introduced the hexameter which was more smooth and flowing in Latin epic, accompanied by a poetic diction which served as a basis for the style of his successors.

The beginning of the *Annals* states that Ennius believed himself to be the reincarnation of Homer who had revealed this fact to him in a dream. Indeed many features of his epic were Homeric: a council of the gods, battle descriptions and similes. Yet in fairness there is much that is very different to Homer in this work, especially at the beginning of the work where Ennius discusses his own poetic activities. There is a further autobiographical passage in Book VII, where Ennius contrasts his own craftsmanship with the crude attempts of his predecessors. In later years his style would also appear crude but it is clear that he devoted some care to his own awareness of his role as a pioneer. There is also a moralizing streak in his work which no doubt helped establish him in the school curriculum until the time of Virgil.

Over half of what survives of the *Annals* (approximately 600 lines) is devoted to the major event of Ennius' own lifetime, the Second Punic War and the subsequent expansion of Roman power, which was in itself a remarkable achievement. Ennius glorifies the military achievements of the Roman nobility while at the same time supports traditional Roman morality. He praises individual virtue as the following example, the famous lines about Q. Fabius Maximus Cunctator shows:

One man by his delays restored our nation.
Our weal he put before his reputation.
Thus now his glory shines more brightly yet
In later years ...

Glorification of an individual was perhaps not in the best Roman tradition but the heroes of the *Annals* displayed virtues that were much admired by Romans. Other passages, for instance show the disruptive effects of war.

> Wisdom is driven out: violence holds sway.
> Sound speakers scorned, rough soldiers have their day.
> No longer with abuse or skilful speech
> Do men express their hatred, each to each.
> But now with weapons, not with writs, they fight;
> They strive to rule, press on with massive might.

Ennius set the tone for Latin hexameter writing for the next century and a half. Lucretius and Virgil were considerably influenced by him, and if more of his work survived then it could perhaps help to shed more light on theirs.

Chapter Ten

Cato (Marcus Porcius Cato / Cato The Elder) (234–149 BCE)

> After I'm dead I'd rather have people ask why I have no monument than why I have one.
>
> (*Quotations*)

Cato was born in Tusculum from an ancient Plebeian family. His ancestors had been named Marcus Porcius but Plutarch tells us that at first he was known by the additional cognomen *Priscus* (the Ancient), but was afterwards called Cato, indicating 'a practical wisdom which is the result of a natural sagacity'. The qualities embedded in the word Cato were acknowledged by the plainer title of *Sapiens* by which he was so well known in his old age; Cicero remarks that it became his virtual cognomen. From the eloquence and number of his speeches he was styled orator, but Cato the Censor (*Cato Censorius*), and Cato the Elder are now the most common names by which he is known.

Cato is famous not only as a statesman and soldier but also as an author. He was an historian, the first Latin prose writer of note, and the first author of a history of Italy in Latin. Some have argued that if it were not for the impact of Cato's writing Latin may have been supplanted by Greek as the literary language of Rome. He was one of the few early Latin authors who could claim Latin as a native language.

Cato attracted the attention of Lucius Valerius Flaccus, a young nobleman of influence from a high Patrician family and he encouraged Cato to go to Rome and take up a political career. In 205 BCE Cato was appointed Quaestor and in the following year he followed Publius Cornelius Scipio Africanus Major to Sicily. Cato's appointment was intended to monitor Scipio's behaviour, and Plutarch (*Life of Cato the Elder* 3) reports that lax discipline of the troops under Scipio's command, and the exaggerated expense incurred by the general, provoked the protest of Cato causing him to return to Rome. At the joint request of Cato and Fabius a commission of tribunes was sent to Sicily to examine Scipio's behaviour, where he was found not guilty of the accusations brought against him.

However, the account provided by Livy (*History of Rome* XXIX 19) indicates that Cato was in the wrong, quitting his post before his time. If Livy is correct the commission was sent because of the complaints of the people of Locri who had been harshly treated by Scipio's legate. Livy does not mention Cato's interference in this matter, but he does note the bitterness of Fabius who blamed Scipio for corrupting military discipline and having illegally left his province to take the town of Locri.

In 199 BCE Cato was chosen as aedile, and with his colleague Helvius restored the Plebeian Games. In 198 BCE he was made praetor and obtained Sardinia as his province with the command of 3,000 infantry and 200 cavalry. The author of the abridged work on the life of Cato, generally considered to be Cornelius Nepos, asserts that Cato after his return from Africa, put in at Sardinia, and brought the poet Quintus Ennius in his own ship from the island to Italy. However, it would seem that Cato and Ennius met much later when Cato was Praetor in Sardinia.

In 195 BCE he was elected consul with his friend and patron Flaccus. During his consulship an odd incident took place, noticeably expounding of Roman manners. In 215 BCE at the height of the Second Punic War, the *Lex Oppia* (Oppian Law) had been passed at the request of the tribune of the plebs Gaius Oppius, to restrict luxury and extravagance on the part of women. The law specified that no woman should own more than half an ounce of gold, nor wear a garment of several colours, or drive a carriage with horses at less distance than a mile from the city, except for the purpose of attending the public celebration of religious rites. The tribunes Marcus Fundanius and Lucius Valerius proposed that it was time to abolish the Oppian law but were opposed by their colleagues Marcus Junius Brutus and Titus Junius Brutus.

The women of Rome crowded the streets and denied access to every avenue to the Forum, pleading with their husbands. They even implored the praetors, consuls and other magistrates. Flaccus hesitated but his colleague Cato was adamant and made an impolite speech which was remodelled and modernized by Livy (*History of Rome* XXXIV 1,8). Finally the women had their way and the hated law was repealed by a vote of all the tribes. On the conclusion of this affair, Cato who had maintained a severe opposition without and caused serious damage to his popularity, set sail for his appointed province Hispania Citerior.

In his campaign in Hispania Cato behaved according to his reputation. He worked hard, lived soberly, sharing the food and labours of the common soldier. His stratagems and manoeuvres were accounted as original and successful. The details of his campaign are supplied by Livy and make it clear that he reduced Hispania Citerior to subjection with great speed and little mercy. The phrase *bellum se ipsum alet* (war feeds itself) was coined by Cato during this period. On account of his achievements in Hispania the senate decreed a thanksgiving ceremony of three days and in 194 BCE he returned to Rome and was awarded a triumph.

However, Cato's military career was not ended. In 191 BCE he was appointed military tribune, under the Consul Glabrio who was dispatched to Greece to oppose the invasion of Antiochus III the great, King of the Seleucid Empire. In the decisive Battle of Thermopylae which led to Antiochus' downfall Cato behaved with his usual valour, the general hugged Cato and attributed the victory to him. From the date of his censorship (184 BCE) until his death Cato held no further public office but distinguished himself in the senate as a persistent opponent of new ideas. In his last years he constantly urged his fellow Romans to destroy Carthage, in what was to become the Third Punic War. Despite the unsuccessful mission he continued to repeat, what has now become his most famous quote:

Ceterum censeo Carthaginem esse delend est
Futhermore I think Carthage must be destroyed.

His manual on running a farm *De Agri Cultura* (On Farming) is the only work of Cato's that completely survives. It is a miscellaneous collection of rules of husbandry and management, and includes snippets on country life in the second century BCE. This work was used as a text book by many Romans who wished to expand their farms and turn them into profitable businesses. The work makes the assumption that the farms would be managed and run by slaves whom Cato treats rather harshly. He laid out advice on how to keep slaves continually at work, and on reducing rations for sick slaves, and that owners should sell any who were too old or sickly. The work was intended to be read aloud and discussed and was very popular and much quoted by later authors.

Probably Cato's most important work was *Origines* a historical work in seven books, which does not survive, except for fragments quoted by later Latin authors. This highly original work was the first prose history in Latin, and among the first prose works of any genre. Along with Livius Andronicus, Naevius, Ennius and Plautus, Cato helped to found a new form of literature.

There were already two historical works in Latin by Naevius and Ennius but they were in verse not prose. Also there were two existing prose histories by Romans, Quintus Fabius Pictor and Lucius Cincius Alimentus, but they were written in Greek. All four works focused specifically on Rome; moreover the two poems wove Roman history inextricably into the adventures of the Greco-Roman gods. In *Origines* Cato chose to do things differently.

I do not care to copy out what is on the High Priest's tablet; how many times grain became dear, how many times the sun or moon were obscured or eclipsed.

(*Origines* frag. 4.1)

According to Cato's biographer Cornelius Nepos the work was divided into seven books. The first dealt with the history of the early Kings of Rome; the second and third books the beginnings of each Italian city, which dealt with each city individually and drew on their local tradition. The final four books dealt with Rome's later wars and growth in the city's power (Nepos, *Life of Cato* 3).

Cato's own achievements were not downplayed, that was not in his nature and the work included several of his own speeches verbatim. He made it a rule not to mention military commanders by name, yet the surviving fragments give the impression that Cato's campaigns were given special mention.

Under the Roman Empire a collection of roughly 150 of Cato's political speeches existed. In them he pursued his political policies, fought verbal vendettas and opposed what he viewed as Rome's moral decline. Not all the titles of these speeches are known but some fragments are preserved. The first one which can be dated was *On the Improper Election of the Aediles* delivered in 202 BCE. The collection included several speeches from the year of his consulship, followed by a self justifying retrospect *On His Consulship* and numerous speeches delivered when he was Censor. It is not clear whether the speeches were published during his lifetime or whether they only became available after his death.

Cato also wrote *On Soldiery*, possibly a practical manual similar to the *De Agri Cultura, On the Law Relating to Priests and Augurs* of which only one brief extract remains, and *Praecepta ad Filium* (Maxims addressed to his son), from which the following extract survives

> In due course, my son Marcus, I shall explain what I found out in Athens about these Greeks, and demonstrate what advantage there may be in looking into their writings (while not taking them too seriously). They are a worthless and unruly tribe. Take this as a prophecy: when those folk give us their writings they will corrupt

everything. All the more if they send their doctors here. They have sworn to kill all barbarians with medicine-and they charge a fee for doing it, in order to be trusted and to work more easily. They call us barbarians, too, of course and Opici a dirtier name than the rest. I have forbidden you to deal with doctors.

(Quoted by Pliny the Elder, *Naturalis Historia* 29: 13–14)

For Cato life was a continual discipline and public life was the discipline of the many. Family life was equated with the life of the state. He used his time economically and accomplished a huge amount of work and expected the same from his dependants making him a harsh husband and father, as well as a severe master. To the Romans there was little in his behaviour that seemed worthy of censure; indeed he was respected as an example of Roman traditional manners. Livy (XXXIX) describes the character of Cato and lays no blame on him for the rigid discipline of his household.

Chapter Eleven

Polybius (c.200–123 BC)

Who is so thoughtless and irresponsible as not to wish to know by what means, and under what constitution, the Romans succeeded in subjugating the whole inhabited world to their sole rule in not quite fifty-three years – an event unique in history.

(*History*, Book I, 1.5)

As an historian Polybius follows his predecessors inasmuch as his choice of the theme, the rise of Rome, is designed to demonstrate the impact of the non-Greek world upon Greece. The theme of Herodotus' *Histories* had been the conflict between the two nations of Greece and Persia, culminating with the battles of Plataea and Salamis which finally eliminated the danger to Greece posed by Persia. Even though Thucydides' work makes little reference to Persia, the Peloponnesian War had brought the Empire back into Greek politics. To most Greeks, however, Philip II of Macedon was to pose an even greater threat to Greek unity. A prophecy by Demetrius of Phalerum had foretold that just as the Macedonians had overthrown the Persian Empire, so they (the Macedonians) would in turn be overthrown and yield their mastery to another country. This is the event that Polybius believed he had witnessed in his lifetime.

Polybius was born at Megalopolis in Arcadia around 200 BCE. His father was a wealthy landowner who was friendly with the leader of the Achaean League, and had travelled as ambassador to Rome and Egypt. When he came of age, Polybius also entered public life and accompanied his father when he visited Egypt. He served as a cavalry officer of the League with the intention of fighting on the side of Rome during the Third Macedonian War

(172–68 BCE), but the Romans distrusted the League and rejected the force, deporting about a thousand Achaeans, including Polybius, to Italy.

Polybius was slightly more fortunate than some of his compatriots for he managed to become a tutor to the two sons of Lucius Aemilius Paullus, building a close friendship with the younger son, Scipio Africanus. During this period of his life Polybius made important connections with the elite of Roman society. He also made important connections with other detainees, one of whom was the future King Demetrius I of Syria, and it seems that with Polybius' instigation and planning Demetrius succeeded in boarding a ship at Ostia and sailed back to claim his kingdom (Book XXXI).

In 151 BCE Polybius left for Spain and North Africa with Scipio and in the following year he and 300 other deportees were finally, after a 16-year exile, allowed to return to Greece. The climate in Achaea was not favourable to those exiles that had made important contacts with the Roman aristocracy, so Polybius may have been in no great hurry to return home. When the Third Punic War broke out in 149 BCE, he went with Scipio to Africa and was there when Carthage fell in 146 BCE, advising on siege operations and exploring the coast of Africa.

Two years later the Romans suppressed the Achaean League and ravaged Corinth, its capital. When the Romans destroyed Corinth and re-founded it as a Roman colony, Polybius was given the authority to reorganize the region under Roman control which he set about doing.

Polybius states his purpose for writing his *History* on many occasions, which was to write a world history that would be of use. He wanted to impress on his fellow countrymen the significance of Rome by giving an explanation of the Roman constitution and growth of power, so that those Greeks who were regularly coming into contact with Roman envoys would have some knowledge of who they were dealing with during a pivotal period of Greek history, when, as Momigliano (*Legacy of Greece* 1981) says, 'for the first time in their history the Greeks realized their complete loss of independence.' The secondary aim was to show the principle of cause and effect. His work is five times the length of Thucydides' *History*, and he would have worked on it for about 50 years.

The *History* comprises about 40 books of which only the first five have survived intact with fragments remaining of the others. Polybius was writing in Greek for a Greek and Roman audience. But although he suggests that Roman readers were his main concern there is one passage which would suggest that they were not. The passage deals with a discussion of the integrity of Aemilius Paullus, a sort of obituary, in Book XXXI, where after saying that Aemilius died a poor man despite opportunities for gaining wealth he continues,

> ... if anyone considers what I say to be incredible he should bear in mind that I am perfectly well aware that the present work will be perused by Romans above all people, because it contains an account of their most glorious achievements, and that it is impossible that they should be either ignorant of the facts or disposed to pardon any departure from the truth.

It seems that this passage is primarily aimed at a Greek audience and other instances of this can be seen in many other references to internal Greek affairs throughout the work. But without a doubt his work was valued in ancient times, especially by the Romans.

His original plan had been to record the rise of Rome to supremacy over the Mediterranean states during the period 220–168 BCE, from the beginning of the Second Punic War to the Third Macedonian War. He later extended the work to include the beginning of the First Punic War in 264 BCE and continue down to 146 BCE to the destruction of Carthage and Corinth.

Polybius was a cautious and practical writer. As a man of action he was very aware of the necessity to gain first hand evidence rather than rely on hearsay. He also made a special study of geography, as he had been so widely travelled himself. Book

XXXIV is almost entirely geographical, recording his visits whether official or unofficial to various countries, where he examined records and documents to make his work correct. In such matters he was always meticulous and generally correct in his conclusions. He was a seeker of truth as he tells us: 'For as a living creature is rendered wholly useless if deprived of its eyes, so if you take truth from history, what is left but an idle unprofitable tale?'

Polybius was a man typical of his age. As a native of Megalopolis, a city which had been founded as an experiment in federal unity, Polybius as an aristocrat had no sympathy with democratic survivals or demagogues. As a statesman he realized that the old idea of Greek freedom and independence, centred round the city-state, was no longer viable. Early on he had seen that Roman power would be inevitable and he attempted to use skilful diplomacy to keep the Achaean League and the Greeks in general on a path that would be acceptable. Polybius was a Stoic and believed that the Roman order of things was part of a divine Providence that ruled the world. Awe of the supernatural, he said, helps maintain cohesion and religion helps pacify the common man's anarchic temper. Rome's patriarchal tradition and its religion Polybius saw as the cohesive factors in establishing Rome's success.

Polybius understood the value that religion played in society, by which example Gaius Flaminius (consul 223 BCE) had failed. He also allotted a dominant role to Fortune (*Tyche*) and in this way he avoided any complete commitment to philosophy or religion, for he recognized the fact that events were often decided by accident. Although interested in causation, he was not attentive enough to economic or social causes.

According to Polybius, discipline provided another prominent factor in securing Roman supremacy. He noted that they were willing to enforce punishments such as executing a sentry for neglecting his duty or beating a soldier with a cudgel for throwing away his weapon, for boasting, or for being a homosexual. Decimation (the killing of every tenth man) in a military unit that had displayed cowardice, he saw as strength of character. He firmly believed that Rome's success was in part the result of its superior institutions and in part the result of its superior people. He believed the Romans had the virtues of moderation, integrity, valour, boldness, discipline, frugality in greater amounts than any other peoples. It was these qualities that enabled the Romans to unite when faced with any threat. Although he saw the Greeks as more literate and educated, their propensity for argument and division had weakened them in the face of danger. Polybius saw the superiority of the Romans belonging only to the aristocrats. Common people whatever their race Polybius viewed as less noble in character, and the rebellion of the common folk of Greece against Rome he viewed as insane folly, believing that despite its abuse, Rome had bestowed great benefits upon the Greeks. . These beliefs were confirmed for him by his close contact with the Romans and their conquests and his *History* expounds the causes and consequences of these actions. Although Rome lies at the heart of Polybius' work, this is not to say that he always held the same view about it throughout his life.

The *History* was divided up into Olympiad years, an idea he got from Timaeus, an earlier historian. This system had advantages in this era for indicating intervals of time. However, if Polybius had used it strictly it would have been disadvantageous because his narrative contains much military campaigning and of necessity they would have had to have been split between two Olympiad years. For modern readers of course there is a further disadvantage because we have no evidence for the dates of the Olympic Games except that they fell at a full moon in high summer.

Whether he recounts a campaign in Spain (Book III), Africa or Italy, Polybius would have enough information to say whether the event fell before or after the Olympic Games in an Olympic year, what was more difficult to ascertain was whether it fell before or after the arbitrary date in summer that separated one year from another Olympiad year. However, what Polybius did was to manipulate the Olympiad year to allow him to continue with a campaign to the end of the summer in which it had begun so to have it all in the same year. This had the added benefit for Greek readers, as each state had its own dating system, of coinciding roughly with the end of Aetolian 'general' year, which was the end of year of the Aetolian magistrate, and the Achaean year as well.

This system proved very useful as Polybius could operate with some flexibility, for example in Books III–IV he recounts the events of Olympiad 140 (220–16 BCE). For Greece and Asia Minor he ends in the summer of 216 BCE, but he concludes with the death of L. Postimius Albinus who fell at the end of 216 BCE when he was consul designate for 215 BCE, but Polybius included it in the Olympiad year 140 BCE to complete the story of the battle of Cannae. Another example can be seen in Book VIII where in order to round of the Sicilian campaign Polybius included events beyond the fourth Olympiad year and even beyond the normal campaigning season. Polybius would usually conclude at the most logical point, the winter quartering of troops at the end of a season's campaign, the end of a campaign, or a decisive battle and then start the next Olympiad year from there.

Polybius divided historians into three classes, those who wrote for pay to accommodate the ideas of their patrons; those who wrote for rhetorical display and those who wrote for truth and the good of mankind. Although he appreciated the use of rhetoric he attempted to avoid it in his work for fear that he may fail to tell the whole truth. He expressed very strong views about the need to reproduce speeches as accurately as possible and he accused other writers, notably Phylarchus, Chaereas and Sosylus of inserting fictitious speeches or as he called it, 'gossip of the barber's shop'. No doubt he knew that in Greek-speaking lands speeches had a marked effect upon actions.

Polybius felt spurred on to write his version of what history should be about; although he declared that only the true words should be recorded he did invent some speeches himself. He also occasionally wrote in an emotive fashion; one example is the account of Hasdrubal's surrender at the fall of Carthage, and the reproach made to him by his wife and fellow citizens (Book XXXVIII: 20). In fact he excuses his emotional outburst in Book XXXVIII where he went to great lengths to show that of all the ruins that had befallen Greece in her long history, nothing was quite as calamitous as that which he had witnessed in his own lifetime.

Polybius had a great deal to say about the historians of the Hellenistic age, whose writings have not survived. He disliked Phylarchus because of his sympathies for Sparta and the emotive way in which he wrote. He also held in low regard any historian who resorted to telling fabulous tales, like Zeno of Rhodes or Ptolemy of Megalopolis. Polybius saw that there was a clear distinction between tragedy and history. As he said

> For the object of tragedy is not the same as history but quite the opposite ... In the one case it is the probable that takes precedence, even if it is untrue, the purpose being to create illusion to spectators; in the other it is the truth, the purpose being to confer benefit on learners

> (Book II, 5)

This was the prime motivation for Polybius to write, to denounce the growing tendency to write history in the style of tragedy.

Overall his vocabulary is ordinary and his statements clear yet because of this his work is rarely remarkable or attractive to the modern reader. Nevertheless he was thought in ancient times to have exemplified every virtue of history, and he was often quoted. His works were compressed into epitomes and reproduced in excerpts. Unfortunately for modern historians what was considered suitable for survival in an epitome for that particular generation cannot necessarily give us a complete picture of the man or his work.

Polybius wrote other minor works. *The Numantine War*, composed sometime after 133 BCE which is now lost and a treatise on *Tactics*, which is referred to in Book IX. Without Polybius' writings we would know very little about the third and second centuries BCE. A sportsman to the end Polybius met his death by an accidental fall from a horse as he was returning from the country; he was 82 years old.

However, most significantly of all, he has supplied posterity with a remarkable account of the rise of Roman power in the Mediterranean. One of his doctrines, that of the mixed constitution, which in his view was responsible for Rome's success, exercised a powerful influence in the early days of the United States of America. John Adams often referred to him and because of Polybius the constitution of the USA contains the separate powers limited by a system of balances and checks that have contributed to its continuing strength.

Chapter Twelve

From Republic to Empire

In 62 BCE Pompey returned victorious from Asia, but the senate refused to ratify the arrangements that Pompey had made, which in effect made Pompey powerless. So, when Julius Caesar returned from his governorship in Spain in 61 BCE he made his own arrangements with Pompey. Caesar, Pompey and Crassus established a private agreement, known as the First Triumvirate, whereby Pompey's arrangements could be ratified. The other agreements were that Caesar would be elected consul in 59 BCE, and would then serve as governor in Gaul for five years, Crassus was also promised a future consulship.

As planned Caesar became consul in 59 BCE and he submitted the laws that he had promised to the assemblies. He came up against opposition from Marcus Calpurnius Bibulus, so Caesar used violent means to ensure their passage. Caesar was then made governor of three provinces. He also facilitated the election of the former patrician Publius Clodius Pulcher to the tribunate in 58 BCE. Clodius set about depriving Caesar's senatorial enemies, especially Cicero. Cicero had testified against him in a sacrilege case and so Clodius attempted to have Cicero tried for executing citizens without trial during the Catiline conspiracy. Cicero went into self-imposed exile and his house in Rome was burnt to the ground. Clodius also passed a bill that forced Cato to lead the invasion of Cyprus which would remove him from Rome for many years. However, Clodius overstepped the mark when he formed armed gangs that terrorised the city. They attacked the followers of Pompey, and soon the political alliance of the triumvirate began to crumble.

The triumvirate was renewed at Luca and Pompey and Crassus were promised the consulship in 55 BCE and Caesar's term as governor was extended for five years. Crassus led an ill-fated expedition with legions led by his son, who was Caesar's lieutenant against the Parthians. This resulted in his defeat and death at the battle of Carrhae. Finally Caesar's daughter and wife of Pompey, Julia, died in childbirth; this event severed the last remaining bond between Pompey and Caesar.

The summer of 54 BCE saw a wave of political corruption and violence sweeping Rome, which reached a climax in January 52 BCE when Clodius was murdered in a gang war with Milo. On 1st January 49 BCE an agent of Caesar presented an ultimatum to the senate; it was rejected and the senate passed a resolution which declared that if Caesar did not lay down his arms by July of that year he would be considered an enemy of the people.

On 7 January 49 BCE the senate passed a *senatus consultum ultimum* which vested Pompey with dictatorial powers. On the 10th January Caesar in defiance of Roman law marched his troops across the Rubicon and marched on Rome. Caesar's rapid advance forced Pompey, the consuls and the senate to abandon Rome for Greece: Caesar entered the city unopposed.

With Pompey vanquished Caesar wanted to ensure that his control over the government was undisputed. The powers that he gave himself would ultimately be used by his successors. Caesar held the dictatorship and the tribunate, but alternated between the consulship and the proconsulship. In 48 BCE Caesar was given permanent tribunican powers. This gave him power to veto the senate and allowed him to dominate the Plebeian Council. In 46 BCE Caesar was given censorial powers which he used to fill the senate with his own partisans, and he raised membership of the senate to 900. This act robbed the senatorial aristocracy of its prestige and made it increasingly subservient to him. Even the assemblies became powerless and unable to oppose him because he submitted all candidates to the assemblies and all bills to the assemblies for enactment.

Caesar was preparing for a war with Parthia, and so he passed a law which allowed him to appoint all magistrates in 43 BCE and all consuls and tribunes in 42 BCE. This transformed the magistrates from being representatives of the people to being representatives of the dictator.

Caesar was assassinated in the senate chamber on 15 March 44 BCE; the conspirators were personal and political and were led by Gaius Cassius and Marcus Brutus. The majority of the conspirators were senators who were angry that Caesar had deprived the senate of much of its power. Others believed he wished to make himself king, so they decided to destroy him before he made himself invulnerable. The civil war that ensued destroyed what was left of the Republic.

THE SECOND TRIUMVIRATE

Following Caesar's death Mark Antony his right hand man formed an alliance with Caesar's adopted son and great nephew Gaius Octavian. With the assistance of Marcus Lepidus they formed the Second Triumvirate and held powers that were almost the same as Caesar had held before his death. The senate and the assemblies still remained powerless. The conspirators were defeated at the Battle of Philippi in 42 BCE.

In 36 BCE Octavian was given the power of a Plebeian Tribune which gave him power of veto over the senate and the ability to control the Plebeian Council. In 32 BCE the triumvirate ended, torn apart by the competing ambitions of its members. Lepidus was forced into exile and Antony, who had joined forces with his lover, Cleopatra of Egypt, committed suicide in 30 BCE after his defeat by Octavian at the Battle of Actium. Octavian annexed Egypt into the Roman Empire.

Octavian was now the sole ruler of Rome and he began a full scale reformation of military, fiscal and political matters. In 29 BCE he was given the authority of a Roman censor and therefore the power to appoint new senators. The senate also granted him a unique grade of proconsular *imperium,* giving him authority over all proconsuls, who were the military governors of the Empire.

These powers were the same that his uncle Caesar had held when he was dictator. The provinces at the frontiers where the vast majority of the legions were stationed were now under the control of Octavian; however their numbers were reduced from 50 to 28 legions. Octavian also created nine special cohorts to keep the peace in Italy, keeping three stationed in Rome who became known as the Praetorian Guard.

In 27 BCE Octavian offered to hand control back to the senate but they refused, they offered him the title of 'Augustus' and also took the title *Princeps* or 'first citizen'. As the adopted heir of Caesar, Octavian, now referred to as Augustus, took Caesar as a component of his name. By the time of the emperor Vespasian (69 CE) the term Caesar had evolved into a formal title.

Augustus invested heavily in reshaping the city of Rome with massive building works that advertised his rule, while poets sang his praises and that of the new Rome. He completed the conquest of Hispania while subordinate generals expanded Roman possessions in Africa and Asia Minor. Augustus' final task was to ensure the succession of his powers and to that effect Augustus granted tribunican powers to his stepson Tiberius in 6 CE, and soon afterwards recognized him as his heir. After ruling the Empire for 40 years Augustus died in 14 CE.

TIBERIUS TO SEVERUS ALEXANDER (14–235 CE)

Historians refer to the period 14–68 CE as the Julio/Claudian dynasty because of the *gens* of Julia (the Julian family) to which Augustus belonged and the *gens* Claudia (from Augustus' second wife Livia, mother of Tiberius). The early years of Tiberius' reign were relatively peaceful. However, the new emperor became paranoid and began a series of treason trials and executions, known as the 'Reign of Terror', which continued to his death in 37 CE. The successor to the much-hated Tiberius was his 24-year-old grandnephew, Gaius nicknamed Caligula. His reign began well enough but deteriorated when after an illness he became tyrannical and insane. In 41 CE he was assassinated by members of the Praetorian Guard and for two days the senate debated the merits of restoring the Republic.

However, the army intervened and installed Caligula's uncle Claudius as emperor, perhaps the first true emperor having been elected by popular demand? Claudius was able to administer the Empire with reasonable ability and during his reign the new Roman port of Ostia was constructed, and the invasion of Britain undertaken.

His family life was not so successful; his second wife Messalina was guilty of trying to have him assassinated, and his last wife, his niece Agrippina, may well have poisoned him in order to install her son Nero in his place.

Nero did indeed succeed him; however he was no more than a tyrant and was forced to kill himself in 68 CE. The Empire was once again plunged into civil war, a period known as the 'Year of the Fours Emperors'.

Augustus had established a standing army, where individual soldiers served under the same military governors over an extended period of time. The consequence was that the soldiers in the provinces developed strong loyalties to the commanders, which they did not necessarily have for the emperor. Therefore, the Empire in a way was nothing more than a series of inchoate principalities. Between June 68 CE and December 69 CE Rome witnessed the successive rise and fall of Galba, Otho and Vitellius. The war came to a close when Vespasian finally became emperor and showed that any successful general could quite legitimately claim a right to the throne.

Vespasian was a successful emperor and established the Flavian dynasty; however, the state continued to weaken despite his sound fiscal policy. During his reign the Jewish Revolt broke out and the Colosseum was constructed. His successor, his son Titus, proved his merit despite his short reign. He captured the city of Jerusalem and put an end to the revolt there, and held the opening ceremonies in the still unfinished Colosseum. He died in 81 CE and was succeeded by his brother Domitian who was also a tyrant and suffered from some kind of insanity. Finally his poor relations with the senate brought Rome to the verge of even more disaster when one of Domitian's slaves murdered him in September 96 CE. Nerva succeeded him and set a new standard; he restored much confiscated property and involved the senate in his rule.

After the disasters of the previous century the second century became known as the period of the 'Five Good Emperors' in which the successions were peaceful and prosperous. Emperors were now adopted by their predecessor, which meant that the best man for the job held power. This period is known as the Antonine period and its first ruler in 101 CE was Trajan, who undertook two military campaigns against the gold-rich Dacia, which he conquered in 106 CE. In 112 CE Trajan marched on Armenia and annexed it to the Roman Empire; then he turned his attention to Parthia, taking many cities en route before declaring Mesopotamia a new province of Rome. During his rule the Empire expanded to its furthest extent. Hadrian's reign was marked by a general lack of major military conflicts, but there was the need to defend the vast territories that Trajan had acquired.

The reign of Antoninus Pius was also fairly peaceful. During the reign of Marcus Aurelius, Germanic tribes launched many attacks on the northern border. The period of the 'Five Good Emperors' (also known as the *Pax Romana* Roman Peace) was finally brought to a close by Commodus, the son of Marcus Aurelius, breaking the tradition of adopted successors that had been so beneficial. Once again another insane and paranoid emperor ruled until his murder in 192 CE.

The Severan dynasty which lasted from 193–235 CE included several troubled reigns. Septimius Severus the first of the dynasty was generally a successful ruler. He cultivated the support of the army and substituted equestrian officers for senators in key administrative positions. His son Caracalla extended full Roman citizenship to all free inhabitants of the Empire. Caracalla was, however, highly unstable and autocratic and was assassinated by

Macrinus who succeeded him before being killed and succeeded by Elagabalus. Alexander Severus the last of the dynasty was unable to control the army and he also was assassinated in 235 CE. The crisis of the third century is the terminology applied to the near collapse of the Empire between 235–84 CE. During this period no less than 25 emperors reigned and the Empire experienced extreme military, political and economic crises. Also the Plague of Cyprian broke out causing heavy mortality which may have reduced the Empire's capacity for defence. This period ended with the accession of Diocletian who reigned from 284–305 CE. Diocletian saw the Empire as unmanageable as a single unit and therefore split the Empire into two halves and created two equal emperors to rule under the title of *Augustus*. In so doing he effectively created what would become the Western Roman Empire and the Eastern Roman Empire.

In 293 CE authority was further divided when each *Augustus* employed a junior emperor called a *Caesar* to provide a line of succession. This constituted what is now known as the 'Tetrarchy' (rule of four). The transitions of this period mark the beginnings of Late Antiquity.

The Tetrarchy collapsed with the death of Constantius Chlorus in 306 CE. Constantius' troops immediately proclaimed his son Constantine I, (also known as the Great), *Augustus*. A series of civil wars then ensued, which ended with the entire Empire being united under Constantine, who legalized Christianity in 313 CE through the *Edict of Milan*.

Chapter Thirteen

Gaius Julius Caesar (100–44 BCE)

> They are like nude figures upright and beautiful, stripped of all
> ornament of style as if they had removed a garment. His aim was
> to provide source material for others who might wish to write
> history, and perhaps he has gratified the insensitive, who may
> wish to use their curling tongs on his work; but men of good sense
> he has deterred from writing.
>
> (Cicero, *Brutus* 262)

Julius Caesar is probably the most well known of all historical
figures, his military skills are renowned and his associations with
some of the colourful characters of the ancient world, Pompey,
Mark Antony and Cleopatra, is the stuff of legend. He came from
a patrician background, but both his father and uncle and been
supporters of Marius who was married to his aunt, Julia, and for
this reason the family were regarded as *populares* (radicals) by the
optimates (good men). The *optimates* were conservative supporters
of the senatorial oligarchy.

Caesar grew up during the time of the proscriptions of Marius
and the dictatorship and proscriptions of Sulla. In 83 BCE he
married the daughter of Cinna and so incurred the hostility of
Sulla. During this early dictatorship Caesar nearly lost his life
because of his connection with the Marian faction; however, he
survived and spent the next ten years without any major incidents,
building up a network of friendships within the nobility until in
73 BCE he was co-opted into the college of priests. Two years later
he was supporting Pompey, who was working against the Sullan
constitution.

Initially he had decided to become a lawyer and had travelled to the island of Rhodes to become a pupil of the rhetorician Apollonius Molon. On his way there he was captured by a group of pirates, and disappointed by the small amount asked for his ransom he negotiated terms for himself, and so obtained his release. Later in 75/4 BCE he captured the pirates and had them crucified. When he returned to Rome he married for a second time, the granddaughter of Sulla, the enemy of Marius, and began to pursue a political career. In furtherance of his career he was backed by the wealthy landowner Marcus Crassus and subsequently became *Pontifex Maximus* (Chief Priest), governor of Further Spain and finally in 60 BCE a member of the First Triumvirate, alongside Pompey and Crassus. Caesar offered his daughter, Julia, in marriage to Pompey to help seal their alliance. Given the province of Gaul, Caesar spent the next nine years there on campaign.

In 53 BCE Crassus was killed in action by the Parthians at Carrhae, which left Pompey and Caesar to vie for the dominant position. In 50 BCE Caesar was ordered by the senate to resign his command in Gaul and disband his army, while Pompey was entrusted with large powers. Civil war soon broke out between them; Caesar had the support of his troops and in 49 BCE moved south and drove Pompey into Greece. In three months Caesar was master of all Italy. After subduing Pompey's legates in Spain, Caesar was made dictator. Meanwhile Pompey had gathered a large force in Egypt and Greece, and his fleet had control of the sea. Finally, at the Battle of Pharsalus in 48 BCE Pompey was routed and fled to Egypt where he was murdered. Caesar was appointed dictator for a year and consul for five years but instead of returning to Rome he went to Egypt and engaged in the Alexandrine War on behalf of Cleopatra VII against her brother Ptolemy.

In 45 BCE he received the title 'Father of his Country' and was made dictator for life after putting down an insurrection in Spain led by Pompey's sons. His person was declared sacred and his statue put in temples, his portrait appeared on coins and the month Quintilis was renamed Julius in his honour. Caesar had many plans to improve drainage of the marshes, making a new harbour at Ostia, founding libraries, etc., but they did not come to fruition. He was murdered on the Ides of March (15th) 44 BCE by a group of aristocrats led by Brutus and Cassius who believed they were striking a blow for the freedom of the Republic. Instead they were plunging the Roman world into a fresh round of civil wars from which the Republic would never emerge.

Caesar was not only a politician and soldier but also a man of letters. His great work, *The Civil War*, is in three parts, and chronicles the first two years of the confrontation with Pompey and his sons. The rest of the work is enlarged by narratives of the Alexandrian War in the autumn of 48 BCE, culminating with the battle of Munda in 45 BCE, and was completed by others, officers of Caesar's staff, notably Aulus Hirtius, for part three does not end with a natural break, like the death of Pompey or Caesar's return to Rome. It has been suggested that the work was put out as propaganda to win over some of the opponents of the new regime, in a similar way to the *Gallic War* which was rushed out in order to pick up votes for his intended candidature for the consulship in 49 BCE. It seems highly likely that the *Civil War* was written during the course of the war and that once the need for propaganda had passed Caesar gave up the work.

Book I charts the outbreak of the civil war starting with the events in Rome in 49 BCE, and the flight of the pro-Caesar tribunes Marcus Antonius (Mark Antony) and Quintus Cassius Longinus to Caesar in Ravenna (1:5–6). While still trying to negotiate a settlement Caesar invaded Italy, according to the historian Plutarch (Greek historian, biographer and philosopher 46 CE – 120 CE) he quoted his favourite poet Menander quoting the immortal words 'the die is cast' as he crossed the river Rubicon and invaded Italy, thus provoking further Civil War (1:7–12). The remainder (1:13–24) deals with his capture of Corfinium and his attempts to block the port of Brindisium where Pompey has taken flight. Pompey refused to meet Caesar and sailed across the Adriatic to

Epirus, so Caesar abandoned his attempt to capture him. Caesar sent Quintus Valerius to capture Sardinia while he set off for Rome to meet with the senate (30–3). When he entered Rome he pardoned instead of massacring his enemies and created a new senate which would authorize his acts. There he defended his actions and spoke about what his enemies had done, suggesting that he might run the state himself, but he was obstructed by the Pompeian sympathisers. Caesar left for Spain, before the senate had assembled and defeated the Spanish rebel army at Ilerda, (43–7) not far from modern Barcelona.

Book II tells of Caesar's capture of Cordoba where two legions under the command of Marcus Terentius Varro surrendered to him (17–21). On his return to Rome after a six-month absence he was made dictator. The remainder of the book deals with the expedition of Curio to Africa and his defeat there at the hands of King Juba. Book III concentrates on the final showdown between Caesar and Pompey, culminating in Pompey's defeat at Pharsalus in Greece (84–104). Pompey fled to Egypt where he was given refuge by the ten year old boy king, Ptolemy XII. However, the king's regents had other plans and had Pompey killed, in the hope of securing Caesar's aid in the quarrel with his sister Cleopatra VII. Caesar had pursued Pompey to Egypt and was furious that he did not have the chance to pardon his old enemy. He then became involved in the dynastic war between the two rival claimants Ptolemy XII and Cleopatra VII, choosing to support the latter. The Commentary ceases at the point where Caesar is fighting against the king's men led by Achillas at Alexandria.

Once Egypt had been pacified Caesar and Cleopatra spent some time together before Caesar once again hurried off to Asia Minor where Pharnaces, son of Mithridates, had challenged Roman authority. He was defeated in a rapid campaign at Zela, where Caesar uttered his famous words, 'veni, vidi, vici' (I came, I saw, I conquered). Finally, in September 47 BCE Caesar was free to return to Rome. However, while he had been dallying with the

Egyptian Queen his opponents, the last Republican diehards, had been able to regroup.

His other great work, the *Gallic War* (sometimes called the *Conquest of Gaul*) provides the only contemporary account of an important Roman foreign war that has survived. Between 58 and 50 BCE Caesar had not only conquered almost the whole of France, Belgium and Switzerland, including parts of Holland and Germany, but had also invaded Britain twice.

There was already a province of Gallia Narbonensis, the rest of modern France, Belgium and some of Switzerland, with the exception of modern Provence was occupied by the Celts who the Romans referred to as Gauls. Caesar spent nine years campaigning in Gaul, slaughtering the tribal armies who opposed Roman domination. His accounts vividly describe the battles and intrigues that took place.

The *Gallic War* is divided into eight books, although only the first seven were written by Caesar; the last book was added after his death by Aulus Hirtius who had served with him. The work is important for the many historical and geographical insights it provides into the region and the lives of the native people. For example chapter 6 tells of the costumes worn by the Gauls (13), their religion (17) and also makes comparisons between them and the Germans (24). The first book of the *Gallic War* describes the country of Gaul and the campaign against the Helvetii, who were a tribe living just outside Provence in Switzerland. They had decided, because of an expanding population problem, to move to the west lowlands in France. This brought them into contact with the tribal regions that were allied to Rome. Caesar declared he would not allow this to happen, and that resulted in an alliance of various tribes to fight against him. The later books describe the various campaigns with the tribes of the Venetii, Aquitani, Bretons and Germans, Caesar's invasion of Britain; the insurrection of Gaul (VII, 4) and the defeat of Vercingetorix at Alesia (VII, 89).

Most of the campaigns began in late summer with the provisioning of grain and construction of fortresses, and ended late in the year when Caesar retuned to Italy for the winter. By the end of the second year the majority of the tribes had been defeated and most of Gaul was under Roman dominion. The war was a costly one and it is suggested that part of the motivation behind Caesar's writing was to provide a reason for the necessity of the campaigns, especially his forays into Britain, to pacify his detractors back in Rome, or to make sure that he did not get recalled early?

Caesar called both his works 'Commentaries' and the word originally meant memoirs or reports. It is one of the earliest to be written in the third person singular (Caesar refers to himself as 'he' instead of 'I'). By giving his work this title Caesar obviously implied that these were straightforward objective reports, notes that one would use to write up a history rather than a piece of literary material. The style is simple yet elegant and as an author Caesar eventually won the praise of Cicero for his work on the *Gallic War*. Cicero had also called his work on his own consulship a commentary.

But it was not only Caesar's written work that gained Cicero's praise, his skill in oratory was also remarked upon. Indeed it was said by Quintilian (35–100 CE, Roman rhetorician) that had Caesar had the time to devote himself solely to oratory he would have been a serious rival to Cicero. The qualities that Quintilian ascribes to Caesar are penetration, energy and elegance of language. It seems that Caesar had his own views on the elegance of language and he wrote a two-volume work entitled *Analogia* (On Selection of Words) which he dedicated to Cicero. The work no longer survives but from ancient references to it, it appears that Caesar advocated careful selection of vocabulary rather than an uncritical acceptance of the everyday colloquial usage. He said that the orator should avoid speech which contained any foreign corruption or bizarre and unfamiliar words, with the aim to use clear and pure Latin. Caesar's works go a long way to fulfil this aim for they are written in a simple style yet are not repetitive and never dull.

Although rendered in direct speech to give them a greater amount of force, the orations contained in Caesar's works are not authentic. Although both the *Gallic War* and *Civil War* provide valuable information they are extremely clever works of self-aggrandisement and personal propaganda. Their real aim appears to have been to avenge personal insults and Caesar often takes the credit for successes that had been won by subordinates, and blames any setbacks such as that at Gergovia (*Gallic War* Book VII) on others. He also explains that his aggression against Britain was needed because they were sending mercenaries to assist the Gauls. He is keen to present himself and his cause in the best possible light in his work. Because of this there are some omissions, anything that may be detrimental to his aims. On the other hand he makes sure that he mentions everything he can that discredits his opponents. He was accused in antiquity, by the Roman orator and soldier Pollio (76 BCE – 4 CE), of being inaccurate.

Some of Caesar's other earlier works were suppressed by his adopted heir the future emperor, Augustus, as unworthy. Lost works that we do hear of are *Anticato* (an answer to Cicero's pamphlet in praise of M. Porcius Cato), a work on astronomy, possibly in connection with his reform of the calendar, and a poem called *The Journey* which appears to have been written on a journey from Rome to Spain which took 24 days. Only six lines survive of his poetry: a literary judgement on Terence (190–59 BC, Roman comedy writer) whom he praises as a lover of pure speech.

Caesar left a great legacy in his writing, which won the praise of many of his contemporaries. They were composed in the city of Rome, in a style which was pure, lucid and compressed, with clear diction, simple but brilliantly chosen, as Grant says, His masterly style raises these works far above the level of ordinary Commentary into literary masterpieces that are unmistakably the work of an intellect of exceptional force and power.

(*Researches into Classical Historians* 1992, 266)

Chapter Fourteen

Sallust (Gaius Sallustius Crispus) (86–34 BCE)

Wealth and beauty can give only a fleeting and perishable fame,
but intellectual excellence is a glorious and everlasting possession.

(Conspiracy of Catiline, Chapter 1, Preface)

Caesar had remedied some of the stylistic shortcomings of
writing Roman history and this trend was to be continued and
expanded upon by Sallust, Livy (59 BCE – 17 CE) and perhaps most
remarkably of all by Tacitus (55–120 CE).

Sallust was born into an upper-class family from north-east of
Rome (Amiternum) and entered into public life after an ill-spent
youth. During the Civil War between Pompey and Caesar, Sallust
had fought on the side of Caesar, who made him *quaestor* for the
second time, restoring his membership of the senate. He had
been *quaestor* in 55 BCE and tribune of the people in 52 BCE but
had been removed from his position in the senate by the censor,
Appius Claudius Pulcher, on the grounds of gross immorality;
most probably the real reason was because of his opposition to the
conservatives, the old aristocracy of Rome.

Having become a partisan of Caesar he served as an officer
under him in Caesar's victory over Pompey in 46 BCE at Thapsus
in North Africa, where he was rewarded by being made the first
governor of the province of Africa Nova (Algeria).

Unfortunately Sallust abused this position and on his return
home was prosecuted for extracting illicit profits from his governorship. Only the intervention of Caesar on his behalf meant he
escaped condemnation. There was little left for him to do but
retire gracefully from public life and devote himself to some
other pastime. He had acquired many fine estates, including
the famous gardens on the Quirinal (Sallustian Gardens) and on

these he lived the remainder of his life until his death in 34 BCE. He devoted his time wholeheartedly to writing history, which he pronounced to be a continuation of political life. Two of his works, *The Catiline Conspiracy* and *The Jugurthine War* have been preserved but there remain only fragments surviving from his larger and perhaps more important work, *Historiae*, a history of Rome from 78–67 BCE which he began in 39 BCE.

Both his surviving works were written between the time of the death of Julius Caesar in 44 BCE and 40 BCE. His first published work *The Catiline Conspiracy* concerns the year 63 BCE when the conspiracy was unmasked. Catiline had been one of Sulla's lieutenants, brave and loyal but also bloodthirsty and brutal. He was indicted for extortion and unable to stand for the consulship in 66 or 65 BCE. He and another man Gnaeus Piso then allegedly became involved in a plan to kill the consuls and take over the state but the conspirators procrastinated and so the chance was lost. Catiline stood against Cicero for the consulship and was defeated, despite extensive bribery on his part. When his ambitions were frustrated by Cicero he turned to insurrection and in this he had the backing of some of Rome's leading families. He began stockpiling an arsenal of weapons and it was only when he approached a Gallic tribe, the Allobroges, that he was unmasked.

Catiline and his followers, mainly disaffected Sullan veterans, were harried from Rome, and while attempting to withdraw to Gaul he was killed in battle at Pistoia by a senatorial army led by Cicero's co-consul Gaius Antonius, and Quintus Metellus Celer. Those conspirators still remaining in Rome were rounded up and executed without trial by Cicero.

Sallust takes the view which was widely accepted that Catiline was the enemy of law, order and morality, but does not give a comprehensive account of his views and intentions. Catiline was a supporter of Sulla and therefore in direct opposition to Sallust's own view. Furthermore it is also highly probable that one of Sallust's intentions was to clear Caesar from any connection with the conspiracy.

Sallust was deeply troubled about the moral decline of Rome, and this is apparent in his work, especially in his descriptions of aristocratic behaviour. His most famous contribution to Roman historiography was to say that the decline of Rome began with the defeat of Carthage. Nevertheless this work gave him the opportunity to show his rhetorical skills at the expense of the old aristocracy and he took great delight in painting their degeneracy in the blackest possible colours. He was of the opinion that all Roman politicians, whether *populares* or senatorial conservatives were ambitious, self-seeking and insincere. The *Catiline Conspiracy* is a masterpiece of dramatic narrative, with a few minor inaccuracies in chronology, and an ideal subject for a writer who was gifted in lively characterization and description.

The *Jugurthine War*, although historically a useful piece, has little to recommend it in the literary sense. It would appear that he collected notes for the work during his governorship of Numidia. The work concerns the hostilities against King Jugurtha of Numidia (111–05 BCE), and the first challenge to the supremacy of the ruling class by a plebeian, Marius. In this work the focus is mainly concentrated upon the feebleness of the senate and aristocracy to the point of distraction and even the military aspects are less than acceptable, with many inaccuracies in geographical and chronological details. Sallust states that his reasons for selecting it as a subject were:

'First because it was a hard fought and bloody contest in which victories alternated with defeats; secondly, because it was at this time that the first challenge was offered to the arrogance of the Roman nobles – the beginning of a struggle that played havoc with all our institutions, human and divine, and reached such a pitch of fury that civil strife was ended only by a war which left Italy a desert.'

(section 5)

He was attracted by this theme because of the chance it gave him to write about exciting incidents and to set against each other the characters of the protagonists, Jugurtha himself, Adherbal, Metellus, Marius, Sulla and Bocchus. About the campaigns themselves he showed less interest, and here the historical defects are more pronounced than in the *Catiline Conspiracy*. This was partly due, as in the case of most ancient historians, to the fact that he lacked the technical knowledge to give accurate details about sieges and battle formations. Although he had lived for some time in Africa he gives little information about the position of towns or battlefields, even the directions of the marches are omitted. The chronology gets even more unsatisfactory as the narrative progresses, either because Sallust has just omitted the details, or because he actually did not know in what year certain events occurred.

The fact is that he may have omitted important details not simply because he forgot them but that he may have lacked access to information. Not only that but Sallust hired secretaries to do most of his historical research and they could have proven less than reliable. This can be borne out from his treatment of the campaigns of Marius, whom Sallust saw as the real victor, a man who had risen from the ranks of the plebs to become the saviour of his country. These campaigns are dealt with in a very sketchy fashion, so making it extremely difficult to fathom out exactly what happened. This cannot have been through lack of interest on Sallust's part. There may have been little tangible information more than 60 years after the events took place, and whatever written sources he did have access to may have been very fragmentary. Later campaigns, in which Sulla played an important part, are more detailed and this suggests that the documents that Sallust had were supplemented here by Sulla's memoirs.

Sallust does show his own bias for the 'popular' side in Roman politics, which was an important factor in his writing. He makes repeated accusations of treason against the senatorial nobles, even putting an abusive attack upon them into the mouth of Marius. For he saw in Marius a man of the people, who was also an able soldier and had a powerful personality that could not be ignored. Marius had risen from obscurity to become consul and brought Rome's struggle with Jugurtha to an end. Following that he went on to repel a far more serious threat from Rome's northern frontier. In this man Sallust saw an opportunity to contrast his view of the corrupt, selfish and incompetent noblemen with a brilliant, capable plebeian who saved them all from the calamity into which Rome and her people had fallen.

Naturally Sallust overplays the contrast, and while he is fair in his judgement of Metellus, the aristocratic commander who was dismissed to make way for Marius, the same cannot be said about Sallust's treatment of other notables. His charges against them of wholesale bribery are totally exaggerated. This is not to say that there were not unscrupulous members of the senate, no doubt money often changed hands, but Sallust would have us believe that Jugurtha had half the members of the senate on his pay roll.

What Sallust fails to realize, or simply will not admit, is that Rome had the soundest of reasons to avoid a war with Africa at that particular time. The German tribes, the Cimbri and Teutones were mobilizing their forces. In 113 BCE, before the war with Jugurtha had commenced, they had defeated a consular army south of the Danube, and were heading to Switzerland and after that Gaul. It would have folly to take on a war with Africa at this moment and after the first campaign in 111 BCE then any sensible senator would have wished to come to terms with the king, even if they did pocket the king's money.

The few fragments that remain of the *Historiae*, some of which were discovered in 1886, are sufficient to indicate Sallust's political partisanship, and he takes pleasure in describing the reaction against the dictator Sulla's policy and legislation after his death. The loss of the work is regrettable for it could have thrown a great deal of light upon an eventful period of Roman history. For example, much more could have been learnt about the war against Sertorius, the campaigns of Lucullus against Mithridates VI of Pontus and the victories of Pompey in the east.

There are two letters which are also attributed to Sallust, *Duae epistolae de republica ordinanda*, these are letters concerning political counsel and advice to Caesar, and an attack on Cicero *Invectiva* or *Declamatio in Ciceronem*; however, they may well be the work of a first-century CE rhetorician.

Sallust's style is highly individual if somewhat artificial. He writes in short terse sentences, eager to impart his ideas and views, and can appear sometimes almost abrupt. His speeches, which obviously are composed by him, are full of rhetoric, in much the same way as the speeches composed by Thucydides, whom he greatly admired. But his works lack accuracy and objectivity which makes him less worthy of the title 'historian'. Yet despite these drawbacks Sallust's success is in part due to the expert organization of his material. As Grants says (*Ancient Historians* 1970 211):

> Small incidents are cunningly linked together into units, and each part grows irresistibly to a conclusion- which in turn looks ahead to subsequent events. The supreme example of Sallust's skill is his Catiline. Every possible advantage is taken of the striking, tragic theme to create an elegant, close knit, diversified structure, leading steadily up to a climax ...

We may have had an opportunity to see his style displayed to greater effect had more of his *Historiae* survived. This management of great exciting episodes had never been so extensively utilized before in Roman history and set a trend which later Roman historians would imitate. Sallust was highly favoured in antiquity: Tacitus calls him an 'eminent historian' (*Annals* III, 30) and he was also highly spoken of by Quintilian (II.5, X. i). He virtually started a whole new line in literature, endeavouring to explain the connexion and meaning of events, and was a successful portrayer of characters. He was often reproached for the high moral stance that he took, considering his own earlier character, but that is not to say that he had not learned from his own mistakes. It is possible that his own weaknesses caused him to view the morality of his fellow men in a similar light and so cause him to judge them severely. His model was Thucydides whom he attempted to imitate in truthfulness and if not in impartiality, introducing philosophizing reflections and speeches. He used old words and phrases, in which he imitated his contemporary the Younger Cato (Roman statesman and orator 95–46 BCE), that caused him to be ridiculed. Nevertheless this was one of the reasons that he became a favourite author from the second century CE onwards.

Chapter Fifteen

Livy (Titus Livius) (c.64 BCE – c.7 CE)

> You may choose for yourself and for your own state what to imitate
> (and) mark for avoidance what is shameful in the conception and
> shameful in the result.
>
> (*History*, Preface 10)

Livy declares in his preface that the chief merit of history is to
provide a model from which leaders can choose to imitate or avoid
past actions. In contrast to Polybius, who focused on institutions,
for Livy, as Luce says (1977 230), 'it is the workings of character
that determine success or failure'. Livy's fame is due to his work,
a staggering 142-volume book entitled *Ab Urbe Condita* (From the
Founding of the City), which he began to compose around 29 BCE
chronicling the history of Rome. The surviving volumes (I–X and
XXI–XLV) cover the period 753–243 BCE and 210–167 BCE, but books
XI–XX and XLVI–CXLII have been lost save only for a few fragments.

In fact Livy came closest to fulfilling the expectation that
Cicero's friends had of Cicero, to produce a readable history
of Rome. Cicero had argued that Roman histories could not be
compared with the Greek because they lacked *ornatus* (attractive
presentation). This comprised variations in tone and colour, an
easy flowing style and good word order, ideally with the rhythm
of the sentences reproducing the rhythm of events. Livy had the
resources of language and style of which Cicero would have
been proud to boast. But Cicero also believed that a good history
required proper chronology, geographical descriptions and a
thorough interpretation of events and policies and in this respect

Livy proved to be defective; he was no interpreter in his treatment of historical detail or of causation. Instead he substituted an imaginative use of emotion and portrayal of human feelings both in his speeches and in the narrative, providing some of the most memorable of all the passages in his histories. This was the tragic approach to history, unlike the pragmatic approach of Polybius.

There are few details known about Livy's early life except that he was born in 64 or 59 BCE in Padua in Cisalpine Gaul. He went to Rome as a young man and spent most of his remaining years writing his *History* until his death in 7 or 12 CE. His family did not belong to the senatorial class and Livy does not seem to have embarked on a political career. He was a man of learning rather than of political or intellectual distinction. Because Livy played no part in politics he was unable to gain access to first hand information concerning historical events, for most official records would have been out of bounds to him. As a consequence he did not seek political explanations for historical events, and this makes his work unique, for he saw history more in personal and moral terms.

Early in his career Livy attracted the attention of the emperor Augustus and was at one point invited to supervise the literary activities of the young Claudius (the future emperor). Augustus called him a 'Pompeian', implying that he had an independent and outspoken personality. Nevertheless, Livy was a man of his time: in keeping with other thinking Romans he looked at history from a moral standpoint. Augustus used both propaganda and legislation to inculcate moral ideals, and to emphasize that it was moral qualities that had made Rome great, and only by keeping those moral standards would Rome remain great, something the poets Horace and Vergil also stressed in their works.

It is Livy's account of the Second Punic War (218–201 BCE) that bears witness to his belief in Rome. Book XXI opens with a passage that is an almost Thucydidean echo about the power and status of Rome and Carthage as they embark on the most 'memorable war in history' (XXI:1). They are described as old antagonists in a conflict fuelled by mutual hatred. Livy begins with an account of the young Hannibal being compelled by his father Hamilcar to take an oath of enmity against Rome. Already we are given an image of Hamilcar's great resentment at the defeat of Carthage during the First Punic War, and his great desire to redress the balance.

By setting his main characters and peoples centre stage Livy provided the opening scene for his account of the Second Punic War; but in order for his account to be effective his characterizations depended upon a number of factors. Hannibal was the most prominent personality and Livy used many indirect means to show the kind of man he was. Hannibal's speeches and speeches referring to him that were made by others, and the way in which other people reacted to his actions, generally leave the reader to make up their own mind about the kind of person Hannibal was. Polybius had expressed strong views about the reporting of speeches and the need for accuracy. Livy's speeches, however, are pure fabrications, even though they are usually well adapted to the circumstances and speakers, showing a remarkable psychological insight into the characters.

Livy also used indirect methods of providing a character sketch (4) to signal Hannibal's importance in the narrative. For example Hannibal exhorts his troops to further efforts when they show signs of flagging before crossing the Alps (30); riding ahead of a struggling column to show them Italy lying at their mercy, 'you are walking over the very walls of Rome' (35); and his tactical ability against mountain tribesmen (34) and the Romans (54). Yet Livy's portrait is not consistent: his character sketch in 4 does not mention the other more positive qualities possessed by Hannibal that appear elsewhere in Book XXI. These other features present a charismatic leader, brave and quick witted, ready to plunge headlong into dangerous situations, yet lacking wisdom and moral stamina.

Here we see Livy giving a view of the virtues he would like Hannibal to have but he fails to maintain this in his narrative, for in his character sketch (4) Hannibal's vices are also enumerated. Hannibal is, according to Livy, cruel, dishonest and impious, with a general lack of honour; even his tactical genius is used against him to render him a barbarian. Livy shows by various methods that the strategies employed by Hannibal are very un-Roman ways of fighting, and they serve to place Hannibal on an equal footing with the barbaric local tribesmen. So, for all Hannibal's success, Livy wishes the reader to see this man as something less than the best sort of leader. His characterizations of other Carthaginians add weight to his assessment; Hamilcar is an embittered man (1), Hasdrubal's peaceful and diplomatic policies strongly contrast with the militaristic approach of Hannibal (2). Indeed Livy shows Hannibal to be displaying an aggressive policy inherited from his father, 'this son of his, with the devil in his heart and the torch in his hand' (10), providing the reader with an image of Hannibal that is both demonic and violent.

By contrast Livy presents the Romans in a more positive light. Although they too have their faults they are by no means as terrible as their opponents. In 21 Livy gives his view of the Roman race which contrasts nicely with the general picture of the Carthaginians and other races, highlighting those aspects of Hannibal's character that Livy was at great pains to demonstrate as less than moral or civilised. Individual Romans, such as Quintus Fabius in the embassy to Carthage (18), are shown as being down to earth and straight talking. However, they are capable of allowing their judgement to become clouded by personal indignation seen in Lucius Manlius' reaction to the mistreatment of the envoys by the Gauls (25).

The central Roman character of the narrative is Publius Cornelius Scipio, who displays foresight in locating Hannibal on the Rhone (26) and in reorganizing his forces once he becomes aware that he cannot prevent Hannibal from reaching the Alps (32). The contrast between the clemency of Scipio toward the surrendered Actinogram and the barbarity inflicted by the Carthaginians on Victumulae (57) once again exemplifies Livy's bias in extolling the virtues that had made Rome great by contrasting them with her enemies. There are other examples. For instance, Scipio is shown as being respectful to the gods (41), while Hannibal's attitude to the divine is inconsistent (4, 21, 45). Furthermore, Livy indicates another significant Roman characteristic in a speech made by Scipio where he appeals to the bond that existed between previous Roman armies and the troops he was now addressing. This solidarity of historical purpose was viewed by Livy as a key factor in Rome's past historical successes.

The stable and successful operation of the Roman state makes a striking contrast with the government of Carthage which is in the nepotistic control of one family (2). Scipio appeals to his men's 'indignation and anger' at the injustice of Carthaginian behaviour (41), while on the other hand Hannibal invokes baser motivations in his troops, 'rousing their greed with the hopes of rich rewards' (11). Livy fails to emphasize that Hannibal's troops were made up mostly of mercenaries and therefore would expect rewards for fighting. Livy presents all the combatants, Carthaginians, Spaniards, Gauls and Romans as capable of great courage, but it is the Romans who are steadfast in their pursuit of carefully considered aims. Although he allows the Allobroges to be powerful and famous (31), such status is kept squarely within the context of Gaul and no comparisons are made with Rome at all.

The good features of the Roman people are always shown by the contrasts that Livy made with the Carthaginians or other peoples. Livy puts into the mouth of Hanno the Carthaginian a speech that the 'Roman demands are mild, their first steps slow and cautious' (10). In all aspects of legalities Rome is always portrayed as honest and just, as opposed to the unreliable and treacherous Gauls and Carthaginians. The calm and deliberate approach taken by the Romans in times of crisis is best seen in the senate's debate over Hannibal's initial move against Saguntum (6) and the diplomatic activities before the final declaration of war (10–11, 18). Livy made the point that despite impending disaster the process of government continued uninterrupted.

However, the picture that Livy created was not one-dimensional characterizations. The inconsistencies of his portrayals of Scipio and Hannibal did not overshadow the aim of his work, which was to 'commemorate the deeds of the foremost people in the world,' even if his approach was Romano-centric. As Usher says (1985,176):

> the negative attributes of Hannibal's personality can be seen as magnifications of general Carthaginian characteristics, while those racial features are themselves closely related to contrasting Roman virtues.

His narrative, which some call novelistic rather than historic because of the high drama and emotion contained in it, presents to the modern reader a wonderful picture of a great nation throughout its history. He was the only historian to compose a full scale history of the growth and expansion of Rome, covering a period of 744 years, and also the only historian to show what the Romans themselves thought about a past that had made them the greatest power in the Mediterranean. The social history contained in his works is abundant, although he himself may not have realized its importance.

Livy was well aware that many of his stories were not factual:

> Events before Rome was born or thought of to have come us in old tales with more of the charm of poetry than of sound historical record, and such traditions I propose neither to affirm nor to refute. (1:1)

Livy therefore not only invented earlier warfare but he also distorted those battles that took place during the Second Punic War, which are for the most part pure invention. This enabled him to shift the war guilt from Rome, but still he does not give us any explanation about why Rome was eventually successful.

He was patriotic and supported senatorial authority. Although he was sympathetic to the *plebs* in their struggle with the patricians, he does show a distinct bias toward the aristocratic hardliners who unwaveringly resisted any concessions to the *plebs* or a break with tradition. The lost books on the fall of the Republic may well have shown Livy believing that the failure of such men actually brought about the Republic's demise. A good example of such a man is Cato Uticensis who opposed Caesar and had already been noted for his selfless devotion to the Republic in Sallust's work *Conspiracy of Catiline.*

Yet as an historian Livy made some glaring errors. First he never checked his sources which meant that he often repeated the same event because he had two separate accounts available to him. For example some of Hannibal's Spanish operations are repeated, and his crossing of the Apennines is reported as an attempt in 218 BCE and then as a fact in 217 BCE, when clearly the accounts concern the same march. A similar situation occurs in Book XXVIII where the expulsion of the Carthaginians from Spain, is dated first in the thirteenth year of the war and then in the fourteenth.

Second, Livy also makes many errors in translation as he relied heavily on Greek sources. As Walsh says (1967 144):

> His most culpable errors are those involving mistranslation, which can be detected by systematic comparison with the account of Polybius ... In some passages Livy has misinterpreted whole sentences ... A clear and somewhat damning picture emerges of a mind rapidly and mechanically transposing the Greek, and coming to full consciousness only when grappling with the more congenial problems of literary presentation.

Livy was not as abrupt as Sallust. He had a fast and varied narrative and used a rich vocabulary. His approach was conservative as most annalistic approaches were, and he produced, in Latin rather than Greek, the last great annalistic history of the Republic. Earlier Roman annalistic historians had written in Greek, for Latin possessed no ready-made style that could be used for such a purpose. However, Livy evolved a flexible and varied style which the ancient critic Quintilian characterized as a 'milky richness'. It is recorded that those who attended his recitations were singularly impressed by his nobility of character and his eloquence. Pliny the Younger, who was particularly fond of historical writing, says that Livy had at one point been tempted to abandon the project but found it so fascinating that he could not give it up. Pliny also tells us that a citizen of Cadiz (modern Spain) came all the way to Rome just for the satisfaction of being able to gaze upon the historian (*Letters* 2.3).

Chapter Sixteen

Augustus (Gaius Octavius) (63 BCE – 14 CE)

> At the age of nineteen on my own initiative and at my own
> expense I raised an army, with which I successfully championed
> the liberty of the Republic when it was oppressed by the tyranny
> of a faction.
>
> *(Res Gestae* 1)

On the death of his father Gaius Octavius was brought up under
the guidance of his mother Atia, whose uncle was Julius Caesar.
Caesar became fond of the boy and introduced him to public life.
At the age of 12 he gave the funeral address for his grandmother
Julia (Caesar's sister) and he accompanied his great-uncle in his
triumph of 46 BCE. On hearing of the murder of Caesar he learnt
that he had been adopted by him and made his heir, from then on
he was to style himself Gaius Julius Caesar Octavianus (Octavian)
and set about recruiting Caesar's veterans in order to take
revenge on the assassins. He allied himself with Caesar's deputy
Mark Antony and allowed him a free hand to murder his political
enemies, including the senator Cicero. It was under Antony's
leadership that the 'Second Triumvirate' (consisting of Octavian,
Antony and Lepidus) crushed the assassins of Caesar at the Battle
of Philippi. There followed a decade of uneasy relations between
Octavian and Antony, finally in 30 BCE Octavian defeated Antony
and his ally Cleopatra of Egypt at the Battle of Actium.

In 27 BCE Octavian took the title of Augustus and assumed
monarchical power under the guise of restoring the Republic;
it could be said that the Roman Empire began at this point.
Augustus brought Egypt in the Roman Empire and ruled over
the entire Mediterranean for two generations. His main aims
were to resettle his vast armies after the civil wars, create a new

administrative and financial structure and secure the succession within the Julio-Claudian family.

Even though he had always been sickly he outlived at least four of his designated successors and died on the 19 August 14 CE at the age of 77. On his death he left behind him four documents which had been entrusted to the Vestal Virgins for safe keeping; Suetonius tells us that they consisted of his will, instructions for his funeral, a catalogue of his achievements, which he wished to be inscribed on bronze tablets and set up in front of his mausoleum, and finally a summary of the military and financial state of the whole Empire.

The catalogue of achievements has survived and is generally known as the *Res Gestae* (*Res Gestae Divi Augusti*, the Achievements of the Divine Augustus). The text is addressed to Roman citizens and especially to the inhabitants of Rome. The document can be seen as an *apologia*, containing informative that Augustus wished to be remembered about his life and omits those points that appeared inconsistent with the image of himself that he was portraying for posterity.

According to the text it was written just before Augustus' death but it would seem likely that that it was written and revised over a longer period of time.

There are three surviving sources for this document. The main one is the *Momumentum Ancyranum*, an inscription in the temple of Rome and Augustus in modern Ankara in Turkey. Inscribed on the walls were the Latin text and accompanying Greek paraphrase. Both texts are damaged but the other two remaining texts enable a good proportion of the damaged or missing sections to be reconstructed. The two other sources are fragments of the Greek text discovered in Apollonia in Pisidia and fragments of the Latin text discovered in Antioch. It is clear that Suetonius and probably other Roman historians had access to the original document or at least a copy in the Imperial archives.

The text is written in the first person and consists of a short introduction where Augustus sets out his agenda (2–14) where he aims to justify his position of pre-eminence. He describes his entry into public life, lists his triumphs and military successes which justify the honours he accumulated. He stresses that the honours were bestowed by the people as well as the senate

> The dictatorship was offered to me by both senate and people in my absence and when I was at Rome in the consulship of Marcus Marcellus and Lucius Arruntius, but I refused it. (5.1)

This is a clever piece of propaganda writing for while it is true that he accepted no individual office or position for which there was no Republican precedent, he did not mention that there was no precedent for any one man holding numerous positions and power at the same time.

The least controversial section of the work (15–24) consists of a list of his expenditure, the donations of money, land and grain to the citizens of Italy and his soldiers, as well as the public works and gladiatorial games that he commissioned. He also speaks of the foreign wars and successes that he wished to be commemorated, and which was a result of his own efforts.

Chapter 34 consists of a statement of the Roman approval for the reign and deeds of Augustus. Augustus had brought an end to the Civil Wars and restored constitutional government for which he received exceptional honours. The result of these honours was pre-eminence in *auctoritas* (influence) which is implied was fully justified. Chapter 35 tells how he received the title *Pater Patriae* (Father of his Country) from the senate and people.

The appendix is written in the third person, so perhaps not by Augustus himself. It summarizes the entire text and lists various buildings he renovated or constructed; it states 600 million denarii from his own funds were spent during his reign towards public projects.

The *Res Gestae* is less objective as a historical text because of the nature of the work, designed to be propaganda for the principate that Augustus instituted. The work glosses over the events between the assassination of Caesar and the victory over Antony and Cleopatra at Actium. Caesar's murderers are not mentioned by name:

> I drove into exile the murderers of my father, avenging their crime through tribunals established by law; and afterwards when they made war upon the Republic I twice defeated them in battle. (*RG* 2)

Likewise Mark Antony and Sextus Pompeius, Augustus' opponents in the east, remain equally anonymous, the former being 'a faction' (1) and the latter 'a pirate' (RG 25).

Augustus also fails to mention his *imperium mius* and his exceptional tribunican powers. Augustus' official position of his government can be seen in his statement that although he surpassed all others in achievements his official powers were no greater than any of his colleagues. This is in keeping with his propaganda that promoted itself as a restoration of the old Republic, with a leader who was nothing more than a 'first among equals' but which was in effect an absolute monarchy backed by the sword.

The *Res Gestae* is valuable inasmuch as it is a first-hand account by Rome's first emperor and how he wished his reign to be remembered. It is also useful as a guide to later historical writing about Augustus who characterized his rule according to the categories he himself constructed. The *Res Gestae* may be considered as a development of a *eulogia*. *Eulogia* would not contain untruths since there would be too many people who could disprove them. However, it imposed limitations on the author who may have wished to have presented himself in a good light to posterity. However, this did not prevent the author from being selective. Therefore, while the historian may rely on factual statements they must be wary of the interpretation of those facts. Indeed what is omitted may be as informative as what is included.

Chapter Seventeen

Flavius Josephus (Joseph Ben Matthias) (c.37/8 – c.100 CE)

The war of the Jews against the Romans- the greatest not only of the wars in our own time, but, so far as accounts have reached us, well nigh of all that ever broke out between cities and nations-has not lacked historians ... ... I-Josephus, son of Matthias, a Hebrew by race, a native of Jerusalem and a priest, who at the opening of the war myself fought against the Romans and in the sequel was perforce an onlooker-propose to provide the subjects of the Roman empire with a narrative of the facts, by translating into Greek, the account which I previously composed in my vernacular tongue.

(*Jewish War* Book I:1)

Toward the end of the first century BCE an encyclopaedic tendency emerged that heralded the closing of a cultural tradition. For modern historians this is an important fact as many of these bulky works managed to survive, driving out their predecessors and offering evidence for reconstructing the historical tradition. The Greek tradition of history writing had, in 350 years, produced most of the styles of history and had tried to analyse most of the political and social problems of the respective time periods. This tradition tried to establish standards of accuracy and approach. However, there had never been any recourse before to explain God's role in history. This would be remedied by the end of the Hellenistic period, when a new religion emerged, Christianity, which necessitated the merging together of the traditions of Greece and Judaea into a new form of history, the working out of God's salvation on earth. The Apocryphal Books of Maccabees and the works of Josephus are products of this fusion of cultural traditions, which would point the way forward to the *Church History* of Eusebius and the Christian world of Byzantium.

Josephus was born Joseph ben Matattyahu (the son of Matattyahu = Matthias) in 37–38 CE. His father was a Jew who belonged to the priestly class, and his mother was related to the former Hasmonean (Maccabee) royal family. Josephus' first language was Aramaic, although he was educated in Hebrew and could write Greek.

When he was young he was eager to know as much as he could about the various sects in Judaism and says that he became in turn an adherent of the three main branches, the Sadducees, Pharisees and the Essenes. He finally decided to become a priest within the Pharisee sect. In 64 CE, at the age of 27, he was sent to Rome to defend some colleagues who had been arrested and were being detained by the emperor Nero. With help from a Jewish actor, Aliturus, and the wife of the emperor, Poppaea Sabina, he successfully undertook his mission and they were released. However, on his return he found the Jewish nation on the verge of revolution against their Roman masters. Josephus was not convinced about the success of such a course of action, but when the rebellion was launched in 66 CE the moderate Jewish leaders at the time dispatched him to Galilee to take command of their force there.

Most of Josephus' time in Galilee appears to have been spent trying to control the internal factions in the area rather than fighting the Roman army. The Roman general and governor of Syria, Vespasian, with his forces gradually approached the Galilee, and soon Josephus and his army were forced to retreat to Jotapata, where they held out for seven months before finally being defeated. Josephus and his supporters hid in a cave where they agreed to enter into a suicide pact. The result was that Josephus managed to evade this pact and went over to the Romans.

According to his own account, the reason he gives for his apparent 'conversion' was because he had had a dream that Vespasian would be emperor and this implied it was the will of God, and so it was Josephus' duty to remain alive to help convince the rest of his countrymen of the futility of their struggle.

As a prisoner of Vespasian, Josephus presented himself as a prophet. He noted that, as the war had been fuelled by an ancient oracle that predicted a world ruler would arise from Judaea, Josephus asserted that this referred to Vespasian, who would be destined to become emperor of Rome and related his dream to him. Consequently, Vespasian spared his life, and when the prediction came true and Vespasian was made emperor he rewarded Josephus handsomely, freeing him from his chains and because he was technically Vespasian's freed slave he adopted the Flavian name – hence Flavius Josephus. During the remainder of the war, Josephus assisted the Roman commander Titus, Vespasian's son.

In the subsequent siege of Jerusalem Josephus acted as an interpreter for Titus and tried to negotiate with the revolutionaries. They, on the other hand, considered Josephus to be a traitor and he was unable to persuade them to surrender Jerusalem to Rome and so had to watch the destruction of the city. After the capture of Jerusalem he went with Titus, first to Alexandria and then to Rome, where he was given a pension and Roman citizenship.

In his apartments that were attached to the emperor's palace Josephus began writing. The oldest surviving work was completed by 79 CE and is a seven-volume history of the Jewish revolt against Rome. 79 CE is a *terminus ante quem* (date before which) the work must have been finished for Josephus tells us that he presented a copy to Vespasian, who died in 79 CE. Were it not for Josephus' work the Jewish War (*Bellum Judaicum*), we would know little about the great conflict of the Jews with Rome, which led to the eventual destruction of the Temple in Jerusalem in 70 CE. The work is written in Greek but Josephus claims that it had originally been written in his native Aramaic, which he had written for 'the barbarians of the interior.' This version has not survived and is only attested to by Josephus.

As Thucydides had done before him, Josephus claimed that the truth of his history was due to the fact that he was a first-hand witness to the events that he portrays, as well as having inside knowledge of the workings of both the Jewish and Roman camps (*BJ* i.6). Josephus thought that the Greeks disregarded historical truth (*BJ* i 16). While his claim of accuracy should not be accepted at face value, it does show that he was at least aware of historical accuracy as a concept. Modern historians have no way of judging the validity of this work. The only other account was given by the Roman historian Tacitus and most has not survived.

The very title of the work shows that Josephus was writing from the Roman rather than the Jewish standpoint. The messianic goal of the rebellion, hinted at by Tacitus (*Histories* v.13) and Suetonius (*Vespasian* 4) and by rebel coins of the period is almost totally suppressed by Josephus. He presents the war as the actions of a few fanatics in order to underplay Jewish hostility to Rome. However, archaeology has provided some evidence to check the validity of Josephus' account especially with regard to the episode at Masada. Here, in this rocky fortress, the last remnants of the rebel army, men, women and children, were under siege from the Roman forces. Rather than surrender to the Roman forces, they chose suicide. This is one of the most moving passages in *War*, especially the speech made by the rebel leader, Eleazar ben Yair. Discoveries in the 1960s at this site revealed the skeletons of 25 of the defenders, plus 11 ostraka on which were carved the names of some of the rebels including one of Ben Yair. This may prove that the event took place, but exactly what happened or what Ben Yair said can still only be conjectured. Perhaps Josephus uses this event to voice his own opinions about the nobility of the rebel cause?

Josephus' largest work was the 20 volume history of the Jewish people, incorporating their laws and customs. The *Jewish Antiquities* (*Antiquitates Judaicae*) was completed around 94 CE and according to him it was something that he had contemplated during the composition of the *War*, but had decided on making *War* a separate volume, returning to the larger project some years later on the encouragement of his patron. (*AJ* I. 6–7). The first 11 books are basically a paraphrase of the *Septuagint* (Greek Bible, known by the abbreviation LXX), which despite his claim neither to add to nor subtract from differs greatly from the original. His knowledge of his own religion is un-profound and at times inaccurate; the accounts of Nehemiah and Ezra are full of inaccuracies. Nevertheless, his work constitutes a remarkable praise of Jewry and Judaism for the benefit of non-Jews in the first century CE.

Books XXII and XIII cover the period of the Maccabean Revolt and the Hasmonean dynasty. Once again, Josephus paraphrases, in a similar way to his treatment of LXX, the Jewish history contained in 1 Maccabees, which he alters to suit his own personal and political aims. The last third of *Antiquities* (Books XIII–XX) covers the second half of the Hasmonean dynasty during the Roman period, the last few books conclude with the war with Rome. For this section Josephus used several Greco-Roman histories, official reports and of course his own eyewitness account of events. Among these sources is the work of Nicolaus of Damascus, biographer of Herod the Great, and it is because of Josephus that we have any account at all of Nicolaus' work. Josephus has parallel accounts in *War* and *Antiquities*. The former is more carefully composed and more stylistically polished. The latter places more stress on the power and influence of the Pharisees.

For centuries the works of Josephus were widely read in Europe, more so than any other book with the possible exception of the Bible. It was believed by many that his works provided an eyewitness account to the foundation and growth of Christianity in the first century CE. Josephus mentions in *Antiquities* events and people that occur in the New Testament accounts, for example Herod, John the Baptist, Pontius Pilate and even Jesus.

> About this time there lived Jesus a wise man, if indeed one ought to call him a man; for he was one who performed surprising deeds, and was a teacher of such people as accept the truth gladly.
> (AJ 18: 3, 3)

In Book XX (9:1), he mentions James, the brother of Jesus:

> Festus was now dead, and Albinus was but upon the road: so he
> assembled the Sanhedrin of judges and brought them before the
> brother of Jesus, who was called Christ, whose name was James,
> and some others ...

The accounts that mention Jesus have been embroiled in controversy since the seventeenth century. Critics have said that no Jewish man, especially a loyal Pharisaic Jew, would have referred to Jesus as *ho christos* (the Christ) and therefore the passage must have been inserted by a later Christian copyist, possibly in the third or fourth century CE. This view was expressed in John Meier's book (1991), *A Marginal Jew*:

> The opinion held that the paragraph was formed by a mixture
> of writers. It parsed the text into two categories: anything that
> seemed too Christian was added by a later Christian writer, while
> anything else was originally written by Josephus.

Over the centuries vast amounts of literature have been produced on the debate of the *Testimonium Flavianum* (Testimony of Flavius Josephus). Most recently (1995) the view has altered. It was pointed out that Josephus' description showed an unusual similarity with another early description of Jesus. It was established statistically that the similarity was too close to have appeared by chance and that both descriptions were based on a Jewish-Christian gospel that has since been lost. Therefore it is possible to prove that the account is not an entire forgery, and also possible to show which parts were written by Josephus and which were added by later interpolation.

The last two works are Josephus' autobiography, *The Life* (*Vita*), which is often considered to be an appendix to the *Antiquities*, published after the death of Agrippa II (CE 100), and *Against Apion* (*Contra Apionem*). *Life* is the oldest extant autobiography to remain in its original form to have come down to us from antiquity. However, most of it is devoted to a single episode in Josephus' life, his command in Galilee. It was written for a particular purpose: to refute the charge of Justus of Tiberias, whose work on the war has been lost. It would appear from the response in *Life* that Justus came to the defence of the city of Tiberias, and had attacked Josephus' religiosity.

Josephus' last extant work has been titled by later historians *Against Apion*, however, its original title has been lost. The title is misleading as what this work does is to refute certain allegations made against the Jews by their opponents. The worked is divided into two books that form an apologetic for the Jewish people. First he examins the antiquity of Jews: He counter-attacks that the Greeks are of more recent origin and that their historians are untrustworthy. In the second part he responds to the opponents of Judaism, many of which apparently accused the Jews of worshipping the head of an ass in the Temple, and of practising ritual murder. The work closes with a summary and defence of the Mosaic constitution with those of the Greeks.

In *Against Apion* there is a problem concerning one large section of the second book where the Greek text is missing and has subsequently been reconstructed from the sixth century CE Latin version, made for Cassiodorus, the minister of Theodoric. Eusebius, one of the early Church Fathers (324 CE), made further useful quotations which are encompassed in the Loeb edition of Josephus work. It is possible that the modern text used differs greatly from the original and once again the problem remains, as with the *Testimonium*, that the work could have been subjected to interpolation.

The audience for the work was most probably the Roman educated elite, who would have been aware of the anti-Jewish libels. Josephus was attempting to answer slander and promote the positive aspects of Judaism. The date of its composition cannot be accurately assessed although Josephus mentions *Antiquities* which puts its composition no earlier than 94 CE.

Grant says that Josephus was a determined Jewish chauvinist, outdoing even the Old Testament in exaggerating Jewish power, strength and importance. (1992 73). He abandons any claim to objectivity by describing those who disagreed with his views as 'tyrants', 'brigands' or 'factious'. Deuteronomy told how the Jews were ordered to remember their past and this is precisely what Josephus aims to do. Although biased and inaccurate in many respects Josephus displayed a great technical skill in the construction of his work. He made intelligible the horrors and brutality of a war which he thought had been useless. While he was at great pains not to upset the Romans, to whom he owed his life and his well-being, he was able to praise Jewry and give a remarkable insight into Judaism in the first century, a century that was an axial time in the development of the history of the Western world. It is no surprise that St Jerome called him 'the Greek Livy'.

Chapter Eighteen

Tacitus (Publius Cornelius) (56/7 – c.117 CE)

> I shall write without indignation or partisanship: in my case the customary incentives to these are lacking.
>
> *(Annals* Book I:1)

We know tantalizingly little about the early life of Tacitus. We cannot even be sure whether the first of his three names was Publius or Gaius. His family probably originated from Cisalpine Gaul (northern Italy) or Narbonese Gaul (Provence), and he may not have had wholly Italian ancestry. His father or uncle may have been procurator in Lower Germany and paymaster for the Roman Rhine army. His date of birth is estimated as being sometime around 56/7 CE during the reign of the emperor Nero. As a member of the provincial upper class he would have received a good education and it is also likely that he came to Rome to study rhetoric and attend the courts as a pupil of one of the leading orators of the day.

By 75 CE Tacitus had become an esteemed orator, at the age of 20 he served in one of the minor civilian posts followed by a short period of military service as a military tribune. In 77 CE he married the daughter of one of the consuls of the year, and Britain's governor designate, Gnaeus Julius Agricola. This was followed by his election to the quaestorship in 81 CE, a post that brought with it membership of the senate. By 88 CE he had moved up the ladder to the position of praetor which may have been the earliest age possible for him to attain this position. We can pinpoint the date with accuracy as Tacitus himself tells us that he held this position in this year:

> This year being the eight hundredth since Rome's foundation, Secular Games were celebrated, sixty-four years after those of

Augustus. The calculations undertaken by the two emperors I omit, since they have been sufficiently described in my account of Domitian's reign. For he too celebrated Secular Games, with which I was closely concerned as a member of the Board of Fifteen for Religious Ceremonies and praetor for the year.

(*Annals* 11.11.1)

Tacitus then left Rome to take up a series of posts in the provinces. From his work the *Agricola* we learn that he and his wife had been absent for a period of four years at the date of Agricola's death in 93 CE. We can conclude that Tacitus held the post of legate for much of this time; under the reign of next emperor Nerva (96–8 CE) Tacitus achieved the rank of consul. We know practically nothing about what Tacitus did for the next 15 years or so. During the latter years of the emperor Trajan, Tacitus was to become the proconsul of Asia; there is an undated inscription which bears witness to Tacitus holding this office most probably in the year 112/13 or 113/14 CE.

Tacitus wrote a number of books, the first two monographs, the *Agricola* and the *Germania* were published within a short time of one another, around 98 CE. The *Agricola* is a semi-biographical, moral eulogy of his father in law, but with the added benefit of historical material and a good deal of geographical material relating to Britain, where his father in law was the governor. The *Germania* is an ethnographical study of central Europe. The agenda of the author seems clear; however, the work does contain many moral implications. Tacitus draws on the contrasts between the decadence of Rome and the crude exuberance of the peoples beyond the Rhine, who posed a potential threat to Rome itself. Presumably the aim was to encourage Romans to return to the moral code of the ancestors. However, that political aims should not be overlooked, it is also feasible that Tacitus was trying to make Romans aware of the continuing threat to Roman security that the German tribes posed.

Section 16–27 vividly illustrates the contrasts between Roman and barbarian and nowhere is his praise for the Germans more eloquently put than in regard to marriage.

> They consider this their closest bond, these their sacred rites, these their marriage gods ... at the outset of their marriage the bride is reminded that she comes to share her husband's toils and dangers; in peace, in battle she will suffer and dare the same ...

> So their life is one of fenced-in chastity. There is no arena with its seductions, no dinner-tables with their provocations to corrupt them. Of the exchange of secret letters men and women alike are innocent; adulteries are very few for the number of the people. Punishment is prompt and is the husband's prerogative.

> Better still are those tribes where only maids marry, and where a woman makes an end, once for all, with the hopes and vows of a wife; so they take one husband only, just as one body and one life, in order that there may be no second thoughts, no belated fancies ...

There is another work *Dialogue on Orators*, which has been attributed to Tacitus. In this work four historical characters, two lawyers and two literary men discuss the claims of oratory against those of literature, and the reasons why eloquence had declined from the time, of Cicero's death a century earlier. One reason put forward was that under the 'new regime' of emperors there was little scope for such activities which had flourished in the clashes of the outgoing Republic.

Tacitus' two major works are *The Histories* and *The Annals*. *The Histories* were written first and cover the period from the death of Nero in 68 CE to the assassination of the last Flavian emperor, Domitian in 96 CE. The opening 11 chapters lay the foundation for the whole work. He draws a distinction between the historians of the Republic who were eloquent and outspoken and the historians of the Empire, who Tacitus believes had their judgement impaired by changed political circumstances: these men reacted to the imperial regime with excessive flattery or hostility. In his narrative Tacitus gives a good deal of prominence to individuals and he also concentrates on the underlying causes of the troubles of that period.

For example, in Chapter 8 Tacitus begins his review of the provinces, where his main interest centres on the commanders and their armies and only insomuch as they influence the power struggle. Tacitus is interested not only in an individual's characteristics but in the whole range of group psychology. A major part of the *Histories* is concerned with the psychology of the army 'which played a sinister role in this process of disintegration.' (Grant, M., *Annals* (reprint) 1996 21).When dealing with the eastern provinces he emphasizes individuals, notably Mucianus, governor of Syria. Vespasian, the future emperor, hardly gets a mention.

Unfortunately the extant portion of *The Histories* provides us with only about one quarter of the entire work, covering 2 of the 28 years that it originally contained. Yet this small portion, up to AD 70, contains some brilliant descriptive writing, surpassing Sallust in speed and brevity, imposing Tacitus' personality on the reader. His invented speeches, following the traditions of ancient historians, he inserted with great skill, using them to underline a person's character and to show how the public *persona* differed from the private personality. Much of the material that he used in the earlier books of the *Histories* was drawn from the same source that was used by both Plutarch and Suetonius, yet Tacitus still manages to stamp his own character upon it.

The Annals, as the name suggests, was a year by year narrative, covering the period 14–68 CE from the accession of Tiberius to the death of Nero. Apart from the work being a yearly account the other main emphasis that determines the structure of the work as a whole is that is appraises the reign of individual emperors. The reign of Tiberius covers six books with only a small section of the fifth book missing. Gaius (Caligula) and Claudius are dealt with in a further six books, of which only the last book and a half of Claudius' reign survives. For Nero three and a half books remain.

Tacitus believed that Tiberius' reign fell into two halves and he organizes his books on the emperor in the same fashion on a year by year basis. The first half of Tiberius' reign was mainly a time of prosperity for state and emperor; the second half saw a rapid deterioration. Only at the end of Book VI is a more detailed subdivision of Tiberius' life offered by the author. According to the passage it is only at the end that the true Tiberius is revealed. Behind this lies an attitude towards an understanding of character that is very different from the modern attitude. In the ancient world people regarded character as immutable, so if a person changed towards the end of their life that could only be because they had concealed this part of their nature from early on, not that events or personal trials may have shaped this change. It was therefore the historian's job to unmask this seeming hypocrisy, and present the reader with the truth, which is what Tacitus attempts to do by revealing that Tiberius character was subject to change:

> His character too passed through different phases: (i) excellent both in achievement and reputation, as long as he was a private citizen or held commands under Augustus; (ii) given to concealment and an artful simulator of virtue, as long as Drusus and Germanicus survived; (iii) a similar mixture of good and evil during his mother's lifetime; (iv) then a period of loathsome cruelty, but concealed lusts, as long as he had Sejanus to love or fear; (v) then, finally, he threw himself into crimes and vices alike, casting aside all sense of shame and fear, following no inclination but his own. (*Annals* 6.51.3)

It has been argued that the work should have begun with Augustus' reign but both historical and dramatic reasons suggest that Tacitus chose Tiberius because it was at that point in the transition of power that dynasty became a reality. There is a school of thought that believes that Tacitus treated Tiberius as though he was Domitian retrojecting his own experiences under Domitian. Tacitus describes what steps Augustus took to secure the succession for one of his preferred relatives but their untimely deaths one after another left him with no other option than to nominate Tiberius. These deaths are hinted at as being the work of Augustus' wife Livia (the mother of Tiberius). The theme of Livia's intrigues occurs many times in the opening few chapters and one is left wondering whether we are dealing with history or mere invention. Tacitus notes that these were rumours but he is obviously aware that the innuendo will leave an impression.

Throughout the final chapters there is a theme emerging which becomes apparent only with the very last words of Book I. The theme is *libertas* (freedom), which in this context means the freedom of the senator to speak his mind. Two passages that demonstrate this are the case of Cnaeus Piso (1.75.1) and statements attributed to Asinius Gallus (1.77.3). But there is another passage (1.75.1) where Tacitus speaks about Tiberius sitting in on judicial proceedings of the senate; Tacitus adds that Tiberius sat in on the praetor's court, where his presence acted as a safeguard against the attempts of the powerful to influence the verdict. According to Tacitus 'this aided truth and justice, but destroyed freedom.' The freedom that Tacitus refers to had been the practice of the Republican aristocrat – to pervert the course of justice if they so wished.

The Histories and *The Annals* show that Tacitus recognized the precariousness of a balance between the principate and senatorial freedom. The *Annals*, written after the accession of Hadrian, should not be seen as a projection of Tacitus' disillusionment with Trajan. He may well have been disillusioned with the path that his own career had taken; perhaps he sought a further term as consul or the coveted post of city prefect. However, he ended his career on a high note with the proconsulate of Asia. Now he was free to devote to his time to the writing of history, the history of the period that had laid the political foundations of the last century and in doing so achieved undying fame.

The writings of Suetonius in Latin and Plutarch in Greek are an important part in the changing nature of the tastes of the period; from this period on biography seems to be replacing history. In many respects they could be ranked as literature, alongside the letters composed by Pliny. However, while the dramatist or satirist could adopt a *persona* to give voice to his feelings without incurring any recriminations, Tacitus needed no reminder about the dangers that threatened anyone who gave any offence to someone in authority. The fact that he was dealing with an earlier period was of no avail for he knew that among his readers there would be those who,

> Having similar characters, think that the crimes ascribed to others are aimed at them; while even fame and integrity have their enemies, for they seem to come too close to criticizing their opposites. (*Annals* 4.33.4)

Tacitus, perhaps obsessively, admired the traditional virtues that had made Rome great and the virtues that a Republican ideal embodied. But at the same time he was realistic enough to know that the Republic was a thing of the past and could not be reinstated. He saw political opposition had now become passive, but that this was now the only honourable course, the middle road, taken by his father in law Agricola or Seneca, men who he admired. Although he appears to approve of Augustus, on further reading this is not the case, for Tacitus believed that an autocrat cannot be good. Although Tacitus is a staunch senator and a supporter of the traditional oligarchic view of society, he has no faith in the senate under imperial rule either.

Tacitus sees absolute power as a very dangerous thing whether it is in the hands of someone inexperienced such as Nero, or someone of great experience. 'In spite of all his experience of public affairs, Tiberius was transformed and deranged by absolute power.' (*Annals* 6. 48)

Tacitus' style was unique; at once it is intense, sombre and surprising, yet it also can seem laboured and dislocated, full of insinuation. Thomas Jefferson considered him to be 'the first writer in the world without a single exception'. In a literary sense this is a very true statement, but it cannot be said that in a modern sense we can consider him to be a great historian. He is far from fair in his judgements, although he is a passionate believer in the nobility of history. His accounts of the 'Year of the Four Emperors' are dominated by wild uncontrollable forces and irrational emotions, lust, greed, mob violence, giving the impression of the futility of human behaviour. For all this Tacitus maintained that human beings were capable of great things.

We do not know how well received Tacitus' historical works were at the time. As Martin says:

> The career and writing of Tacitus thus presents a paradox, unique in his time, that a man who had advanced without hindrance through all the stages of a senatorial career should write of the political system under which he himself prospered in a way that starkly underlined how that system tended to bring out the worst in both princeps and senate ... there will often be mention of an element of ambiguity in his attitude to situations and persons. That (it seems to me) is the product of his awareness of the paradox within himself. That awareness, unique among his contemporaries, is perhaps one of the chief reasons why the writings of Tacitus makes so immediate an appeal to our own age.
>
> (Martin, R., *Tacitus* 1981 38)

Chapter Nineteen

Dio Cassius (Cassius Dio Coccianus) (c.163/4 – c.235 CE)

Although I have read pretty nearly everything about them that has been written by anybody, I have not included it all in my history, but only what I have seen fit to select. I trust moreover, that if I have used a fine style, so far as the subject matter permitted, no one will on this account question the truthfulness of the narrative, as has happened in the case of some writers; for I have endeavoured to be equally exact in both these respects so far as possible.

(*Roman History* Book I:1)

Dio Cassius was born in Nicaea in Bithynia sometime between the years 163–4 CE.

He was a related to, perhaps even the grandson, of the famous orator Dio Chrysostom, after whom he was named. His father was Cassius Apronianus, a Roman senator, who served as a governor of Cilicia and Dalmatia. The only information we have regarding his early life comes from the statements that he makes throughout his writing.

We learn from him that he accompanied his father during the latter's governorship of Cilicia and that on his father's death in around 180 CE he went to Rome where he held successfully all of the high offices of state. He became praetor under the reign of the emperor Septimius Severus (193–211 CE), a reign which won the praise of Dio who believed that this heralded a new age. He wrote and published a little book containing an account of the dreams and portents which had foretold Severus' future greatness, which he presented to the emperor. He was twice consul (c.205, 229 CE).

He appears to have withdrawn from public affairs for the remainder of Severus' reign and retired to his estate in Capua, where he spent his time gathering material for his *History*. It is possible that the reign of Severus which he initially believed heralded a new age had not progressed in the way he thought it would and so, disillusioned, he withdrew from public life. Under the emperor Caracalla, Severus' successor, Dio went along as a member of his retinue in 216 ACE in his Eastern expedition, and spent the following winter in his home city Nicomedia. As a member of the local elite he was expected to contribute to the entertaining and feeding of the emperor and his troops. However, he did not accompany Caracalla to the Parthian war. Following this he returned to Italy until 218 CE, when he was appointed by the new emperor Macrinus to be curator (overseer) of Pergamum and Smyrna. He remained in this position during the reign of the succeeding emperor Elagabalus. He enjoyed the intimate friendship of the next emperor, Severus Alexander (222–35 CE), who appointed him proconsul of Africa (Tunisia), and also sent him as legate to the imperial provinces of Dalmatia and Pannonia with two legions under his command.

In 229 CE he returned to Rome and became consul for a second time with Alexander himself as his colleague. However, his disciplinary methods in Pannonia had made him extremely unpopular with the Praetorian Guard and he found it in his best interests to stay away from Rome as much as possible. He finally obtained permission to retire to his native city and presumably spent the rest of life there; as he was past the age of 70 we can conclude that he may have died not longer after his retirement.

The work for which is well known is his *Roman History*, originally comprising 80 books, covering the period from the landing of Aeneas in Italy down to the year of his (Dio's) second consulship in 229 CE. A considerable proportion of the work survives and further sections are preserved in part or in epitomes. The last seven years are treated summarily and were possibly added as an afterthought. He tells us that he spent ten years gathering his information, reading everything of importance and 12 years actually writing the work. Dio tells us how he came to write his *History*:

> After this there occurred very violent wars and civil strife, and I wrote an account of these for the following reason. I had written and published a memoir about the dreams and portents that led the emperor Severus to hope for imperial power, and after he had read the copy I sent him he wrote me a handsome acknowledgement. Receiving the letter in the evening, I soon went to sleep, and as I slept the divine power commanded me to write history. Thus I came to compose the present account. And since it found great favour, not only with others but with Severus himself, I felt the desire to put together the whole history of the Romans; therefore I decided not to leave my composition as a separate work but to incorporate it into this present history ... . I spent ten years collecting everything that the Romans did from the beginning until the death of Severus, and another twelve years in working it up; later events will be recorded as fortune allows.
>
> (*History* 1.73.23 1–3, 5)

The span of the history covers nearly a thousand years and falls into three divisions. The first is the period of the Republic when political power rested with the senate and the people. The second period extended from the establishment of the monarchy to the death of Marcus Aurelius. According to Dio, under the emperors action was no longer taken openly, and the versions that were given to the public were received with suspicion. He wrote interestingly about imperial secrecy which made accurate information even harder to obtain:

> In later times most events began to be kept secret and were denied to common knowledge, and even though it may happen that some matters are made public, the reports are discredited because they cannot be investigated and the suspicion grows that everything is

said and done according to the wishes of the men in power at the time and their associates.

In consequence much that never materializes becomes common talk, while much that has undoubtedly come to pass remains unknown. And in pretty well every instance the report which is spread abroad does not correspond with what actually happened.

(*History* 70: 19)

Dio knew that it was impossible to master the vast problems of the Empire but the size and complexity of it put any acquisition of accurate knowledge out of reach. So, he had to content himself with giving the published report of events, now and again giving his own comments based on what he had heard or read. The third period covers his own time and he could now write about events of which he had some first-hand knowledge.

He probably began writing during the reign of the emperor Caracalla, one of the most despicable and autocratic emperors of any age. Caracalla's father on the other hand, Septimius Severus, shared many traits in common with the first emperor Augustus for he had also come to power after a period of civil war. Like Augustus, Severus' power was based on the loyalty of his soldiers and attention to the welfare of the ordinary people of Rome. But Severus, and certainly his son after him, never concealed that theirs was a military despotism, with the senate merely a tool to validate their actions.

Dio's reaction was most probably typical of men of his class; describing Severus' entry into Rome he says:

Entering the city in this way, he made some fine promises to us like the emperors of old, that he would put no senator to death; and he took an oath to this effect, and furthermore ordered it to be confirmed in a joint decree that the emperor and anyone who aided him in such a deed, both themselves and their children, were to be declared public enemies. Yet he himself was the first to transgress and not keep this law, executing many senators ... He did many things that we disliked, and he was blamed for disturbing the city with the numbers of his soldiers, and for burdening the state with excessive expenditure, and most of all because he placed his hopes of safety not in the goodwill of his companions but in the strength of his army.

(*History* 75.2.1–3)

Dio obviously saw that this was no way for an emperor to behave; he seems to have taken the emperor Augustus as a role model. Dio paints a very favourable picture of Augustus, although he occasionally includes some discreditable items. He outlines the period of transition from Republic to Empire and shows how, if used correctly, such imperial power could benefit all citizens no matter what their status. For Dio Augustus is a benefactor of mankind. His sense of the importance of this 'new regime' can be seen in the way he structured Books LII and LIII.

Dio's own political views are expressed clearly in the fictitious speech of Maecenas (Book LII) in answer to Agrippa, and shows that Dio approved, in principle at least, of the monarchy.

Ponder these thoughts and the rest of the advice I have offered, be persuaded by me, and do not let slip this fortune which has singled you out from mankind and set you over them as their ruler. For if, in reality, you prefer the fact of monarchical rule yet fear the name of king as accursed, you need not accept that title, but can still rule under the style of Caesar. If you need other titles besides, the people will give you that of imperator as they did your father Julius, and they will pay homage to your august status by yet another form of address. In this way you can enjoy to the full the reality of kingship without the stigma which attaches to the name.

(*History* 52:40)

Dio chose men like Maecenas as his mouth piece because he was one of the most influential and important of Augustus' advisors.

Dio wrote in the annalistic fashion, which was very popular among the Romans. All the events of the year no matter where in the world they took place were grouped together. The consuls for each year are regularly named at the appropriate point in the text and prefixed to each book is a table of consuls for the time period covered. When he writes about the Imperial period he is careful to specify to the day the exact duration of each emperor's reign. However, despite this attention to detail it is often very difficult to extract a consistent chronology, for in trying to examine the causes or results of a given event he exceeds the limits of a single year by a considerable margin. In other words he uses an annalistic framework but sometimes puts events in the wrong year. With regard to this he misdates an Augustan conspiracy (see Millar, F., *A Study of Cassius Dio* 1964 97).

Dio held two theories about historical writing. While he conceded that the true value of history demanded that details and personal anecdotes should give way to the larger aspects and the significance of events, at the same time the historian was also a rhetorician. This meant that if the facts lacked ascertain lustre they could be adorned or modified in the interests of dramatic presentation. Unfortunately, these two principles have greatly diminished the work of Dio for modern historians, for the very data which is required is often lacking or confusing; exact dates and names are often omitted, geographical details too vague to be useful and battles lose some of the individual elements in favour of generalizations. However, Dio is the main source for much of the second and third centuries CE and he can sometimes be useful for the first century CE when giving details from sources not used by Suetonius or Tacitus.

Chapter Twenty

Arrian (Lucius Flavius Arrianus) (c.86 – c.160 CE)

No matter who I am that make this claim. I need not declare my name though it is by no means unheard of in the world; I need not specify my country or my family, or any official position I may have held. Rather let me say this: that this book of mine is, and has been from my youth, more precious than country, kin and public advancement- indeed for me it is these things.

(Anabasis tr. De Selincourt 1976)

Lucius (or Aulus) Flavius Arrianus came from a family at Nicomedia, a Hellenized city in Bithynia where he was born, educated and where he held the priesthood of Demeter and Kore. An inscription records his name and this provides evidence to show that he was a Roman citizen; it appears that his father or grandfather had received the honour from one of the Flavian emperors (CE 69–96). In Greek-speaking cities citizenship was rarely granted except to members of the local ruling elite, and that fact that Arrian held a priesthood would also suggest wealth and high birth.

In his earlier years he had attended the classes of the Stoic teacher Epictetus at Nicopolis and was so impressed that every day he wrote down extensive notes of the lectures, to try to preserve a word for word account. He published these notes many years later entitled *Discourses of Epictetus* of which eight books survive. He also wrote a manual summarizing Epictetus' teaching (*Enchiridion*) which is still extant. References that he makes in the *Discourses* indicate that he was a pupil during the first half of the second century CE. Arrian in his own day was considered a philosopher for he also composed a little book on meteorology, which was then considered philosophy, and this also survives.

From inscriptions as well as from information in his work we know that he was governor of Cappadocia from circa 132–7 CE; he had previously held the office of consul (c.129 CE). It has been argued that he was admitted to the senate and rapidly promoted by the emperor Hadrian (117–38 CE) as a reward for his literary works. There are no details concerning Arrian's early career in Rome. As governor of Cappadocia he had the task of protecting the upper Euphrates frontier with an army that possibly consisted of two legions. It could be possible that he had some military experience before he held this position, although high military commands could be entrusted to civilians. Arrian reported officially to Hadrian in Latin, but he also presented him with a small work in Greek entitled 'Voyage round the Black Sea' (*Periplous Euxini*). He had during his time as governor inspected the forts in this area, and while on official duty had taken time to compile a dossier on the works of art and antiquity in the area which he knew the emperor would be interested in.

He was later confronted with a serious danger of an Alan invasion and wrote a short description of his preparations to repel it (*Ectaxis contra Alanos*). His fellow countryman Dio Cassius, who composed a biography of Arrian, now lost, says in his *History* (1:xix) that Arrian did in fact deter the Alans from attack. In 136/7 CE he wrote a third treatise on *Tactics* which includes an account of contemporary methods of training cavalry. Both of these works are useful for an historian for the evidence they provide on the Roman army in the provinces and on their marching and fighting tactics.

Arrian composed many works but perhaps the most famous of all is the *Anabasis Alexandrou* (The History of the Campaigns of Alexander, The Anabasis of Alexander), which is the best evidence we have for Alexander the Great. There are some drawbacks, however, because Arrian plunges straight into a narrative of Alexander's campaigns without giving us any information about the condition of Persia, Greece or Macedon, what Alexander's military resources were or indeed how he came into this position in the first place. Nevertheless by comparison with other works on Alexander, Arrian's comes out as the best.

Arrian chose to use two eye witness accounts in compiling his work on Alexander, one by Aristobulus, an architect and one by Ptolemy, a commander of Alexander's who went on to become the founder of the Egyptian successor kingdom.

He says in his introduction:

> Wherever Ptolemy son of Lagus and Aristobulus son of Aristobulus have both given the same accounts of Alexander son of Philip, it is my practice to record what they say as completely true, but where they differ, to select the version I regard as more trustworthy and also better worth telling.
>
> (Book I:1)

He adds that he has also recorded, but only as tales, statements he found in other writers, which he sometimes rejects as being utterly incredible.

He says that Alexander marched to the Hellespont in 334 days with not many more than 30,000 foot and over 5,000 horse soldiers. But Arrian is often unreliable concerning detail; although he often refers to individual units when he describes the employment of the army in great battles, he does not give any particulars of the strength of those units. It seems incredible that his sources, especially Ptolemy, would never have given any breakdown of the various units deployed.

However, Arrian's account is in general more clear and coherent than those given by some others (Diodorus, Curtius), containing less trivia. Because little of the works of Aristobulus and Ptolemy survive, Arrian's usage of them provides us with an idea of their value as source material and justifies Arrian's dependence upon them. If there is a flaw it is that Arrian was too much of an admirer of Alexander to notice that these sources were often apologetic. Likewise that Ptolemy's version may well have been coloured by the feuds that occurred after Alexander's death in which he had played no small part.

In the *Anabasis* he writes in the old Attic (Greek dialect), while in the *Indica* he seeks to reproduce the Ionic of Herodotus. No doubt this was no mean feat and may explain his claim that he was master of Greek speech. Arrian was a prolific writer, included in his works was a ten-volume *History of Affairs after Alexander* (now lost), a *History of Parthia* and a *History of Bithynia* (both also lost). Apart from the *Anabasis* and the *Indica*, the only work to have survived is his essay on Hunting (*Cynegeticus*). He also appears to have written biographies of Dion and Timoleon and a biography of a bandit named Tilliborus.

There is no evidence that Arrian was employed by Rome after his governorship of Cappadocia. He retired to Athens where he was a citizen and became *archon* (chief magistrate) in 148/9 CE. He is said to have lived into the reign of Marcus Aurelius (161–80 CE) but was dead when Lucian wrote his *Alexander the False Prophet* shortly after 180 CE. It is assumed that most of his writings date from his period of retirement.

Arrian said Alexander's greatness was worthy of praise and should be known by future generations, he wanted to make Alexander a legend. However, some historians disagree with his ambition. Bosworth criticized his work:

> Arrian is prone to misread and misinterpret his primary sources, and the flow of his narrative can obscure treacherous quicksands of error (1980)

One of his principal sources Ptolemy had been an interested party, Bosworth says:

> Not only has it been virtually disproved that Ptolemy constructed

his history from archival material, but it appears that he inserted his own propaganda to exaggerate his personal achievements under Alexander and to discredit those of his rivals.

Modern scholars agree that Arrian's work is to a great extent a reworking of Ptolemy; using material from other writers particularly Aristobulus. However, the main drawback is that Alexander as a political leader and a man are not reflected in Arrian's work clearly or indeed reliably. Arrian was primarily a military historian and here he followed his great model Xenophon, from whom he earned his nickname. He says little about Alexander's personal life, political ideologies or the reasons why he campaigned against Persia. However, Arrian's work does give a reasonably full account of Alexander's life during the Persian campaign and he offers an assessment of Alexander that is neither totally flattering nor totally condemning.

Chapter Twenty One

Men of Letters: Cicero and Pliny the Younger

Although these men are not classed as historians their work is invaluable for gaining an insight into the political and social issues of their times. This is especially true of Cicero whose letters give an almost daily account of the last days of the Republic.

CICERO (MARCUS TULLIUS) 106–43 BCE

> From the day I arrived in Rome all my views, words and actions were increasingly directed towards peace. But a strange madness was abroad.
>
> (Cicero, *Ad familiares* 146 XVI 12)

Marcus Tullius Cicero was born into a wealthy family in Arpinum (Southern Italy) on 3 January 106 BCE. He studied law and oratory at Rome, also Greek philosophy and literature. He also served during the Social war of 90–88 BCE under the command of Pompeius Strabo, the father of Pompey the Great. The Social war was followed by terrible internal struggles. In 88 BCE the consul Sulla, who was also a brilliant general set a fateful precedent by marching his army on Rome as revenge for a personal injustice. Most of his opponents were killed except Marius who escaped into exile. Sulla set of for the east to Pontus to deal with the troublesome king Mithridates and while he was away Rome was besieged by the forces of the exiled Marius. Marius was to take his revenge upon the aristocracy in a brutal way: on his orders, 4,000 slaves carried out murders for five days and nights. Finally Marius and Cinna were elected consuls for the year 86 BCE.

Marius was to die only a few months after taking Rome and a fortnight after being elected to the consulship, leaving Rome and Italy under the control of the consul Cinna. Once again on Sulla's return a bloodbath ensued but now Sulla emerged as the victor. Although he was ruthless and showed no mercy to his enemies, he was seen to be the restorer of the Republic and as dictator he produced a new constitution which was to remain in place for almost 30 years.

Despite having Marian connections Cicero seems to have disliked the regime of Cinna and only started his public career as an advocate after Sulla's victory. When he was 26 years old he made his first successful public speech which was in defence of a client Roscius the victim of a persecution by an influential freedman and favourite of the dictator Sulla. After a tour of Athens and Asia Minor in 76 BCE he was elected *quaestor* and obtained an appointment in Sicily. In 70 BCE he secured a successful impeachment at the request of the Sicilians of the corrupt governor Gaius Verres. In 66 BCE he was praetor and supported in a great speech (*Pro Lege Manilia*) the appointment of Pompey to conduct the war against Mithridates VI.

In 63 BCE he was consul and foiled the plot by the conspirator Catiline. Catiline was a patrician champion of the bankrupt and disinherited. Catiline had left Rome and joined his armed followers but was defeated and killed. Five of the conspirators were brought back in front of the senate and after a memorable debate were executed on Cicero's orders. He was hailed as 'father of his country'; however, in foiling the plot Cicero had transgressed the constitution, for no Roman citizen could suffer capital punishment save by the sentence of the people in a regular assembly.

In 62 BCE Pompey the general returned to Rome after his brilliant defeat over Mithridates and the King of Armenia. Pompey made two requests of the senate, the ratification of his terms in the East and land for his veterans. The senate under the influence of the consul Cato distrusted his motives, and there were several senators who held personal grudges against him; his requests were vetoed. Pompey struck up an alliance with two prominent politicians who were also both out of favour with the establishment, M. Crassus and Gaius Julius Caesar. This alliance was known as the First Triumvirate although it had no official status.

In 59 BCE Caesar became consul. Despite senatorial opposition and constitutional precedence he pushed through a legislative programme that gave him a five-year command in northern Italy and Gaul and passed laws that suited his allies. Before leaving Rome to take up his command he had arranged to personally have Cicero eliminated, however, the tribune Publius Clodius who had a personal grudge against Cicero was allowed to press the charge that he had acted unconstitutionally in the killing of the five conspirators.

In 58 BCE Cicero took refuge in Thessalonica: he was condemned to exile and his houses in Rome and Tuscany were plundered, but one year later the people apparently called for his return. Cicero was now no longer a power in politics and the incident had made him reticent to accept popular opinion. He could not decide whether to support Pompey and the aristocracy or Caesar and his party. Because of his hesitancy he lost the esteem of both parties. In 52 BCE he defended Milo who had killed Clodius in a riot. The following year he was in Cilicia as governor. In 49–8 BCE he was with Pompey's army in Greece but the defeat of Pompey at Pharsalia in August 48 BCE by Julius Caesar saw him throw himself on Caesar's mercy.

In September 47 BCE he was back in Rome. Caesar was outwardly friendly toward him and he was on sociable terms with many of Caesar's followers but his advice was no longer sought and he made few appearances in the senate. In 46–44 BCE he composed most of his chief works on rhetoric and philosophy, living in retirement plagued by disappointments. Cicero had no prior knowledge of the conspiracy against Caesar, despite the fact that when Caesar was assassinated, Brutus, one of his murderers, waved his dagger and called out Cicero's name. The act did meet with Cicero's approval, but unfortunately the Republic was still threatened by Mark Antony, who had escaped assassination and now planned to take Caesar's place.

In 43 BCE, after the death of Caesar, Cicero's famous speeches against Mark Antony (the *Philippics*) were delivered in the senate, and these were to cost him his life. Caesar's heir was Octavian and at first Cicero professed great confidence in Octavian's loyalty to the Republic. Soon after the defeat of the assassins Octavian, Antony and Lepidus formed themselves into a second triumvirate and they set about proscribing their old enemies; Cicero's name was on the list. Antony's troops overtook his carriage while he was fleeing to his home in Tuscany. Bravely Cicero stepped from the litter and told the assassins to do their work, which they did. He was 63 years old.

Cicero excelled in oratory. His speeches before the senate and the people indicate that he had the ability to present issues in different ways to different audiences, invariably with great success. While he was consul he was able to persuade the populace against measures of land redistribution and corn relief even though there were genuine shortages of both. Who else but an orator like Cicero could have persuaded the senate to vote official powers to a man (Octavian), who was a revolutionary with a private army?

The most difficult type of oratory to master is known as 'forensic'. In this type of oratory arguments derived from law and fact counted less than appeals to the emotions. In this aspect Cicero dominated the courts for at least 20years. He was particularly famed for his ability to arouse and calm the emotions of both jurors and spectators and was regularly asked to give concluding speeches for the defence.

He wrote a history of Roman oratory in 46 BCE entitled *Brutus*. In this work as in his earlier work *De Oratore* Cicero laid great stress on the proper training for an orator. According to him it was not enough to be able to master the techniques of oratory but also to acquire a broad education based on Greek culture. Cicero himself had been an apprentice to L. Licinius Crassus who as censor in 92 BCE had opposed the opening of schools in Latin rhetoric; he insisted that Greek was a much richer language with an established tradition of great oratory that needed to be studied.

While advocating history and law as essential components of the orator's education, Cicero fervently believed that Greek philosophy was the essential ingredient of any orator's education. First because it imparts wisdom and second because it offers training in argument. Cicero chose his philosophical sect with care. He rejected Epicureanism mainly because it involved abstention from public life; a philosophy that suited his friend Atticus very well.

Cicero preferred the teachers of the New Academy. This was name given to a section of the Platonic school who taught that certain knowledge was unattainable but that probability was an intellectually respectable basis for practical life. These people were committed to the Academic tradition of arguing both sides of a question, which was excellent practice for a life of public speaking. Their beliefs allowed Cicero the freedom to choose whatever philosophical tradition he found most convincing regarding different issues. Cicero always believed that public service took precedence over study and writing; however philosophy remained his great passion. This was fortuitous for him when the political climate became difficult. This is evidenced in 46 BCE by two minor works that show his enthusiasm for philosophy. The first and by far the most impressive was *The Paradoxes of the Stoics* is Cicero at his rhetorical best. He defends the extreme formulations of the Stoic doctrine, for instance that virtue is the only good, and that all bad deeds are wicked whatever the cause. The work was dedicated to Cato's nephew, Brutus and opens with praise of Cato, who was leading the Republican forces in Africa at the time. One year later Cato was to commit suicide and Cicero delivered a moving eulogy for him.

By the following year Cicero embarked on what he termed as a plan 'to provide for my fellow citizens a path through the noblest form of learning.' Over the next couple of years he produced a dozen works. Mostly these were in the form of dialogue similar to the kind invented by Plato and Aristotle, which covered three branches of philosophy. The series began with *Hortensius*, a work that is now lost; other works were *On the Nature of the Gods, On Divination, On Fate* and a moral philosophy *On Ends* and a work that defended the Stoic view of happiness and duty *On Moral Obligations*. It was not Cicero's intention to expound particular doctrines; rather he advocated that there was no specific truth but defended his right to find different views more convincing according to the argument used on each occasion. His main contribution was his ability to reproduce Greek philosophy in Latin and to create Latin philosophical literature for Rome to rival that of Greece. Among his many admirers was the elder Seneca (55 BCE – 40 CE) the Roman rhetorician.

This period of history that begins with the dictatorship of Sulla in 82 BCE and closes with the death of Caesar in 44 BCE covers the political life and death of the later Roman Republic. The works of Cicero give the historian a tremendous amount of insight into this period. From the abundance of letters and speeches that survive some light is cast on the men who were remaking the history of Rome. The correspondence that Cicero maintained throughout his life is probably the most valuable of all historical source material for this period. Many of his letters were private and not intended for public consumption; others were written with a more general circulation in mind. In all, there are over 900 letters focusing on a variety of issues which provide insight into the public and private views of the time. The most candid of his letters were written to his friend Atticus.

Atticus (Titus Pomponius) was an old school friend who came from an equestrian family. After his father's death in circa 86 BCE he made his home in Athens, hence the cognomen Atticus. In 65 BCE he returned to Rome but made frequent visits to his estate in Epirus, and it is these absences that resulted in the correspondence between the two friends. From his many letters to Atticus we can glimpse how the events of Cicero's life affected him for example he writes from his exile in Thessalonica in May 58 BCE:

Clearly I have every reason for apprehension, but I don't know what to write. I'm afraid of all manner of things, and nothing seems too bad to happen to us in our present plight. As for my unhappy self, plunged in dire woes and afflictions of my own and now with this added fear [events taking place in Rome], I am staying for the present at Thessolonika, in suspense and not daring to make any move.

(*Letters* to Atticus 53. III.8)

Another written in April 55 BCE from his estate at Cumae also indicates his weariness with the political events in Rome and his desire to indulge his passion for philosophy:

At Puetoli there is a strong rumour that Ptolemy [Egyptian king father of Cleopatra VII] is on his throne. If you have any more reliable information, I should be glad to know. I am living here on Fautus' library, you perhaps think it's on these Puteolan and Lucrine commodities [seafood for which the bay of Naples was famous]. But seriously, while all other amusements and pleasures have lost their charm because of my age and the state of our country, literature relieves and refreshes me. I would rather sit on that little seat you have underneath Aristotle's bust than in our Consuls' chairs of state, and I would rather walk with you at your home than with the personages in whose company it appears that walk I must.

(*Letters* to Atticus 85.IV.9)

There are other letters written by Cicero to a variety of people in the *Letters to Friends,* consisting of almost all private letters written with no thought of later publication. Nearly all of the letters were written in the last 20 years of his life. Atticus preserved his letters dating from his consulship in 63 BCE in 11 papyrus rolls. It seems possible that they were not published until the middle of the first century CE even though the rest of the correspondence was published earlier. The *Letters to Friends* appears to have been arranged and published separately or in groups during the Augustan period, possibly by Tiro, Cicero's secretary. In all there are 16 books of letters; some books consist entirely of letters to a single correspondent; Book I, Lentulus Spinther; Book III Appius Claudius. Books X–XII consist of correspondence relating to the struggle with Mark Antony in 44–3 BCE. The 'friends' are a differing bunch: some like Trebatius were familiar to Cicero and he could write as informally to them as he did to Atticus; others like Cato and Spinther were powerful aristocrats, and Cicero adopted a more elaborate style; high sentiments and flattery were the mark of more 'official' correspondence.

When read in conjunction with the historical background Cicero's letters provide a unique and educational glimpse into the political world of late Republican Rome: in addition his works in general hold a special place in the cultural history of his time, as Qunitilian the Roman rhetorician (35–100 CE) said: Cicero was 'the name, not of a man but of eloquence itself.'

PLINY THE YOUNGER (C. PLINIUS CAECILIUS SECUNDUS)

> You have frequently pressed me to make a select collection of my Letters (if there be any which show some literary finish) and give them to the public. I have accordingly done so; not indeed in their proper order of time, for I was not compiling a history; but just as they presented themselves to my hands.
>
> (*Letters* Book I. Letter To Septicius)

As Pliny himself says he was not compiling a history, so it may seem a little out of place to include him among the ancient historians of this book. However, the contribution of Pliny's work to the modern historian cannot be overlooked, for Pliny supplies a unique insight into his own time and culture. There are many aspects in his *Letters* which are of enormous value when attempting to understand the social and political history of Rome at the turn of the first century CE.

Pliny the Younger, as he is known, to distinguish him from his maternal uncle, known as Pliny the Elder and author of the *Natural Histories*, was born at Novum Comum (Como) in 61 or 62 CE. Both his father and mother belonged to the provincial nobility and were very wealthy. On the death of his father when Pliny was still quite young, he was left to the guardianship of Verginius Rufus. He received a good education which was completed in Rome, where he studied rhetoric under Quintilian, possibly supervised by his uncle.

Pliny the Elder, keen to witness the eruption of Vesuvius in 79 CE, which obliterated the town of Pompeii, got so close to the eruption that he succumbed to the overpowering vapours and died. On his uncle's death in 79 CE, Pliny was left as sole heir, being adopted by him in his will, so according to custom, Pliny took his adoptive father's name and was known as C. Plinius Caecilius Secundus. The same year, while just 18 years of age, Pliny made his first appearance at the bar; he was to become one of the most eminent advocates of his time. He worked his way through the various stages of an official career; in 89 CE he became quaestor, as Domitian's personal nominee; praetor in 93 CE and was also appointed by Domitian prefect of the military treasury in 94 CE.

His public life was successful, despite Domitian's reign of terror. Pliny himself believed that he had always been in danger from the emperor, because several of his friends, Helvidius, Rusticus and Senecio had been the emperor's victims, but the evidence suggests that Pliny never actually fell foul of Domitian. Pliny seems to have played a prudent role during that troubled period, although he never appears to have been dishonourable. He managed to conceal his sympathies with those who were the object of Domitian's persecutions. However, he did like to portray himself as one who narrowly escaped martyrdom under the tyrant.

Pliny was greatly valued both by the emperors Nerva and his successor Trajan. At the close of Nerva's short reign he made Pliny prefect of the treasury of Saturn, which was apparently the only time that this important post was given to a man who had held the prefecture of the Military Treasury. The emperor Trajan (98–117 CE) nominated him for the consulship in 100 CE. Three years later he received the office of augur and in 105 CE, he was given the 'curatorship of the bed and the banks of the Tiber and of the city sewers'. This was a demanding position requiring great administrative abilities and was the last public office that Pliny held at Rome.

The emperor Trajan decided to send Pliny to the province of Bithynia. This province had been placed by Augustus among the senatorial provinces, that is to say a province administered by the senate through proconsuls chosen by lot. The organization of this province had been a failure; political disturbances were rife and the cities' finances disorganized. Trajan decided to take matters in hand and so sent Pliny in circa 111 CE as his legate with full powers to reform and reorganize. Pliny held this post for about two years when he presumably died. After his last letter to Trajan, where he speaks of sending his wife home to Italy, there is no trace of him. The inscription erected to him at Comum records that he held no other office and that he died before 115 CE, inferred from the fact that Trajan is not given the official title Parthicus, which he assumed in that year.

The correspondence between him and Trajan can be found in the tenth and last book of his collection, and was probably published after Pliny's death. These official letters were not written with an eye to publication but the rest of his *Letters* were. This can be seen especially in comparison with the letters of Cicero, who was writing 'real' letters to his friends and discussed the events of his day in an open-hearted and sometimes highly allusive way. Pliny's letters by comparison are pieces of graceful prose, exercises on a variety of subjects and events. The chronology of the first nine books has been much disputed as none of the letters are dated, but it is probable that Pliny published them in groups, the first group in 97–98 CE and the last in 108–109 CE.

Pliny was married three times but had no children. Nothing is known about his first wife; his second died about 97 CE and he married again, a young woman named Calpurnia who was the granddaughter of his fellow townsman Calpurnius Fabatus. Pliny was well over 40 years of age by now and his wife probably about 14. Pliny's description of his third marriage has been criticized for being patronizing and cool but we need to remember that Roman marriages were based on convenience rather than affection, and from his many letters we see that he was a devoted husband. He describes his feelings for his wife, and hers for him, in the language of romantic love.

> … I am persuaded with infinite pleasure, that she behaves in a manner worthy of her father, her grandfather, and yourself. She is incomparably discerning, incomparably thrifty; while her love for her husband betokens a chaste nature. Her affection to me has given her a turn to books; and my compositions, which she takes a pleasure in reading, and even getting by heart, are continually in her hands. How full of solicitude is she when I am entering upon any cause. How kindly does she rejoice with me when it is over! When I am pleading, she stations messengers to inform her from time to time how I am heard, what applauses I receive, and what success attends the cause. When at any time I recite my works, she sits close at hand. Concealed behind a curtain, and greedily overhears my praises. She sings my verses and sets them to her lyre, with no other master but Love, the best instructor.
>
> From these circumstances I draw my most assured hopes, that the harmony between us will increase with our days, and be as lasting as our lives. For it is not my youth or my person, which time gradually impairs; it is my glory of which she is enamoured …
>
> (To Calpurnia Hispulla *Letters* 4:19)

The value of Pliny's *Letters* for an historian is that they supply a great deal of interesting detail about Roman life and manners. The characteristics of Pliny himself also give us a much insight into the social values of the elite at this period. For example the civilized attitude of men like Pliny to their freedmen and slaves, on whom they depended for responsible staff in their households.

> As I know how mildly you treat your own servants I the more frankly confess to you the indulgence I show to mine ... But were I of a rough and hardened temper, the ill state of health of my freedman Zosimus would suffice to soften me. He is honest and well educated; but his profession, his certified accomplishment is as a comedian, wherein he highly excels. He speaks with great emphasis, judgement, propriety and some gracefulness; and also plays the lyre more skilfully than a comedian need do. To this I must add, he reads history, oratory and poetry, as well as if he had singly applied himself to that art .... .
>
> He is besides adhered to me by long-standing affection, which is heightened by his present danger. For nature has so formed our hearts, that nothing contributes more to raise and inflame our love for nay object than the apprehension of being deprived of it; a sentiment which Zosimus has given me occasion to experience more than once.
>
> (To Valerius Paulinus *Letters* 5:19)

Pliny's behaviour is perhaps a little more tolerant than the normal behaviour toward slaves and freedmen but his horror at the murder of Larcius Macedo at the hands of his slaves, even though the man was brutal towards them, shows that even while some men could be indulgent toward their servants, generally they were still considered to have few human rights.

> The horrid barbarity which the slaves of Larcius Macedo, a person of Praetorian rank, lately exercised upon their master, is

so extremely tragic, that it deserves to be the subject of something more considerable than a private letter; although at the same time it must be acknowledged, theirs was a haughtiness and severity in his treatment of them, which showed him little- nay I should rather say too- mindful that his own father was once in the same station.

Thus you see to what indignities, outrages and dangers we are exposed. Nor is lenity and good treatment any security from the villainies of your servants; for it is malice, and not reflection that arms such ruffians against their masters. So much for this piece of news.

(To Acilius *Letters* 3:14)

Generally Pliny preferred to stay in the country engaging in quiet study or other country activities. He gives us some valuable insights into the work and leisure time of Romans of his class.

One cannot be surprised, that take any single day in Rome, the reckoning comes out right, or at least seems to do so; and yet if you take them in the lump the reckoning comes out wrong. Ask anyone how he has been employed today? He will tell you perhaps, 'I have been at the ceremony of assuming the manly robe; this friend invited me to a betrothal, this to a wedding; that desired me to attend the hearing of his cause; one begged me to be a witness to his will; another called me to sit as co-assessor'. These are offices which, on the day one is engaged in them, appear necessary; yet they seem bagatelles when reckoned in your daily occupation- and far more so when you have quitted Rome for the country.

(To Minicius Fundanus *Letters* 1:9)

In the country, on his estate, Pliny begrudgingly indulged in the pursuits of a country gentleman, as this letter to the historian Tacitus shows.

Certainly you will laugh (and laugh you may) when I tell you that your old acquaintance is turned sportsman, and has taken three noble boars. What! (I think I hear you say with astonishment) Pliny! Even he. However, I indulged at the same time my beloved inactivity, and while I sat at my nets, you would have found me, not with spear and dart, but pen and tablets by my side. I mused and wrote, being resolved if I returned with my hands empty, at least to come home with my pocket-book full. Believe me this manner of studying is not to be despised; you cannot conceive how greatly exercise contributes to enliven the imagination.

(To Cornelius Tacitus *Letters* 1:6)

However, the *Letters* do not just provide a source book for the social and political events of the day; they also paint perhaps the fullest self portrait of any Roman to have survived, with perhaps the possible exceptions of Cicero and Horace. Through his letters Pliny, consciously or not, reveals himself. He was tolerant (8:22) but not vain, he was a devoted husband and son-in-law and a loyal friend; in fact his qualities were often positive. If there is failing it is probably his intellectual snobbery and this is shown in his attitude towards the Games, an attitude which is incidentally shared by Cicero and Seneca.

I have been spending all the last few days among my notes and papers in most welcome peace. How could I-in the city? The Races were on, a type of spectacle which has never had the slightest attraction for me. I can find nothing new or different in them; once seen is enough, so it surprises me all the more that so many thousands of adult men should have such a childish passion for watching galloping horses and drivers standing in chariots, over and over again. If they were attracted by the speed of the horses or the driver's skill one could account for it, but in fact it is the racing-colours they really support and care about, and if the colours were to be exchanged in mid-course during a race, they would transfer their favour and enthusiasm and rapidly desert the famous horses and drivers whose names they shout as they recognize them from afar. Such is the popularity and importance of a worthless shirt-I don't mean with the crowd, which is worth less than the shirt, but with certain serious individuals. When I think how this futile, tedious, monotonous business can keep them sitting endlessly in their seats, I take pleasure in the fact that the pleasure is not mine. And I have been very glad to fill my idle hours with literary work during these days which others have wasted in the idlest of occupations.

(To Calvisius Rufus *Letters* 9:6).

Pliny's *Letters* act as a foil to his contemporary Juvenal's castigation of society's faults, Tacitus' analysis of the corruption of power, Martial's malicious attacks on individuals and their vices. Pliny lives in a different world from the idle rich or irresponsible aristocrat in a period of history about which Gibbon said; 'during which the condition of the human race was most happy and most prosperous.'

Chapter Twenty Two

The Biographers: Plutarch and Suetonius

Biography was an important sub-category of the monographic tradition of historiography, and these works are invaluable to the historian. It is always useful to combine biography with other historical writing on the period concerned. Two of the most important biographers of the ancient world were Plutarch and Suetonius.

PLUTARCH. (L. MESTRIUS PLUTARCHUS) *c*.50 – *c*.120 CE

> Fond of seeing and learning, having adequate means and not thinking it worthwhile to acquire more, he employed his leisure for such travels and assembled information (historia) to be the material of what he himself called 'philosophy with theology as its goal.
>
> (Plutarch, *The Decline of the Oracles*)

Plutarch was born sometime around 50 CE at Chaeronea in Boeotia (central Greece, part of the Roman province of Achaea), to one of the principal local families. He spent most of his life in this region, although he travelled widely in Asia Minor and Egypt. He also spent time in both Athens, where he went to study philosophy, and Rome, where he was sent on a political mission. He became a Roman citizen and adopted the family name of Lucius Mestrius Florus, who was consul in 72 CE and whom he accompanied on a visit to Bedriacum. While in Rome Plutarch gave lectures in Greek on philosophical and rhetorical subjects. He was to lecture in Rome again in the 90s when he had become famous.

Despite becoming a Roman citizen, Plutarch was intensely proud of his Greek heritage. He held a long tenure of priesthood at the shrine of Delphi near his home. He was a writer and thinker and had received the best possible education in philosophy and rhetoric, topics on which he lectured. Although he became something of a celebrity throughout the Roman Empire he continued to live and work in his native land, participating in local affairs, even serving as mayor.

His main interest was philosophy and on his country estate guests from all over the Roman Empire would congregate for serious conversations presided over by Plutarch in his marble chair. Many of these dialogues were recorded by him. The 78 essays and other works which have survived are known collectively under the general heading of the *Moralia*, written in Greek, perhaps the most famous of these being *On the Malice of Herodotus*.

In the *Moralia* Plutarch expresses his belief in reincarnation as a bad thing preventing the soul from joining the stars. His letter to his wife consoling her after the death of their 2-year-old daughter offers a glimpse of his philosophy:

> The soul, being eternal, after death is like a caged bird that has been released. If it has been a long time in the body and has become tame by many affairs and long habit, it will immediately take another body and once again become involved in the troubles of the world. The worst thing about old age is that the soul's memory of the other world grows dim, while at the same time its attachment to things of this world becomes so strong that the soul tends to retain the form that it had in the body, until liberated, quickly recovers its fire and goes onto higher things.

Plutarch also stands out among ancient moralists for his sympathetic attitude to marriage and children. He composed another work for Clea, the daughter of some friends, on the occasion of her wedding entitled *Advice on Marriage*.

However, perhaps his most savage account is the one reserved for Herodotus whom he put on trial in a literary sense in his work. The main complaint that was made about him was his emphasis on the pro-Persian sympathies of the Boeotians. This, according to Plutarch, was an example of his general malevolence. Plutarch says 'by not recording good deeds and not omitting bad, he confirms the view that jealousy and gloating over misfortune spring from the same vice'. Plutarch, in the Introduction, elaborates on the ways in which an historian can display malice. Plutarch was expressing something that was genuinely of concern to him, and he appears to be trying to establish some sort of writer's code of conduct. He says:

> Since it is difficult, or rather perhaps impossible, to display a man's life as pure and blameless, we should fill out the truth to give a likeness where the good points lie, but regard the errors and follies with which emotion or political necessity sullies a career as deficiencies in some virtue rather than displays of viciousness, and therefore not make any special effort to draw attention to them in the record. Our attitude should be one of modest shame on behalf of human nature, which never produces unmixed good or bad character of undisputed excellence.
>
> (*Cimon* 2.4–5)

Plutarch also became interested, in his later years, in character, which was one of the motives behind his composition *Parallel Lives* or *Greek and Roman Lives,* as they are alternatively known where his aim was to write a philosophical biography of one famous Roman and one famous Greek who were in some way comparable. These works established Plutarch as a leading thinker during the golden age in the reigns of the emperors Trajan and Hadrian (98–138 CE). These biographies are his best known works and were mostly written between the years 105–115 CE. In total these volumes amount to more than 800,000 words and give 46 portraits of Greek and Roman heroes. They are accounts of military men and politicians, many of which were grouped in pairs. However, in the Penguin editions the parallel structure has been removed and Roman and Greek lives are dealt with separately.

In writing biography Plutarch found a literary genre that suited his talents and also disguised some of his limitations. Plutarch considered the *Lives* as the major enterprise of his career and because of that he often expounded his motives and methods. His intention was not to write a chronicle of historical events, but to examine the character of great men as an object lesson in life. He stated this was his purpose at the beginning of his *Life of Alexander*, 'my intention is not to write histories but lives'.

Throughout the *Lives* Plutarch pauses to deliver penetrating observations on human nature illustrated by his subjects, which makes it difficult to classify these works as philosophy, history or biography. However, what the work does symbolize is an essential feature of Plutarch's own life. He was Greek and proud of it, yet he was able to accept Rome as the dominant power over his country and indirectly advocated the joining together of the two cultures.

The Greek heroes of the *Lives* had been dead for a least 300 years and Plutarch had to rely heavily on older source material, much of which is now lost. But Plutarch says at the beginning of the account of the life of Theseus that even legends may contain a fragment of truth and it is up to the reader to elucidate it by means of the power of abstraction, which is in Plato's words 'passing from a plurality of perceptions to a unity gathered together by reason' (*Phaedrus* 249). In the ancient world the boundaries between myth and history were not so well defined. Plutarch himself had no faith in the accuracy of the materials he had at his disposal; he said:

> It is so hard to find out the truth of anything by looking at the record of the past. The process of time obscures the truth of former times, and even contemporaneous writers disguise and twist the truth out of malice or flattery.
>
> (Preface *Life of Pericles*)

However, the ancient idea of what a biography should contain was not the same as the modern concept. To describe the *bios* (Greek = life) of a great man was to say what sort of man he was.

There are three characteristics of ancient biography. The first was that chronology and development in time were of secondary concern, even though the whole arrangement was chronologically straightforward. In the writings of Plutarch the hero and the general historical conditions have a fixed nature, remaining comparatively static. The biography is composed of various elements, childhood stories, education, how the hero emerged into the public arena, conflicts and challenges that the hero faced and his responses to them. However, the underlying question throughout all the works is what sort of man was he? The facts are used to support a general judgement. In the preface to the *Life of Pericles* Plutarch says that:

> These men resembled each other generally in their virtues, but especially in their mildness and uprightness. Both did the greatest service to their countries by their capacity to endure the foolishness of their peoples and their colleagues in office. Whether this is right judgement or not can be decided on the basis of my narrative.
>
> (Preface to *Pericles*)

The second characteristic was that these biographies made moral assumptions. The answer to what sort of man the hero was necessarily involved an examination of both his virtues and his vices and the reader was asked to make a decision to praise or blame the individual. The flaw here is that this approach does not take into account that what may have been considered a vice in Plutarch's time may not have been seen in the same way in earlier periods and there is no attempt to empathize with the standards of earlier periods or cultures.

The third limitation is connected to the previous two. Plutarch was not concerned with his characters as decisive figures that shaped history; any historical interpretation that stressed the influence of great men or showed events as a sum of their contribution is not found in these writings. Although Plutarch hardly notices the wider historical influence of his characters, there are a few exceptions; Lycurgus and Solon the lawgivers, and Numa and Publicola, who affected their countries by conscious planning. But above all Plutarch's concern was with character and individual human qualities.

Before he began composing *Parallel Lives*, Plutarch appears to have written a few other lives, notably those of the Caesars, and of which only Galba and Otho survive. They must have been written before 96 CE as they did not include the Flavian emperors.

The theories and researches of the philosophers had made a moral biography possible but these theories were also limiting as the characters could be seen as examples of emotions or virtues and Plutarch is often guilty of portraying his characters in such a fashion. His characters tend to be representational figures in whom one set of qualities dominates to the exclusion of everything else that could be said about them. Often the quality is that of ambition but there are other variations – for example, *Pyrrhus* on always wanting more, *Cimon* on the use of wealth, *Coriolanus* on anger, and *Antony* on the dangers of love.

All classical historians had been concerned with the actions and characters of great individuals but few writings came close to the kind of biography that Plutarch produced. However, some monographs on the lives of great men existed in Hellenistic times, and among them there survives a Latin adaptation in the form of the *De Viris Illustribus* (On Illustrious Men) by Cornelius Nepos (99–24 BCE). The idea of a parallel treatment of foreigners was probably taken from Marcus Terentius Varro's (116–27 BCE) *Imagines*, Which was a series of 700 Greek and Roman biographies. However, Nepos is not of the same stature as Plutarch for he is an apologist for all things Hellenic, whereas Nepos made no moral judgements whatsoever. Twelve of Nepos' 23 'famous generals of foreign nations' are among the subjects singled out by Plutarch for his work.

Of all the extant pairs of *Lives* all but four have formal comparisons appended. They do not particularly add anything to the narratives but can be seen more as a rhetorical exercise, which is the better man and which the worse? A good example can be seen in the comparison of Alcibiades with Coriolanus.

We have now set out all the actions that we regard as worth mentioning and recording. It is evident that their actions in war show no decisive difference in favour of either party. Both alike exhibited many acts of soldierly daring and courage and in their commands many acts of skill and forethought. One might perhaps adjudge Alcibiades the more perfect general, because he was consistently victorious and successful both by land and by sea. Both shared the characteristic of manifestly giving success to their own side by their presence and generalship and even more manifestly damaging it by their desertion. As to their political life, Alcibiades' pretentious style, with the tasteless and vulgarity that came from his playing to the mob, disgusted decent folk; while Marcius' totally graceless, overweening and oligarchic manner earned the hatred of the Roman people. Neither is to be commended.

Plutarch continues to say that less blame is attached to the favour-seeking demagogue than to the politicians who insult common people in order not to be thought of as demagogues. Plutarch clearly condemned Coriolanus for his attitude to public life.

The criteria that Plutarch employed to choose the pairs are uncertain, as is the development of his plan for the work. There are some fixed points – for example Demosthenes and Cicero are paired together (Book V), Pericles and Fabius (Book X), and Dion and Brutus (Book XII). Most of the gaps in the first 12 books can be plausibly filled but any cross reference to determine the order of the series gives a very inconsistent picture. Solon, the lawgiver was a suitable subject and Plutarch chose to parallel him with Publicola.

The *Lives* give the impression of being written not to a precise formula but within well-defined patterns. However, there are clear differences of style and treatment between one collection of *Lives* and another, for example the contrast between Romulus and

Theseus (myth) and Alexander and Caesar (history), and these are due mainly to the differences in the available source material. Sometimes Plutarch makes it clear that he is aware of the problem. He had a retentive memory and was widely read and a good deal of what he wrote was loaded with allusion; his evocation of the past was both factual and linguistic and this often makes interpretation difficult.

Nevertheless as Grant says:

> ... one of his strengths is the inclusion in his biographies of a vast range of actions, sayings and minor peculiarities that seemed to him significant ... His special gift lies in his choice of intimate anecdotes, calculated to catch the attention of his readers and to bring out the moral character of his subjects.
>
> (*Readings in the Classical Historians* 1992 405)

Plutarch died a famous man. His reputation in society was assured by his learning and the moral tone of his writings. There were many second century followers of his style; Aulus Gellius drew on both the *Lives* and other works. During the reign of Marcus Aurelius a certain Amyntianus wrote 'parallels' in imitation of him. Plutarch continued to be read throughout the later Empire, down to the sixth or seventh century CE especially in the schools of Athens. And this popularity did not wane throughout subsequent centuries, exerting an enormous influence on Western civilization. Plutarch's work appeared in English translation in 1579 and this work was the text that would have been read by William Shakespeare. Although there were many distortions from the original, Shakespeare used Plutarch to full effect in plays such as *Antony and Cleopatra*, *Coriolanus* etc.

Plutarch is highly readable as de Montaigne (1993) observed: 'I cannot easily do without Plutarch. He is so universal and so full that, on every occasion, however extraordinary your subject, he is at hand to your need.'

SUETONIUS (GAIUS SUETONIUS TRANQUILLUS) *c*.70 – *c*.140 CE

Very well then, you win! Take him! But never forget that the man whom you want me to spare will one day prove the ruin of the party which you and I have so long defended. There are many Mariuses in this fellow Caesar!

(*Lives* Caesar 1)

Suetonius was born to a family that belonged to the knightly rank (*equites*) from Hippo Regius in North Africa (now Algeria). His father was a senior officer in a regular legion and took part in the Battle of Betriacum during the reign of Otho. Suetonius writes about this in his work *Lives*:

My own father Suetonius Laetus, a colonel, served with the Thirteenth legion in this campaign. He often said afterwards that Otho had so deeply abhorred the thought of civil war while still a private citizen that he would shudder if the fates of Brutus and Cassius were mentioned at a banquet. And that he would not have moved against Galba to begin with unless in the hope of a bloodless victory.

(*Lives* Otho 10)

We know little of his early years except that he came to Rome where he was perhaps a teacher of literature and also a lawyer. By 110–12 CE he was working on the staff of Pliny the Younger when Pliny was governor of Bithynia-Pontus (northern Asia Minor). Pliny helped him secure a small property in Italy.

From then on Suetonius held a succession of different posts at the imperial court; first he held the position of the 'secretaryship of studies', of which the precise functions are uncertain. These two posts he held under the emperor Trajan (98–117 CE). Next he became the director of the imperial libraries, and finally he was placed in charge of the emperor Hadrian's (117–38 CE) correspondence. In 122 CE it is reported that he was dismissed from this post because of his rudeness to the empress Sabina. It has been suggested that one of his lost works, *On Public Office*, was the last of his works to be written. The subject, chosen at a time of the administrative reforms of Hadrian, may suggest that he did have a partial return to imperial favour.

Suetonius began the first of his works during the reign of the emperor Trajan. He wrote in Latin, the *Lives of Famous Men*, which were brief sketches of Roman literary personalities. Most of the work has been lost, except for a few sections, with only a portion remaining of the section devoted to historians. The section on grammarians included 15 orators (*De Grammaticis et Rhetoribus*), 33 poets (*De Poetis*), of which 6 survive including Terence, Vergil, Tibullus, Lucan, Flaccus and Horace, and 6 historians, of which only Pliny the Elder and Passienus Crispus survive.

He then composed his *Lives of the Caesars*. These are biographies of the 12 Caesars from Julius to Domitian (d. 96 CE), all of which save for a small section on Julius Caesar survives. The work was dedicated to Gaius Septicius Clarus, who was prefect of the Praetorian Guard and who had been dismissed along with Suetonius in 122 CE.

Suetonius adopted a different style to his predecessor Tacitus whose style he felt was too grand for him to compete with. He also thought that Plutarch's chronological method was not appropriate. So he adopted the method, which had been used before in Greek and Latin, where the straight narrative was interrupted by material classified by subject matter that illustrated the chief characteristics of his subjects. This approach made it possible for him to satisfy the general curiosity about his subjects by the general public. By interspersing the text with the personal and occasionally trivial details about the subjects' lives he made them appear as ordinary human beings. He then left the reader to make up their own mind about the character in question. This was something that many historians felt was beneath them to do.

A good example comes from the section on Augustus:

> In winter he wore no fewer than four tunics and a heavy woollen gown above his undershirt; and below that a woollen chest protector; also underpants and woollen gaiters. In summer he slept with the bedroom door open, or in the courtyard beside a fountain, having someone to fan him; and could not bear the rays even of the winter sun, but always wore a broad brimmed hat when he walked in the open air, even at home.
>
> (*Lives* Augustus 82)

Such inside information on his subjects makes them appear human with all their strengths and weaknesses displayed.

Suetonius also included material about Augustus in his lives of subsequent emperors. The following extract comes from his *Life of Claudius*, who was Augustus' great nephew (Livia's grandson) and emperor from 41–54 CE. As a child Claudius was sickly and his behaviour was often odd, prompting Augustus to discuss him in a number of letters to his wife Livia, from which Suetonius quotes:

> To show what opinions, favourable or otherwise, his great-uncle, Augustus, held of Claudius, I quote the following extracts from the imperial correspondence.
>
> My dear Livia as you suggested I have now discussed with Tiberius what we should do about your grandson Claudius at the coming Games of Mars. We both agreed that a decision should be taken once and for all. The question is whether he has-shall I say?- full command of his senses. If so I can see nothing against sending him through the same degrees of office as his brother; but should he be deemed physically and mentally deficient, the public (which always likes to scoff and mock at such things) must not be given the chance of laughing at him and us.
>
> (*Lives* Claudius 3–4)

Suetonius' major contribution, however, was his high degree of objectivity. The old idea of eulogising a person was replaced by a more clinical appraisal of their character. Suetonius achieved this by writing without style or eloquence in a straightforward if rather abrupt manner. Therefore his principal contribution to biography, and also to historiography, was this new impartiality that reflected both well and badly upon those whom he was writing about. Whether or not this had been attempted in the past is impossible to say, for nothing of this kind survives to the present day. We may possibly conclude that in this respect Suetonius was innovative. He chose the rulers of Rome for his subject matter and gathered information about them which would be both praiseworthy and damning, without adding any personal judgement, most notably without any moralization, something that had been the hallmark of previous Greek and Roman biographers and historians.

The most remarkable aspect of his work is his power to create dramatic narrative; the death of Nero is notable with regard to this. While Nero hesitated about whether he should flee or commit suicide, a runner brought him a letter from Phaon (an imperial freedman) which said that the senate had declared him a public enemy and that when arrested he would punished in 'the ancient style'. Nero asked what that meant and was told that he would be stripped naked, his head would be thrust into a wooden fork and then he would be flogged to death. Terrified, Nero picked up the dagger, and begged his servants to mourn for him, insisting one of them should commit suicide first as an example; all the time he bemoaned his own cowardice.

> Then with the help of his secretary, Epaphroditus, he stabbed himself in the throat and was already half dead when a centurion entered, pretending to have rushed to his rescue, and staunched the wound with his cloak. Nero muttered: 'Too late! But, ah, what fidelity!' He died with his eyes glazed and bulging from their sockets, a sight which horrified everyone present. He had made

his companions promise, whatever happened, not to let his head be cut off, but to arrange in some way that he should be buried all in one piece. Galba's freedman Icelus, who had been imprisoned when the first news came of the revolt and was now at liberty again, granted this indulgence.

(*Lives* Nero 49–50)

In this instance Seutonius probably got the information from Epaphroditus. Suetonius also quotes verbatim from his sources, giving citations from official records and documents, although it should be noted that this only applies to the documents concerning the life of Augustus and we must infer that after writing this (the second of his 12 biographies) he may have been dismissed from court and so lost access to the majority of useful documents.

He often quotes Augustus' letters to his family:

I had a snack of bread and dates while out on my drive today …

(*Lives* Augustus 76)

My dear Tiberius,

Not even a Jew fasts so scrupulously on his Sabbaths as I have done today. Not until dusk had fallen did I touch a thing and that was at the baths, before I had my oil rub, when I swallowed two mouthfuls of bread.

(*Lives* Augustus 76)

And a surviving letter written by Antony to Augustus before they had quarrelled:

What has come over you? Do you object to my sleeping with Cleopatra? But we are married; and it is not even as though this were anything new–the affair started nine years ago. And what about you? Are you faithful to Livia Drusilla? My congratulations if when this letter arrives, you have not been in bed with Tertullia, or Terentilla or Rufilla or Salvia Titisenia- or all of them. Does it really matter so much where, or with whom, you perform the sexual act?

(*Lives* Augustus 69)

The historical period about which Suetonius wrote is one of the most significant periods in the history of the Western world. Suetonius and Tacitus are the only sources for this period, if we discount the Greek Dio Cassius, who was writing much later and whose work is often anachronistic and incomplete. However, by accepting what Suetonius writes the reader can run the danger of neglecting what was happening in the wider historical arena. On the other hand the emperors played a crucial role in the development of the Western world. The old Republic may have broken down with or without Caesar but the outcome may have been very different if there had been no Augustus to take up Caesar's legacy.

While Tacitus often distorts his facts by his colourful method of writing, Suetonius often corrects the errors and certainly Tacitus does not supply the reader with the interesting facts and stories that centre on the human qualities of the characters. It is these personal touches that give us a broader picture of the history of the period and those responsible for making that history.

Pliny the Younger described Suetonius as most scholarly or learned, yet this is not what his writing shows. His *Lives* in particular indicate that his aim was to reveal in a straightforward manner that people's personalities are made up of contradictions. He is often accused of compiling material without any critical application and many have dismissed the more scandalous material as mere gossip.

I cannot believe that Gaius Octavius, his (Augustus') father was

also a money changer who distributed bribes among the voters of
electoral assemblies and undertook other electioneering services.

(Lives Augustus 3)

However, Suetonius shaped his material to leave a definite
impression and he left the reader to make judgements on character
and moral issues. He used a variety of material; much of it
gleaned from archival records and always stated what he knew to
be gossip even though he included it.

Suetonius appears to have lived to a ripe old age, probably
dying around 140 CE. He wrote many other books apart from *Lives*
including *Lives of Famous Whores; Roman Masters and Customs; The
Roman Year; Roman Festivals; Roman Dress; Greek Games; Offices of
State; Cicero's Republic; The Physical Defects of Mankind; Methods
of Reckoning Time; An Essay on Nature; Greek Terms of Abuse;
Grammatical Problems; Critical Signs Used in Books.* None of these
works survive.

One of the twentieth century translators of his work, Robert
Graves says of Suetonius:

The younger Pliny, who persuaded the emperor Trajan to grant
Suetonius the immunities usually granted only to the father of
three children, though he had none, wrote that the more he knew
of Suetonius, the greater his affection for him grew; I have had the
same experience.

(Penguin edn, *Lives*. Trans. R. Graves 1957)

Chapter Twenty Three

The Later Roman Empire

The transformation of the Roman Empire into an oriental monarchy began when Diocletian became sole ruler in 284 CE. The Empire had become so vast that it was almost impossible for one man to rule effectively, so Diocletian took as a colleague Maximianus and shared with him the title of *Augustus*. The two *Augusti* had equal authority, all edicts and laws were issued in their common name. However, in practice the Empire was divided into two: Diocletian ruled the east, with his headquarters at Nicomedia while Maximianus ruled in the west from his headquarters at Mediolanum (Milan).

Nine years later the two *Augusti* appointed two *Caesars* who stood next to them in rank and dignity; however, they had no authority other than that which was conferred upon them by their superiors. The main purpose of the institution of the *Caesars* was to provide for the succession: if one of the *Augusti* died then the plan was that one of the *Caesars* would take his place. However, by 308 CE there were four *Augusti*: Constantine, Galerius, Licinius and Maxentius. A series of wars followed and eventually Constantine defeated Licinius at the Battle of Adrianople and became sole ruler. Constantine ruled alone until his death in 337 CE, after which his three sons, Constantinus II, Constantius II and Constans, were declared *Augusti*.

War soon broke out between the brothers which left Constans as sole ruler in the West. When Constans died in 350 CE three usurpers appeared and it was not until three years later that Constantius finally defeated the last of the usurpers, Magnentius, to become sole ruler until 361 CE. The fourfold division of the Empire into the East, Illyricum, Italy and Gaul was continued.

The divisions were called prefectures and were governed

by praetorian prefects, resident at Constantinople, which had become the new capital of the Empire under Constantine the Great; at Sirmium; Mediolanum (Milan); Treveri (Treves) or at Eboracum (York). The prefectures were divided into dioceses and the dioceses into provinces under the charge of a governor. There were 13 dioceses and 101 provinces; later this number was increased to 120. The reason for these divisions was to prevent any officer from becoming too powerful and starting a revolution. However, a consequence of the action was to remove the emperor from his people; although the emperor was all powerful in fact he was merely a tool in the hands of a hierarchy of powerful ministers and real control was handled by those in the highest military or civil offices.

In 361 CE after further episodes of civil war Julian became emperor. His edict of toleration in 362 CE ordered the reopening of pagan temples, and more problematically for the Christian Church the recalling of the exiled Christian bishops. Julian eventually resumed the war against Shapur II of Persia and died in battle in 363 CE. His officers then elected Jovian as emperor. Jovian ceded territories won from the Persians as far back as Trajan's time and restored the privileges of Christianity before his death in 364 CE.

Upon his death Valentinian I, the first of the Valentinian dynasty was elected *Augustus* and chose his brother Valens to serve as his co-emperor. In 365 CE Procopius managed to bribe two legions who then proclaimed him *Augustus*. War between the two rival Eastern Roman emperors continued until Procopius was defeated; although in 367 CE the 8-year-old Gratian was proclaimed emperor by the other two. In 375 CE Valentinian I led his army in a campaign against a Germanic tribe but died shortly afterward. The succession did not go as planned Gratian's infant brother Valentinian II was proclaimed emperor by the troops.

The Eastern Empire faced problems with the Germanic tribes, one of whom had fled their lands and sought refuge in the Eastern Empire. Valens let them settle in the southern bank of the Danube in 376 CE but they soon revolted. In 378 CE Valens led a campaign against them which proved disastrous for the Romans. The two armies met near Adrianople but Valens was over confident of his superior strength. Eager to obtain the glory for himself, Valens rushed into battle and on 9 August 378 CE the Battle of Adrianople resulted in a crushing Roman defeat and the death of Valens. Ammianus Marcellinus estimated that two-thirds of the Roman soldiers on the field were lost in battle.

The battle had far reaching consequences, as veteran soldiers and administrators were among the casualties. This left the Empire with the problem of leadership. Gratian was now responsible for the whole Empire. He sought a replacement *Augustus* for the Eastern Roman Empire, and in 379 CE chose Theodosius I.

Theodosius proclaimed his 5-year-son Arcadius an *Augustus* in 338 CE in an attempt to secure the succession. The Hispanic Celt general, Magnus Maximus, stationed in Roman Britain, was proclaimed Augustus by his troops in 383 CE and rebelled against Gratian when he invaded Gaul. Gratian was assassinated and following his death Maximus had to deal with Valentinian II, who was only 12 at the time, as senior *Augustus*. Maximus entered into negotiations with Valentinian II and Theodosius, attempting, and ultimately failing, to gain their official recognition. Theodosius campaigned in the West and was victorious against Maximus who was executed. In 392 CE Valentinian was murdered, and shortly afterwards Eugenius was made emperor.

The Eastern emperor Theodosius I refused to recognize Eugenius as emperor and invaded the West and killed Eugenius. He re-united the entire Roman Empire under his rule. Theodosius was the last emperor to rule over the whole Empire. He made Christianity the official religion of the Empire and after his death in 395 CE he bequeathed the Empire to his two sons Arcadius and Honorius. The Roman state would continue to have two halves and two emperors and two different seats of power throughout the fifth century CE.

The Western Empire declined after 395 CE; the year 476 CE is generally accepted as the formal end of the Western Roman

Empire. As the Western Empire declined the Eastern Empire would be relieved of much destruction and in the mid sixth century the Eastern Roman Empire (known as the Byzantine Empire) under the emperor Justinian I reconquered Italy and parts of Illyrica from the Ostrogoths, North Africa from the Vandals and southern Hispania from the Visigoths.

Of the many dates accepted for the end of the Roman classical state, the latest is 610 CE. This is when the emperor Heraclius made sweeping reforms that changed the face of the Roman Empire forever. Greek was re-adopted as the official language of government and Latin influence waned. However, the Empire was never known as Byzantine by its inhabitants; they used terms such as *Romania*, *Basileia Romaion*, or *Pragmata Romaion*, meaning 'Land of the Romans' or 'Kingdom of the Romans', and who still saw themselves as Romans, and their state as the rightful continuation of the ancient Roman Empire.

Chapter Twenty Four

Ammianus Marcellinus (c.330–95 CE)

So far as I could investigate the truth, I have, after putting the various events in clear order, related what I myself was allowed to witness in the course of my life, or to learn by meticulous questioning of those directly concerned. The rest, which the text to follow will disclose, we shall set forth to the best of our ability with still greater accuracy, feeling no fear of critics of the prolixity of our work, as they consider it; for conciseness is to be praised only when it breaks off ill-timed discursiveness, without detracting at all from an understanding of the course of events.

(*History* 15:1)

Ammianus Marcellinus lived during the reigns of the emperors Constantius II, Julian, Jovian, Valentinian and Valens, in the second half of the fourth century CE. This was one of the most uncertain periods in history that saw the Roman Empire on the wane. All the information that we possess about the life and times of this historian is gathered from his own writing. Ammianus Marcellinus was born into a prosperous Greek speaking family in Syrian Antioch (now south-east Turkey). It is highly probable that he was a member of the 'curial' class, a rich hereditary element of society whose ancestors consisted of city councillors. At that time Antioch was one of the principal cities of the Roman Empire and was very cosmopolitan, its inhabitants included Greek, Jews, and Syrians as well as many other different races. Ammianus was proud of his city, if not of some of its inhabitants.

Next Syria spreads for a distance over a beautiful plain. This is famed for Antioch, a city known to all the world, and without a rival, so rich is it in imported and domestic commodities; likewise

for Laodicea, Apamea and also Seleucia, most flourishing cities
from their region.

(Book XIV, 8, 8)

Nevertheless, Greek was the dominant force in intellectual
leadership and education and it would seem likely that
Ammianus would have had a Greek based classical education.
Antioch produced other men of distinction who wrote in Greek,
including Libanius, a fourth century professor of rhetoric, and
John Chrysostom (347–407 CE), one of the early Church fathers.

It was during the reign of Constantius II (337–61 CE), the son
of Constantine the Great that Ammianus became an officer of
the *protectores domestici* (the household guard). In 353 CE he
was attached, by the emperor's order, to the staff of Ursicinus,
the general who commanded the Roman garrison at Nisibis
in Mesopotamia (now Nusaybin in Turkey). This garrison was
situated on the frontier of the Roman Empire facing Persia.
Ammianus became personally attached to his general, immortal-
izing him in his works.

He was in fact a warrior, having always been a soldier and a leader
of soldiers, but far removed from the wrangling of the forum.

(Book XIV, 9,1)

While the war between Constantius and Magnentius raged,
Constantius had conferred the rank of Caesar on his cousin Gallus
and sent him to the East to carry on his war against Persia. The
opening part of the surviving section of Ammianus' narrative
begins with Gallus' cruelty and arrogance at Antioch.

After the survival of the events of an unendurable campaign
when the spirits of both parties, broken by the variety of their
dangers and hardships, were still drooping, before the blare of
trumpets had ceased or the soldiers been assigned to their winter
quarters, the gusts of raging Fortune brought new storms upon

the commonwealth through the misdeeds, many and notorious, of Gallus Caesar

(Book XIV: 1)

He continues with a catalogue of cruel acts instigated by Gallus and his wife who was as 'insatiable as he in her thirst for human blood'.

In 354 CE Ursicinus, who had become an object of suspicion to the emperor, was dispatched to Gaul, accompanied once again by Ammianus, to quell the rebellion there started by Silvanus. Although the mission was successful, Ursicinus received no commendation from the emperor; in fact he was accused of embezzling some of the Gallic treasure.

> And so far was he from praising conscientious service, that he [Constantius] actually wrote that Ursicinus had embezzled funds from the Gallic treasury, which no one had touched. And he ordered the matter to be closely examined, questioning Remigius, who at that time was already auditor of the general's office of infantry supplies, and whose fate it was, long afterwards, in the days of Valentinian, to take his life with a halter because of the affair with the embassy from Tripoli.

(Book XV, 5, 36)

Ammianus remained in Gaul with his general until the summer of 357 CE when he participated in the first German campaign of the newly appointed Caesar, Julian the brother of Gallus.

In late 357 CE Ammianus was once again accompanying his general back to the eastern frontier, where he took part in the warfare against the Persians. In 359 CE he was under siege from the enemy and shut up in Amida (Diyarbakir, in south-east Turkey). He tells of his experiences getting to the city of Amida:

> Here, mingled with the Persians, who were rushing to the higher ground with the same effort as ourselves, we remained motionless until sunrise of the next day, so crowded together that the bodies of

the slain, held upright by the bodies of the throng, could nowhere find room to fall, and that in front of me a soldier with his head cut in two and split into equal halves by a powerful sword stroke, was so pressed on all sides that he stood erect like a stump. And although showers of weapons from all kinds of artillery flew from the battlements, nevertheless the nearness of the walls saved us from that danger, and when I at last entered the city by a postern gate I found it crowded, since a throng of both sexes had flocked to it from the neighbouring countryside.

(Book XVIII, 8, 11–13)

Eventually he escaped from Amida when the city fell, and after many further adventures finally met up with his general at Melitene in Armenia and together they safely made their way back to Antioch.

After the deposition of Ursicinus in 360 CE we know little of Ammianus' career. He did serve in Julian's campaign against Persia but in what capacity is uncertain. By now Julian had become emperor but his reign was short-lived, dying of wounds he received in 363 CE. After the death of Julian and the succession of Jovian the Roman army returned to Antioch and Ammianus seems to have remained there for some considerable time since his account of the treason trials there in 371 CE implies that he was a witness to these events.

However, Jovian died the following year and the Roman Empire was finally split into two halves, Eastern and Western. After Gratian (the son of Valentinian I) succeeded to the throne in 378 CE in the Western sector of the Empire, with its capital initially at Mediolanum (Milan), Ammianus took up residence in Rome where he was to spend a good part of his remaining life. He also travelled widely, visiting Greece and Egypt as well as revisiting Antioch, now part of the Eastern Empire, and it was probably here that he did much of the preparation for the writing of his history. It was during the later years of his life that Ammianus began composing his *Roman History*, a work that covered the period between the accession of Nerva in 96 CE and the death of the Eastern emperor Valens at the Battle of Adrianople (Edirne) against the Visigoths in 378 CE.

After the events of 378 CE, Ammianus went to Rome. He travelled via Thrace where he inspected the battlefields in order to gather material for his history. In Rome he acquired a certain position within the city, making several influential friends in the process. Ammianus set himself the task of succeeding Tacitus as an historian. His work was divided into 31 books of which the first 13 are lost. The remaining books deal with the period of 25 years from 353 CE (the seventeenth year of the reign of Constantius II) to the Battle of Adrianople.

Libanius implies that Ammianus published his work in 391 CE, and quite possibly recited parts of his work in Rome, receiving a very favourable reception. It is also highly possible that he intended to extend his work beyond the death of Valens, for he promises to tell of the fate of Maximinus (Book XXVIII: 1, 57) but his failure to do so may be just be an oversight on his part. When Ammianus died is uncertain but it seems likely that he was still living in 393 CE.

Ammianus appears to have made careful preparation for his work and used a variety of sources. He read Latin literature extensively and made copious notes; in particular he made a special study of Tacitus' *Histories* and imitated him as much as possible. He also read Livy and Sallust, and for information on Gaul he consulted the works of Caesar. He also made use of the poets, Virgil, Horace, Ovid, etc. To improve his Latin he read Cicero, quoting him 30 times in the course of his work. Having been a soldier he knew Latin as the official language of the army.

This is evident in his style, which is decorated with all kinds of ornamentation drawn from a variety of sources and imitations, especially Tacitus. He appears to have made a first draft of his work in Latin and when he was asked to recite or publish it he reworked it, paying particular attention to stylistic effect, using the copious notes he had collected.

In addition to his literary sources Ammianus also relied upon his own personal experiences and observations. He wanted to write history rather than follow a biographical treatment of history that had been popular since the time of Suetonius. But it was difficult to escape this influence; so, rather than have any fixed form of biographical composition he includes a brief biographical sketch of all the emperors and Caesars included in his work.

Ammianus wanted to write the truth to withhold nothing or to indulge in deliberate invention, something he criticized in the official reports of the emperor Constantius. He recognized the dangers of speaking too openly about current events or persons but was brave enough to allocate blame where it was due, even to his hero the emperor Julian. Ammianus wrote for readers in Rome, in particular for the leading literary circle of the day and for that reason alone he wrote in Latin and not his native tongue.

The significance of his work lies in the fact that he supplies information about a period of history that we have little other information on. Also of significance is the fact that Ammianus is moderate in his partisanship, a quality that is not often encountered among ancient historians.

His work is also interesting because Ammianus had the strong conviction that the Roman Empire would last forever. He was not alone in this view which was to be proven wrong, but Ammianus provides a unique insight into this turbulent period. He is also unusual inasmuch as despite his pro-Roman attitude he was a Greek, who like Plutarch had done before advocated the merging of the two cultures.

It is clear that Ammianus was not a Christian for he speaks of *their* rites and customs as someone who is not familiar with them. However, he shows a great deal of liberality in his attitude toward religion, even praising the simple life of the provincial bishops (Book XXVII 3, 15), and in general prefers religious tolerance. He appears to have held some belief in astrology, divination and dreams.

In ancient times his work was not well known, but Gibbon found his work refreshing and Syme noted that: 'Ammianus was an honest man in an age of fraud and mendacity and fanaticism' (Syme, R. Ammianus and the *Historia Augusta* 1968 p. 94).

Chapter Twenty Five

Tertullian (Quintus Septimius Florens Tertullianus) (c.160 – c.220 CE)

> Truth asks no favour in her cause, since she has no surprise at her present position.
>
> (*Apology* 1:2)

Tertullian was a prolific early Christian author from the Roman province of Carthage. He was the first Christian author to produce an extensive corpus of Latin Christian literature, and has been named the father of Latin Christianity, and the founder of Western theology. He is perhaps most famous for being the oldest extant Latin writer to use the term Trinity, and giving the oldest formal exposition of a Trinitarian theology.

There is little reliable evidence concerning his life except from passing references in his and others writings. He was believed to be the son of a Roman centurion, and he was credited with being a trained lawyer and an ordained priest. Jerome states (*De viris illustribus* 53) his father was a *centurio proconsularis* (although no such position appears to exist in the Roman military) in Africa. Roman Africa was famous as the home of orators and this is evident in his style. He was obviously a scholar and his principal study was jurisprudence; Eusebius says that he shone among the advocates of Rome (*Ecclesiastical History*).

His conversion to Christianity probably occurred around 197 CE and the conversion appears to have been sudden. He said that he could not imagine a truly Christian life without a conscious breach, a radical act of conversion: Christians are made, not born (*Apol.* XVIII). Around the year 207 CE he was attracted to the New Prophecy of Montanism and split from the mainstream church.

Jerome says that Tertullian lived to a great age but there is no reliable source confirming his survival beyond the year 220 CE. In spite of his break from the mainstream church he continued to write against heresy, especially Gnosticism. Though his doctrinal works he became the teacher of Cyprian and the predecessor of Augustine who in turn became the chief founder of Latin theology.

Thirty-one of his works remain, together with other fragments. Roughly 15 works in Latin and Greek are lost, some as late as the ninth century CE. His writings cover the whole theological field of the time and can be divided into two periods, the Catholic and Montanist, or according to their subject matter. The former division shows the change of views that Tertullian had, while the latter is subject to further division, apologetic and polemic writing.

Among his apologetic writings the *Apologeticus*, addressed to Roman magistrates is a defence of Christianity and the Christians against the reproaches of the pagans, it is an important legacy of the ancient Church proclaiming the principle of freedom of religion as a human right.

He argued that the gods have no existence and therefore the Christians could not offend them. He also stated that Christians do not engage in emperor worship, that they did better by praying for them; Christians can afford to be tortured and put to death, for the more they suffer the more they grow: 'the blood of martyrs is seed' (*Apologeticum* 50).

The five books against Marcion written 207/8 CE are the most comprehensive and elaborate of his polemical works, and are invaluable for gauging the early Christian view of Gnosticism. His extensive writings give a picture of the religious life and thought of the time which is of great interest to the church historian.

Chapter Twenty Six

Eusebius (Eusebius Of Caesarea) (c.260–340 CE)

> To work at this subject I consider especially necessary, because I am not aware that any Christian writer has until now paid attention to this kind of writing and I hope that its high value will be evident to those who are convinced of the importance of a knowledge of the history.
>
> (*Ecclesiastical History* 1.1)

Eusebius came from Palestine and was educated in Caesarea Maritima, the city of which he was later to become bishop. He was a Roman historian, exegete and Christian polemicist, who became bishop of Caesarea in Palestine around the year 314 CE.

There is little evidence about the life of Eusebius; a work by his successor at Caesarea, Acacius, on his life has been lost. Eusebius' own works were probably many of which many survive.

By the third century CE Caesarea was a pagan city of approximately 100,000 inhabitants; it had been a pagan city since the time of Pompey during his command of the eastern provinces in the 60s BCE when control had been given to the gentiles. The city also had a large Jewish and Christian contingent, although there was no Christian bishop attested to the town before 190 CE.

Through the activities of Origen (185/6–254 CE) and the school of his follower Pamphilus (later third century) Caesarea became a centre of Christian learning. Soon after Pamphilus settled in Caesarea he began teaching Eusebius who was then a young man in his early 20s.

Eusebius succeeded Agapius as bishop of Caesarea soon after 313 CE and played a prominent role at the Council of Nicaea in

325 CE. Because he was a learned man and author he enjoyed the favour of the emperor Constantine, and so was called upon to present the creed of his own church. However, the anti Arian creed from Palestine prevailed which became the basis for the Nicene Creed.

The theological views of Arius were problematic. Eustathius of Antioch strongly opposed the growing influence of Origen's theology as the root of Arianism. Eusebius, who was an admirer of Origen, was reproached by Eustathius for deviating from the Nicene faith; however, Eusebius prevailed and Eustathius was deposed at a synod in Antioch.

Anthanasius of Alexandria was a more powerful opponent and in 334 CE he was summoned before a synod in Caesarea, which he refused to attend. In the following year he was once again summoned this time to a synod in Tyre at which Eusebius presided. Athanasius went to Constantinople to bring his cause before the emperor. Constantine called the bishops to his court and Anthanasius was condemned and exiled. Throughout this period Eusebius held the emperor's favour and more than once was exonerated with the emperor's approval. After Constantine's death Eusebius wrote the *Life of Constantine*, an important historical work because of the use of eye witness accounts and primary sources.

Eusebius extensive literary activity has resulted in a large proportion of his works being preserved. His comprehensive and careful excerpts from original sources saved his successors the labour of original research. Therefore much has been preserved, quoted by Eusebius that might otherwise have been destroyed.

Soon after he joined Pamphilus he began assisting his master to expand the library's collections and widen access to its resources. It was about this time that Eusebius began compiling a *Collection of Ancient Martrydoms* as a reference work. In the 290s CE Eusebius began work on his *Ecclesiastical History*, a narrative history of the Church and Christian community from the Apostolic Age to Eusebius' day. At the same time he also worked on his *Chronicle*, a universal calendar of events from the creation onwards. In his Church History Eusebius provided the first chronological history of the Christian Church. It is based on earlier sources complete from the period of the Apostles to his own era. This history contains much of Eusebius' own theological agenda interwoven with factual text.

The work consists of ten books covering the period from the foundation of the Church to the defeat of Licinius by Constantine the Great in 324 CE. Eusebius has sometimes been called the 'Christian Herodotus' and is the definitive historian of Christian antiquity. He is valuable for the many documents he quotes about which we would have no other information. Photius, the ninth-century scholar and Patriarch of Constantinople, said of him:

> His style is neither agreeable nor brilliant, but he was a man of great learning.
>
> (Photius, *Bibliotheca* 13)

At the beginning of the work he writes that Matthew composed the gospel according to the Hebrews. The time scheme correlated the history with the reigns of the Roman emperors and had a broad scope. Also included were the bishops and other teachers of the Church; Christian relations with the Jews and those believed to be heretical, and finally the Christian martyrs. Eusebius used *Acts*, Justin and Iranaeus to portray heretical teachers and to understand the foundations for heresy.

Among his other works is a *Life of Constantine* (*Vita Constantini*), which is a eulogy or panegyric. However, it was not suitable for reading as a continuation of the *History* because the facts are affected by its purpose. The historian Socrates Scholasticus said:

> Also in writing the life of Constantine, this same author has but slightly treated of matters regarding Arius, being more intent on the rhetorical finish of his composition and praises of the emperor, than on an accurate statement of facts.

The work is so exaggerated in its praise for Constantine that many scholars even doubt some of the less controversial material in it; for example Constantine's legislation. His histories can be seen as apologetic works intended to persuade the reader of the virtue of the Christian church and most of all, its patron Constantine. However, Averill Cameron and Stuart Hall (*Life of Constantine* 1999) have pointed out that the most controversial letter in the *Life* has since been found among the papyri of Egypt. His works, however, had an enormous influence on others, and the value of his works lie mainly in the fact that he used copious quotations from other sources many of which are now lost

Chapter Twenty Seven

Other Roman and Early Christian works

These are only a few of the other lesser histories from antiquity; some remain almost complete while others are lost, and of the lost histories there are a further 20 that have been referred to in other writings, some of which were so poorly written that this probably accounts for them not surviving.

GNAEUS NAEVIUS (*c*.270 – 201 BCE)

Gnaeus Naevius was a Roman epic poet and dramatist of the Old Latin period. He had a notable literary career at Rome until he angered the Metelli family by his satirical comments and was imprisoned. After he was freed by the tribunes he was exiled to Tunisia where he wrote his own epitaph and committed suicide.

He had served as a soldier during the Punic wars and it was probably during his exile that he composed his epic poem on the First Punic war *Bellum Punicum*. By combining the representation of actual contemporary history with a mythical background, it may be said that he created the Roman type of epic poetry.

The poem was one continuous work, but was later divided into seven books. The first part of the work dealt with the adventures of Aeneas in Sicily, Carthage and Italy and borrowed from the first book of Homer's Iliad the interview of Zeus and Thetis (in this case Jupiter and Venus); which Virgil later made one of the important passages in his *Aeneid*. The rest of the work dealt with the events of the First Punic War in the style of a metrical chronicle. The few remaining fragments give the impression of a vivid and rapid narrative, and from what little we know about him, the conclusion is that he was firmly placed among the makers of Roman literature.

QUINTUS FABIUS PICTOR (*c*.200 BCE)

Quintus Fabius Pictor grandson of Fabius Pictor a painter was one of the earliest Roman historians and considered to be the first of the annalists. He became a senator and fought against the Gauls in 225 BCE, and against Carthage in the Second Punic War. He was selected to travel to the Delphic oracle for advice after the Roman defeat at the battle of Cannae (206 BCE).

He wrote in Greek not Latin and although he is often referred to as an annalist there is little evidence in his remaining work of annalistic history. He used the chronicles of his own and other important families as source material and his work began with the arrival of Aeneas in Latium and ended with his own recollections of the Punic War, which he blamed on Carthage. Fabius' work made use of the writings of the Greek historian Diocles of Peparethus, who allegedly wrote an early history of Rome.

Fabius was used as a source by Plutarch, Polybius, Livy and Dionysius of Halicarnassus, and by the time of Cicero his work had been translated into Latin.

CORNELIUS NEPOS (*c*.99–24 BCE)

Cornelius Nepos was born in Cisalpine Gaul He was a biographer rather than an historian. He wrote a number of works on different subjects, although they hardly rank as serious pieces of research. Many of the lives in the series *De Viris Illustribus* (On Illustrious Men) that he composed are still extant.

This work was the first surviving biography written in Latin. He took the idea, probably from Marcus Terentius Varro's *Imagines*, to parallel the lives of foreigners.

The *Oxford Classical Dictionary* (2nd edition) states:

His defects are hasty and careless composition (perhaps less marked in his first edition) and lack of control of his material. He is mainly eulogistic, with an ethical aim, but also gives information about his hero's environment. As a historian, his value is slight: he names many sources, but rarely used them at first hand. His style is essentially plain, but contains colloquial features and many archaisms, not used for artistic effect, but from indifference. His rhetorical training appears in attempts at adornment, neither uniform nor discriminating.

(*OCD* 728)

Nepos himself declared that he was no historian. He was an apologist of Greekness, and may have been deceived by propaganda against the Gracchi. He was a contemporary of Cicero, Atticus and Catullus, and his *Life of Atticus* is quite an important piece of source material. He also wrote about Cato, as well as a book of love poems and a book of anecdotes (*Exempla*). He also had the intelligence to lament the fact that Cicero's death had deprived the world of the chance to have a written history of Rome of literary merit.

QUINTUS CURTIUS RUFUS (FIRST CENTURY CE)

Quintus Curtius Rufus may have written during the reign of the emperor Claudius (41–54 CE). His work, the *History of Alexander the Great*, is the only surviving history written in Latin concerning Alexander from antiquity that we possess, and even this work is not complete. The first and second books of the ten are completely lost and there are gaps at the end of Book V and beginning of Book VI.

During Alexander's expedition two official accounts were compiled, the *Ephemerides*, a daily account of events, and a history by Callisthenes of Olynthus. After Alexander's death several other accounts were written, the most important being those of Aristobulus and Ptolemy, who based their accounts on Callisthenes (see Arrian). Several later authors composed works on the campaigns of Alexander based on these and other sources; the best of the Greek works is that of Arrian.

Curtius' principal source is Cleitarchus, son of Dinon, who accompanied Alexander's expedition and wrote a colourful account of it. For Cleitarchus the expedition was a great adventure and he saw Alexander as a tyrant who was spoiled by good luck. Curtius used his work in a slightly changed and contaminated form, perhaps through Timagenes who he mentions in connection with Cleitarchus and Ptolemy (VIII. 5.21).

Curtius' *History* appears to be the work of a rhetorician rather than an historian. One of his main aims was to insert brilliant speeches and romantic incidents into the work. He made many errors both historically and in matters concerning geography. However, his speeches are carefully prepared and of a high quality. He modelled his style on Livy, but at times seems to resemble the orator Seneca more. He did not see himself as an historian and in this respect he is quite right, for he indulges in many sensational distortions of the truth. The most outlandish is his description of the Persian landscape which includes a river (the Medus) which did not exist.

VELLEIUS PATERCULUS (*c*.19 BCE – AFTER 30 CE)

Velleius Paterculus was of Campanian origin. All the information we have about him comes from his own writing. He had some notable ancestors including his paternal grandfather who served as *praefectus fabrum* (superintendent of engineers) under Pompey. Paterculus served as a military tribune in Thrace and Macedonia accompanying Gaius Caesar in 1 CE on his visit to the eastern provinces. He later served for eight years under Tiberius, first as prefect of the horse and then as *legatus*, participating in the German and Pannonian campaigns. In 6 CE he was elected *quaestor* and while still quaestor designate led troops to reinforce Tiberius in Pannonia during the mutiny there.

In 13 CE he and his brother, who was also a *legatus* of Tiberius in the Dalmatian campaigns, were awarded honours at Tiberius' triumph. In 15 CE both brothers were praetors for the year; after that date he appears to have held no further posts, although he may have had a provincial posting. It may have been during this period of his life that he indulged his passion for literature.

Velleius wrote the *Historiae Romanae*, a brief account of Roman history in order to celebrate the consulship of his friend M. Vicinius, to whom he dedicated the work. The work covers two volumes into which are compressed the events from the fall of Troy and ends with the events in Rome in 29 CE. He was a writer of summary history and he draws attention to this throughout his work (1.16, 2.29 et al.).

The whole of Book I is lost and there are many gaps in the history of Rome from the time of Romulus to 168 BCE. Book II begins with the destruction of Carthage, which Velleius sees as an axial moment in Roman history, as did Sallust. The following 59 years are dealt with in the next 40 chapters. However, when Velleius deals with Julius Caesar, Augustus and Tiberius he supplies a more lengthy account. It was his intention to write a full length history and he promises this on several occasions (2.48. 5, 89. 1, 96. 3, 103. 4, 114. 4, 119. 1).

The work climaxes with the reign of the emperor Tiberius and in keeping with the noble values of patriotism toward the emperor of the day, Velleius presents an adulatory account of him, much to the criticism of modern historians. However, this does not render his account worthless for it shows the psychological attitude toward the new regime of the administrative officers of the period. There are slight traces of unease with the system, especially in regard to the rise of Sejanus and the political crisis of 29 CE.

Velleius has received much criticism in modern times, some of it justified. As an historian he does not weigh his evidence carefully and makes little attempt to scrutinise his sources. He often makes errors with chronology and forgets to include certain events which he then later inserts out of sequence. In fact he appears to be more of a journalist than an historian. Nevertheless his character portraits of such people as Sulla, Pompey, Caesar and Lepidus are among some of the best pieces of his work and add to human interest.

Grant says:

> The work is chiefly of interest today because Velleius so greatly admired Tacitus (under whom he had served), in contrast to Tacitus, to whom he therefore provides a counterpoise. He also believed in the phoney resituta republica of Augustus. His evidence and interpretations, when he has not been an eye-witness have to be used with care. He can, for example, plausibly forge a date.
>
> (1995 103)

Yet, with all his faults Velleius makes for interesting reading: the content, the biographies and human interest make this work valuable at least for a contemporary version of the reign of Tiberius and the effects of that reign upon those who were in a position to experience it first-hand.

NICOLAUS OF DAMASCUS (*c.*64 BCE – 16CE?)

Nicolaus was a Greek historian and philosopher form Syria who lived during the Augustan period. According to Sophronius, he became a close friend and teacher to Herod the Great of Judaea, and had been tutor to the children of Mark Antony and Cleopatra. His chief work was his *Universal History* in 144 books which is lost, except for fragments of the first seven books (history of Assyrians, Medes, Greeks, Lydians and Persians). These were preserved in the *Excerpta* which was compiled at the request of Constantine Porphyrogenitus. Josephus probably used this work for his history of Herod the Great.

He also wrote comedies and tragedies none of which survive. However there are some portions of his biography of Augustus. This was written after Augustus' death in 14 CE and two long portions remain; the first concerns Octavian's youth, and the second concerns Caesar's assassination.

Nicolaus went to Rome in 4 BCE with Herod Archelaus (Herod's son) to plead Herod's case when he had displeased the emperor. Nicolaus had said that his wished to retire but evidently he continued to work in Rome. It is not certain exactly when he died.

ALEXANDER POLYHISTOR (FIRST CENTURY BCE)

Lucius Cornelius Alexander Polyhistor was a Greek scholar who was enslaved by the Romans after the Mithridatic war and was taken to Rome as a tutor. He was so productive a writer that he earned the name 'polyhistor'. He wrote historical and geographical works on nearly all the countries of the ancient world, including five books on the history of Rome. His works only survive in references and quotations by other later authors. Eusebius extracted a large section of his work for use in his Chaldean Chronicle.

He died in Laurentum in a house-fire; it is reported that when his wife heard the news she hanged herself.

PLINY THE ELDER (GAIUS PLINIUS SECUNDUS) (23 BCE –79 CE)

Pliny the Elder was a Roman author, naturalistic and natural philosopher as well as a naval and army commander of the early Roman Empire. He was also a personal friend of the emperor Vespasian. Pliny died on 25 August 79 CE while attempting to rescue by ship a friend and his family from the eruption of Mt Vesuvius that had just destroyed the towns of Pompeii and Herculaneum. The prevailing wind prevented the ship from leaving the shore; Pliny collapsed due to the toxic fumes and died.

He is known primarily for his encyclopaedic work *Naturalis Historia* which became the model for all subsequent works. His nephew was Pliny the Younger who said of his uncle in a letter to the historian Tacitus.

For my part I deem those blessed to whom, by favour of the gods it has been granted either to do what is worth writing of, or to write what is worth reading; above measure blessed these on whom both the gifts have been conferred. In the latter number will be my uncle, by virtue of his own and of your composition.

(*Letters* VI 16)

His first work was *De jaculatione equestri*, a work on the use of missiles on horseback. His second published work was a biography of his old commander Pomponius Secundus. When Nero became emperor in 54 CE Pliny was working on two military writings. The *History of the German Wars* in 20 books is the only source quoted in the first 6 books of Tacitus' *Annals* and was probably one of the principal sources for the *Germania*. He completed the historical work of Aufidius Bassus and added to it in 30 books.

Bassus had created something of a stir according to Seneca the Younger, and was a man much admired at Rome. He had begun his history at some unknown contemporaneous time ending with the reign of Tiberius. Bassus suddenly died of illness leaving his work unfinished.

Pliny's Bassus' History was one of the sources used by Suetonius and Plutarch; Tacitus also cites Pliny as a source He is mentioned concerning the loyalty of Burrus, commander of the Praetorian Guard, whom Nero had removed because of his disloyalty. Tacitus gives part of Pliny's view of the Pisonian conspiracy to kill Nero and make Piso emperor as absurd and says that he could not decided whether Pliny's account or that of Messalla was more accurate concerning some details of the Year of the Four Emperors. It appears that Pliny's extension of Bassus' work went from the reign of Nero to that of Vespasian. Pliny reserved this work for publication after his death presumably because he thought it would be controversial.

Pliny's last work was the *Naturalis Historia* an encyclopaedia which utilizes some material from his memories of earlier times and from his prior works, such as the one on Germany. The

Naturalis Historia is one of the largest single works to have survived from the Roman Empire and purports to cover the entire field of ancient knowledge based on the best sources available to Pliny. The work encompasses the fields of botany, zoology, astronomy and mineralogy as well as the exploitation of these resources. It became the standard work for the Roman period and some technical issues he discusses are the only sources for these inventions, such as hushing in mining technology or the use of water mills for crushing and grinding corn. It is interesting to note that much of what he wrote about has subsequently been confirmed by archaeological excavations. It is also a reference work for the history of art, as it is virtually the only work that describes the artists of the time.

This work became a model for subsequent encyclopaedic works in terms of breadth of subject matter, the need to reference individual authors, and a comprehensive contents list. It is the only work of Pliny's to have survived, and he is still remembered in vulcanology where the term *Plinian* refers to a very violent eruption of a volcano.

APPIAN (*c*.95 – *c*.165 CE)

Appian was born in Alexandria, probably during the reign of the emperor Domitian (81–96 CE). All that we know about him comes from his own writings and from letters of Fronto the tutor of the future emperor Marcus Aurelius (161–80 CE). It is suggested that he may have died in about 165 CE. A fragment of his work speaks about a war against the Jews in Egypt in which he had some adventures. This was probably the war waged by the emperor Trajan in 166 CE to suppress an insurrection in the country.

Appian tells us:

> I am Appian of Alexandria, a man who has reached the highest place in my native country, and have been, in Rome, a pleader of

causes before the emperors, until they deemed me worthy of being made their procurator.

(*History of Rome* Preface 15)

In order to have obtained this position he would have to have been a Roman citizen of equestrian rank. The time of his writing of the Preface to his *History* he gives as 900 years after the founding of the city, which dates it to the reign of Antoninus Pius (138–61 CE). There is a surviving letter from Fronto to Antoninus asking for the appointment of his friend Appian as procurator for merited distinction in his old age. Fronto vouches for his friend's honour and integrity.

Appian wrote his *History of Rome* on an ethnographical rather than chronological basis, corresponding to the wars carried on by the Romans with other nations and also those waged among themselves. His plan is sketched out in section 14 of the Preface.

As there are three books which treat of the numerous exploits of the Romans in Italy, these three together must be considered the Italian-Roman history.

But the division into books has been made on account of the great number of events which they contain. The first of these will show that events that took place in successive reigns while they had kings, of whom there were seven and this I shall call the history of Rome under the kings. Next in order will be the history of the rest of Italy except the part along the Adriatic .... The next will be named according to its subject. The order of these histories with respect to each other is according to the time when Romans began to be embroiled in war with each nation ... Internal seditions and civil war will be designated under the names of their chief actors.

Eleven books of this *History* have survived, some of them named after wars, the Spanish, Punic, Illyrian, Syrian, Mithridatic and five books of the civil wars. Extracts from other books have been preserved in two Byzantine compilations made by order of the emperor Constantine.

Appian was a narrator of events rather than a philosophical historian. There is no ornament to his style but the rhetorical passages are at times quite forcible and eloquent. Perhaps the introduction to the history of the civil wars is a good example of the best of his writing. His treatment of the events leading up to the tragedies of the Gracchi brothers had many imitators among later historians and is the only account by an ancient author where both sides of the agrarian controversy have been given.

Perhaps the most important books among Appian's work are the first book of the civil wars and the third Punic war with Carthage. This is the only detailed account to have come down to us. Appian's source may well be the lost book of Polybius from whom a quotation is given:

> Being asked by Polybius in familiar conversation [for Polybius had been his tutor] what he meant by using these words, Polybius says that he did not hesitate frankly to name his own country, for whose fate he feared when he considered the mutability of human affairs. And Polybius wrote this down just as he heard it.
>
> (Book VII, 19:132)

The greatest criticism of Appian's work is that of inaccuracy; however, in this respect Appian is no better or worse than many other ancient historians. White (Loeb edn) quotes Schwartz as saying that his account of the struggle between Antony and the senate in Book III of the Civil Wars was not history but 'novel writing' and indeed this criticism could be applied to a large proportion of Appian's work.

Appian also followed the fashion of inventing speeches, putting into the mouths of leading characters the author's moral lectures that present ideas that moved people or political factions. This had been Thucydides' legacy to history and many other ancient historians followed his example. Ironically the speeches are perhaps the best part of his work in terms of style. He shows himself as a practised debater, and a trained pleader of causes in the imperial courts. The edict of proscription of the triumvirs is a good example of this (*The Civil Wars*. Book V, 8:67).

Grant says that:

> Appian has brought together some useful material, including a certain amount of economic information. But he is too devoted to Rome and is unreliable about Republican institutions and conditions.
>
> (1992 104)

Appian is a far better historian than most scholars will accept. He identified good sources and used them critically. He is the only ancient author who actually recognized the causes of the Roman civil wars, for which he remains one of the most important sources. He is a good writer who describes events vividly and who knows how to manipulate the smaller and larger tragedies that define history.

HERODIAN (170–240 CE)

Herodian was a Greek historian born in Syria. He lived in Rome and wrote a history of the Roman emperors in eight books from the death of Marcus Aurelius (180 CE) to the accession of Gordian III (238 CE).

Very little is known about the life of Herodian but some elements can be reconstructed from his *History of the Roman Empire* since Marcus Aurelius. He states in his work (2.15.6) that he is describing the reigns of those emperors which he knew through personal experience, over a period of 70 years. This would put his date of birth possibly in the 170s CE and quite possibly he place of residence was Antioch because he writes for a Eastern audience, explaining Roman customs and beliefs.

As a youth it is also possible that he lived in Rome because it appears that he was an eyewitness to Commodus' performance in the gladiatorial arena (1.15). Herodian may have served in some minor capacity in the Roman government; his Introduction suggests that he was an *apparitor* (a procurators or prefects assistant) during the reign of the emperor Maximinus (235–8 CE), which in turn suggests that he was the son of a freedman or knight.

Herodian tells a good story, and his work covers what must be considered one of the most chaotic and fascinating periods of Roman history. He describes the reigns of 17 emperors of which only one died a natural death, one a very old man, another, a boy of 13, and one a priest of the sun god Elagabal. His work is alive with plagues, fires, foreign enemies and earthquakes. Nevertheless he was shocked by all the bloodshed; the central scene in the middle of the book is Caracalla killing Geta in the arms of their mother Julia Domna.

However, Herodian is not the equal as an historian to his contemporaries Arrian, Appian and Cassius Dio. These men knew how to check and select their sources; nowhere does Herodian demonstrate that he has any understanding of historical methodology. He merely wrote down what he witnessed during his years of office in Rome.

Modern scholars have regarded Herodian as unreliable. However, this criticism is not altogether fair, for his lack of literary and scholarly pretensions make him less biased than the senatorial historians. His description of the cultic reforms and religious innovations by the emperor Heliogabalus who wanted to introduce the cult of the Syrian sun god, is far less hostile than Dio's account. Certainly he gives a less biased account of the role of the empresses Julia Soamias, Julia Maesa and Julia Mammaea. Today many regard him as an independent and unbiased author who offers some colourful insights into the period concerned.

Herodian's influence is greater than expected. The anonymous author of the *Historia Augusta*, the historians Eutropius, Aurelius Victor and Ammianus Marcellinus all used his work.

HISTORIA AUGUSTA

This work is a collection of biographies of the emperors from Hadrian to Carinus and Numerianus (117–284 CE) and is popularly known as the *Historia Augusta* or *Scriptores Historiae Augustae*. The collection comprises some 30 biographies most of which concern the life of a single emperor, while some include a group of two or more, classed together either because they were related or were contemporary. It is not only the lives of the emperors that are contained in this work but also the heirs presumptive the Caesars and the various claimants to the Empire the 'Tyranni'.

According to tradition the biographies are the work of six different authors who lived during the time of Diocletian and Constantine. Some of the biographies are addressed to these emperors, others to important people in Rome. The biographies of the emperors from Hadrian to Gordian are attributed to four authors. In the section of the *Historia Augusta* which includes the emperors between Hadrian and Severus Alexander, to the life of the emperor is attached the life of the heir presumptive making a double set of biographies. There are some contradictions in the claims to authorship because four of the 'supposed' authors, Aelius Spartianus, Julius Capitolinus, Vulcacius Gallicanus and Aelius Lapridius say that they have written more biographies than appear in the present compilation. Two authors, Trebellius Pollio and Flavius Vopiscus do not profess to have written more than the extant biographies.

According to the testimony of two of the authors the model for their work was Suetonius (Max-Balb IV.5; Prob., II.7; Firm., I.2). *The life of Antoninus Pius* shows this method in its clearest form. The *Life* falls into the following divisions: ancestry (I.1–7), life before accession to the throne (I.8-VII.4), policy and events of his reign (V.3-VII.4), personal traits (VII.5–XII.3), death (XII.4–9), personal appearance (XIII.1–2), honours after death (XIII.3–4). The categories are extended or reduced depending on the importance of events or material available. Therefore the section on cults to which Commodus was addicted consists of a detailed list of acts of cruelty (*Com.* IX.6–XI.7), while nearly one half of the life of Elagabalus is devoted to his acts of extravagance. Suetonius included in his work gossip and anecdotes and with regard to this, the *Historia* also uses such material, although in some lives it is used less sparingly than by Suetonius. The lives of those emperors whose reign was short are padded out with a variety of trivial anecdotes about their private lives. It would appear that the model for this was not Suetonius but Marius Maximus, the author of a series of lost imperial biographies from Nerva to Elagabalus or Severus Alexander. In fact his lives are cited by the authors as their sources for gossip, scandal and personal details:

> Finally he was instantly restored to a friendship with Trajan that was closer than ever, and he took to wife the daughter of the emperor's sister- a marriage advocated by Plotina, but according to Marius Maximus, little desired by Trajan himself.
>
> (*Hadr.* II. 10; XXV.3)

The other more spurious element contained in the *Historia* is the insertion of documents, speeches and letters. Some of them may have been authentic but references in the *Historia* suggest that they were numerous. Another author Aelius Junius Cordus also includes similar material, but to judge from the specimens in the *Historia* these are even more dubious.

Grant says the *Historia Augusta*:

> Quotes documents that are manifestly spurious and contains, at best, a few facts. This is perhaps done partly with tongue in cheek, with the intention of providing amusement, since Junius Tiberianus, prefect of the city, is quoted (no doubt fictitiously) as taking a wholly sceptical view about history, which the writer of this work evidently accepts, or at least does not agree with.
>
> (Grant, 1992 196)

Dessau contended that the work was compiled during the reign of the emperor Theodosius (AD 379–95) and that there was only one author (H. Dessau in *Hermes* 1887, 337ff.). Modern research has shown that the style of work was uniform leading to the conclusion that the work is indeed of one author. There is also general agreement that the documents, letters and other evidence are largely unauthentic. There is also some question about the aims of the writer. The work shows senatorial sympathies, and does not approve of hereditary monarchy, or interference by the army in politics. R. Syme has seen the author as a 'rogue grammarian who warmed to his task becoming more inventive and humorous as he continued' (Syme, R, *Ammianus and the Historia Augusta* 1968).

Nevertheless in spite of its drawbacks as a piece of historical source material it has provided some useful information for the history of the second and third centuries

MARCUS TERENTIUS VARRO (116–27 BCE)

He was a Roman scholar and author probably born in Reate. He studied at Athens and saw military service under Pompey. During the Civil Wars he was legate in Spain. He awaited the result of Pharsalia with Cicero and Cato at Dyrrachium and was kindly treated by the victor, Caesar who appointed him librarian. His property was at one point confiscated and his villa plundered and his books burnt, as well as having his name put on the list of the proscribed. But he was soon exempted and the emperor Augustus restored his property. His prose writings embraced oratory, history, jurisprudence, grammar, philosophy, geography and husbandry. His numerous works included a social history of the Roman people (*De Vita Populi Romani*), an encyclopaedia of the liberal arts (*Disciplinarum Libri XI*) and *Imagines*, a series of 700 Greek and Roman biographies. Some of his works survive.

GAIUS ASINIUS POLLIO (76 BCE – 4 CE)

Pollio was a Roman orator, poet and soldier. In the Civil War against Pompey he sided with Julius Caesar; in 39 BCE he commanded in Spain and was appointed by Marcus Antonius (Mark Antony) to settle the veterans on the land assigned them. He founded the first public library in Rome and was a patron of Vergil and Horace.

He retired from politics to devote his time to literature, especially history. His orations, tragedies and history of the civil wars have all perished save only for a few fragments. He composed the *Historiae* which covered the period from 60–42 BCE. He criticized Cicero and Caesar, disliked Sallust's archaism, and found Livy too provincial. However, his own work was far from perfect and he wrote with little regard for accuracy. Even accounts of his own doings were inaccurate.

Tiberianus in a conversation with Pollio said that much of his work apart from being too brief was careless, but Pollio replied:

> But when I said, in reply, that there was no writer, at least in the realm of history, who had not made some false statement, and even pointed out the places in which Livy and Sallust and Cornelius Tacitus and finally Trogus could be refuted by manifest proofs, he came over wholly to my opinion, and throwing up his hands, he jestingly said besides: 'Well then, write as you will. You will be safe in saying whatever you wish, since you will have as comrades in falsehoods those authors whom we admire for the style of their histories.
>
> (*Scriptores Historiae Augustae*, Aurelian II,1)

DIO CHRYSOSTOM (c.40 – c.120 CE)

Dio Chrysostom, also known as Dion of Perusa, or Dio Cocceianus, was a Greek orator, writer, philosopher and historian of the

Roman Empire. He was born at Perusa in the Roman province of Bithynia (modern-day Turkey). He held important offices in his native town where he composed speeches and rhetorical essays before devoting himself to the study of philosophy. He did not belong to any particular sect or school of thought but applied the doctrines of philosophy to practical purposes and especially the administration of public affairs in order to bring about a better state. However, he does seem to have been influenced by the Stoic and Platonist philosophies in particular.

He arrived in Rome during the reign of the emperor Vespasian (69–79 CE) by which time he was married with one child. He became a critic of the emperor Domitian, who in 82 CE banished him from Rome, Italy and Bithynia for advising one of the conspiring relatives of the emperor (*Orat* XIII.1). Heeding the advice of the Delphic oracle he wore beggar's clothes and carrying only a copy of Plato's *Phaedo* and Demosthenes' oration on the *Embassy*, he lived the life of a Cynic philosopher, and journeyed to the countries north and east of the Roman Empire.

He became a friend of Nerva and when Domitian was murdered in 96 CE, Dio used his influence with the army stationed on the frontier in favour of Nerva. Only then when Nerva became emperor did his exile end and he was able to return home to Perusa. He adopted the name Cocceianus in later life to honour the support that Nerva (Marcus Cocceius Nerva) had given him. Nerva's successor, Trajan held Dio in the highest esteem and granted him many favours. Indeed his kindly disposition won him many eminent friends such as Apollonius of Tyana and Euphrates of Tyre. During his later years he held considerable status in Perusa and there are records of him being involved in an urban renewal lawsuit about 111 CE (Pliny *Epistles* X.85, 86). He probably died a few years later.

Of his works 80 orations are still extant; they appear to be written versions of his oral teaching comprising essays on moral, philosophical and political subjects. They include four orations on kingship addressed to Trajan; four on the character of Diogenes of Sinope; essays on slavery and freedom and political discourses addressed to various towns, among others essays on ethics and mythology.

There also exist fragments of 15 other orations as well as 5 letters. Dio also wrote many other philosophical and historical works none of which survive. Of these *Getica* was on the Getae which the Suda incorrectly attributes to Dio Cassius.

MARCUS JUNIANUS JUSTINUS (JUSTIN) (SECOND CENTURY CE)

Nothing is known about the personal history of Justin, except that he lived sometime during the second century CE. He wrote the *Historiarum Philippicarum libri XLIV,* a work that he describes in his preface as a collection of the most important and interesting passages from the *Historiae philippicae et totius mundi origins et terrae situs,* written during the time of the emperor Augustus by Pompeius Trogus.

Justin must have lived after Trogus because he writes that the Romans and Parthians had divided the world between them; while this is presumably from Trogus, it would be an anachronism after the rise of the Sassanian Empire in the third century CE. The historian Ronald Syme (*Historia* 37 358–71 1988) proposes a date around 90 CE, immediately before the compilation of the Augustan history, and dismisses the anachronism as unimportant.

Trogus' work is lost; however the *prologi* or arguments of the text are preserved by Pliny and other writers. Trogus' main theme was the rise and history of the Macedonian monarchy. Justin made many digressions and produced an idiosyncratic anthology instead of a mundane summary (epitome).

The *Encyclopedia Britannica* (11th edn) concluded that his history contained a great deal of valuable information, and his style, although not perfect, is clear and on occasion elegant. The book was used frequently during the Middle Ages when the author was sometimes confused with Justin Martyr.

SEXTUS JULIUS AFRICANUS (*c*.160 – *c*.240 CE)

He was a Christian historian and philosopher from Jerusalem (Roman Aelia Capitolina). Julius calls himself a native of Jerusalem which some scholars believe was his place of birth. Little is known about his life and all dates are uncertain. One tradition places him under the emperor Gordianus III (238–44 CE), others mention him under Severus Alexander (222–35 CE).

He travelled widely to Greece, Rome and Alexandria attracted by the fame of its catechetical school. In 222 CE he travelled to Rome on an embassy for his city Emmaus to ask for the restoration of the city. His mission was successful and Emmaus was known by its new title of Nicopolis. While there he impressed the emperor Severus Alexander (222–35 CE) so much with his erudition that the emperor entrusted him with the building of his library at the Pantheon in Rome.

He was a typical antiquarian: he knew Hebrew, Latin and Greek in which language he wrote. He compiled a chronicle of world history *Chronographiai* in five books, as well as large miscellany similar to the elder Pliny's *Natural History*. He was the first Christian writer whose works were not concerned with the faith. He harmonized the gospel genealogies, and also noted that the History of Susanna contained an atrocious Greek pun. He also made the claim that Biblical monotheism was the oldest of all religions.

It is uncertain whether Julius was a layman or a cleric; statements referring to him as a bishop only appear in the fourth century CE. He had at sometime been a soldier and a pagan although he wrote all his works as a Christian.

THEODORET (c.393 – c.457 CE)

Theodoret was an influential author and theologian who was bishop of Cyrrhus (Syria) from 423–457 CE. He was born in Antioch in 393 and the majority of facts concerning his life are found in his works *The Epistles* and *Religious History*. He was brought up under the care of the ascetics and acquired an extensive knowledge of the classics. He became a lector among the clergy of Antioch, then he resided in a monastery, in 423 CE he became bishop of an insignificant town. However, he converted more than 1,000 Marcionites as well as many Arians and Macedonians in his diocese.

Theodoret is principally noted for his stand against Cyril of Alexandria in the Christological controversies that he aroused. He may have prepared the Antiochan symbol which was to secure the emperor's (Theodosius II) true understanding of the Nicene Creed and he was a member and spokesman of the deputation of eight from Antioch called by the emperor to Chalcedon.

In his writings he concentrated mainly on exegesis; however, he also wrote apologetic and historical works. Among the apologetic works (now lost) was the *Ad quaestiones magorum* (429–36 CE), in which he justified the Old Testament sacrifices as alternatives in opposition to the Egyptian idolatry and exposed the fables of the Magi who worshipped the elements (*Church History* V. 38).

The *Church History* begins with the rise of Arianism and ends with the death of Theodore in 429 CE. As a historical work it lacks any chronological accuracy and contains a great deal of bias. Nevertheless it does contain many sources otherwise lost, especially letters on the Arian controversy.

The *Religious History* contains the biographies of 30 ascetics held up as religious models. It is of significance for the understanding of the complexities of the role of the early monasteries both in society and the church. It is also remarkable for presenting a model of ascetic authority which runs strongly against Athanasius' *Life of Antony*. Theodoret's correspondence is a primary source for the development of Christological issues between the Councils of Ephesus and Chalcedon and illuminated current administrative and social issues.

All that is known about him after the Council of Chalcedon

is a letter of Pope Leo charging him to guard the Chalcedonian victory (*PG* IXXXIII 1319 sqq.).

ZOSIMUS (*c*.490S – 510S CE)

Zosimus was a Byzantine historian who lived in Constantinople during the reign of the emperor Anastasius I (491–518 CE). According to Photius he was a *comes* and held the office of advocate of the imperial treasury. His work the *Historia Nova* (New History) is written in Greek and comprises six books. He used several sources for his work; for the period 238–70 CE he used Dexippus, for the period 270–404 CE he used Eupanius; after 404 CE he used Olympiodorus. This dependency on his sources is abundantly clear in the change of style and tone between the sections, especially by the confused gap between them. A good example can be found in the Eupanian section where he is pessimistic and vague about Stilchio, while in the Olympiodoran section he offers transliterations from the Latin and generally favours Stilchio.

Book I gives a brief history of the early Roman emperors from Augustus to Diocletian (305 CE). The second, third and fourth deal in greater detail with the period from the accession of Constantine Chlorus and Galerius to the death of Theodosius I. However, the most useful books for historians are the last two which cover the period 395–410 CE, when Pricus Attalus was deposed. For this period he is the most important surviving non-ecclesiastical source; although the work is apparently unfinished as it breaks off in the summer of 410 CE at the beginning of Book VI.

Zosimus selected as his theme the decline of Roman Empire, and perhaps it was his ambition to imitate Polybius, whose theme had been the rise of Rome, which led him to introduce various matters connected with Greek, Persian and Macedonian history, which appear to be out of focus with his main theme. It appears that some of the accounts have either been lost or perhaps more likely that Zosimus did not live to finish it.

Zosimus was a pagan and is therefore not sparing of the crimes and faults of the Christian emperors. As a consequence of this he was attacked by several Christian writers, while on the other hand he has been defended simply because his history tended to discredit many leading persons in the Christian party.

Zosimus did not always adhere to the judgements of his sources with regard to events and characters. For instance he differed from Eupanius in his account of Stilchio and Serena. There are no doubt many errors of judgement to be found in the work, and sometimes, especially concerning Constantine exaggerated opinions which distort the truth. However, this does not mean that he deliberately invented stories or indeed any malicious misinterpretation. It is perhaps understandable that a pagan should attribute the downfall of the Empire to the religious innovations brought about by the spread of Christianity.

Photius characterizes his style as concise, clear and pure; other historians have judged his accounts muddled and confused and only valuable because he preserves information from lost histories.

SOZOMEN (SALMINIUS HERMIAS SOZOMENUS) (*c.*400 CE – *c.*450 CE)

Sozomen was born in a small town near Gaza (Palestine) into a wealthy Christian family. His early education was directed by monks from his native town and it would appear that he was well versed in Greek from the evidence of his writings. He studied law in Beirut and went to Constantinople to work as a lawyer, possibly at the court of Theodosius II. It was during this period *c.*443 CE that he decided to write a history of the Church. He wrote two works on the history of the Church, the second only is extant.

The first work covered the period from the Ascension of Jesus to the defeat of Licinius in 323 CE, contained in 12 books.

The second extant history continued from where he left off, and was written during the years 440–3 CE and dedicated to the emperor Theodosius II. He used as his sources Eusebius of Caesarea, Hegesippus, and Sextus Julius Africanus. The work is contained in nine books arranged along the reigns of the Roman emperors; however, Book IX is incomplete. Sozomen stated that his intention was to cover the period up to the 17th consulate of Theodosius II (429 CE) but his work ends about 425 CE. There is some disagreement about why the end is missing. One theory is that Sozomen suppressed the end of his work because in it he mentioned the empress Aelia Eudocia, who later fell into disgrace because of her alleged adultery. It would appear, however, that some earlier writers such as Nicephorus, Theophanes and Theodorus Lector read the end of his work, according to their own histories.

Sozomen's writing is valuable for several reasons: first he pays more attention than older historians to the missionary activity of the Christians and gives valuable insight into the introduction of Christianity among the Goths, Saracens and Armenians among others. Second the history is full of information about the rise and spread of monasticism and the toils of the early founders and communities. Although the treatment of affairs in the Western Church is by no means complete his work gives us facts and insights not found elsewhere.

In Late Antiquity there was a great amount of *breviaria* (short historical works) that were published (see Aurelius Victor, Eutropius, Festus, Epitome de Caesaribus). They all had a common source, the so called *Enmannsche Kaisergeschicte*, which is now lost

Chapter Twenty Eight

Alexander the Great: A Case Study

There are many ancient sources on the career of Alexander the Great, not all of them are complete or indeed accurate. There are also two traditions of writing on Alexander, the 'vulgate' so-called because they use as their source Cleitarchus, and the 'good' tradition whose writers take their sources from Ptolemy. The *Library of World History* by Diodorus of Sicily, and *The History of Alexander the Great of Macedon* by Quintus Curtius Rufus, are the two main 'vulgate sources, while a *Life of Alexander* by Plutarch and the *Anabasis* by Arrian are considered 'good' tradition of Alexandrian historiography. All of these authors lived more than three centuries after the events they describe, but they used older, nearly contemporary sources, that are now lost. The texts referred to as the 'good' tradition most probably contain the most accurate of all histories that we have of Alexander.

In Alexander's company was a professional historian named Callisthenes of Olynthus (*c.*370–327 BCE). During the campaign Callisthenes' main duty was to write the Deeds of Alexander; however, he was also sent on scientific missions. For example while Alexander was in Egypt he sent Callisthenes to Nubia, where he discovered the cause of the annual flooding of the Nile; and in Babylon Callisthenes supervised the translation of the *Astronomical Diaries* which were used by Callipus of Cyzicus to reform the Greek calendars. However, Callisthenes voiced protests against the introduction of *proskynesis* (an aspect of Persian court ritual) among the Macedonians and lost him Alexander's favour. It is not clear what happened to Callisthenes; either he died in prison or was crucified according to the two differing accounts by Alexander's generals, Ptolemy and Aristobulus.

His work the *Deeds of Alexander* is now lost but underlies much of what was written later. It would appear to be the work of a professional flatterer who knew how to please a king that had had a life-long rivalry with the mythical Achilles. For example it contained many allusions to Homer's *Iliad*, a calculation of the date of the fall of Troy (exactly a thousand years before Alexander's visit to the sacred city) and references to towns mentioned by Homer.

Callisthenes made a point of stressing Alexander's manly behaviour against the effeminate weakness of the Persians. There is one incident that deserves particular mention. When the Macedonian army moved along the Lycian coast the soldiers noticed that the waters seemed to recede to let them pass. Callisthenes, although he must have been aware that this was a purely natural phenomenon, chose to present the receding of the sea in his narrative as the sea doing Alexander obedience. It was the first step toward the later belief that Alexander was the son of a god.

It is unclear when the work was published but secondary authors do not quote it to describe events after 329 BCE, and it is possible that Callisthenes considered the death of Bessus, the last leader of the Persians, to be a fitting climax to his work. However, unlike Caesar's campaigns, this work was not published in yearly instalments to inform those remaining at home. It was published as a whole unit and this can be gleaned from the fact that he consistently portrayed Parmenion, Alexander's right-hand man, as over-prudent. Before 330 BCE there would have been no need to portray Parmenion in such a manner: however, in the November he had been executed because his son Philotas was suspected of a coup.

It also appears that later historians (Arrian in particular) had access to a later sequel to the *Deeds*, possibly based on the Royal diary and this is quoted by several authors who describe the death of Alexander. This no doubt explains why we have such detailed information on chronology and appointments. We know that Alexander died on 3 June 323 BCE, which can be deduced from the *Astronomical Diaries*, a Babylonian source.

These two works by Callisthenes were primary sources, sadly now lost. They were used by secondary authors like Cleitarchus and Ptolemy, who share the same chronology and mention the same officials. Their works are also lost but can be reconstructed from tertiary sources mentioned earlier.

The *Anabasis* by Arrian is the most important source, partly because he ignored Cleitarchus' immensely popular *History of Alexander* and used other sources. Arrian in his prologue explains the reason why:

> It seems to me that Ptolemy and Aristobulus are the most trustworthy writers on Alexander's conquests because the latter shared Alexander's campaigns and the former-Ptolemy in addition to this advantage, was himself a king, and it is more disgraceful for a king to tell lies than for anybody else.

This may well be a quote from Ptolemy's own work, as it was used as by Synesius of Cyrene (*In praise of baldness*, 15), and who cannot have read the *Anabasis*.

This remark of Arrian's may be criticized by scholars, yet they agree that Arrian chose the right sources for the right reasons. Arrian also knew what it was like to fight a war; he had been a provincial governor and had lived at the imperial court. The Roman war against the Parthians had allowed him an opportunity to visit Mesopotamia and he most certainly would have visited those places associated with Alexander's campaigns.

Arrian attempts to give something of Alexander's character but in this he is at odds with Cleitarchus who presented Alexander as a young prince who was corrupted by his constant successes. Arrian, on the other hand, admires Alexander, although sometimes he is critical of his behaviour as can be seen in Book IV. However, the three incidents he mentions here did not take place at the same time, so he obviously wished the reader to be appalled by Alexander only once throughout the work. Nevertheless Arrian is considered by most scholars to be the best source on Alexander's campaigns.

Although Ptolemy's account is entirely known from the *Anabasis* we can still come to some conclusions about them. In the first place he uses Callisthenes' accounts, and a sequel, because he has the correct chronology and events, and knows the names of appointees. Second he sometimes exaggerates his own role, and third the work was biased against Antigonus Monophtalmus, one of Ptolemy's rivals in the war that followed Alexander's death. Finally Ptolemy concentrated solely on the war, there are no digressions: in Ptolemy's view Alexander had been a rational expansionist.

In one place Ptolemy corrects Cleitarchus' account, and this proves that Ptolemy's history was published after the *History of Alexander* which can be dated between 310–301 BCE. There are, therefore indications that Ptolemy's work was published before 301 BCE because in that year Antigonus was killed and so there would have been little point in criticizing his rival.

The other notable source is Plutarch who writes in the prologue of his life of *Alexander/ Life of Julius Caesar.*

> It is not histories I am writing, but lives; and in the most glorious deeds there is not always an indication of virtue or vice, indeed a small thing like a phrase or jest often makes a greater revelation of character the battle where thousands die.

This is a good description of what Plutarch has to offer. There is no in-depth comparative analysis of the causes of the fall of the Achaemenid dynasty or the Roman Republic, but a series of anecdotes with a moral point. The *Life of Alexander* should be read as a collection of short stories, in which virtues and vices are shown. Plutarch took elements from all the traditions, and is interesting because he includes many stories from Alexander's childhood days, which he seems to have acquired from a book called *Alexander's Education* written by a Macedonian named

Marsyas, who went to school with Alexander. In Plutarch's work we get a glimpse of Alexander as a human being rather than just an imitation of Achilles.

The other tradition of writing about Alexander is known as the 'vulgate' tradition and in this category are the historians, Diodorus of Sicily and Quintus Curtius Rufus. These historians are a tertiary source that elaborated a secondary source, the *History* of Cleitarchus.

Scholars criticize Diodorus who, in their opinion, is uncritical of his sources. This is slightly unfair as modern research has offered something of rehabilitation to this author; his theme is well worked out and was certainly appreciated by his contemporaries. Alexander played an important role in Diodorus' *World History*; in this work Alexander was pivotal in bringing four great civilizations in closer contact with each other, Egypt, Libya, Greece and Persia.

There are some minor Roman authors who composed works on Alexander, and of these Quintus Curtius Rufus' is the only writer whose work *History of Alexander of Macedon* has survived. Originally the work consisted of ten books; now only eight remain. They contain events between the accession of Alexander and the death of Memnon of Rhodes. The remaining manuscripts start with the march through Phrygia in the spring of 333 BCE and the last book ends with the burial of Alexander's body in a golden sarcophagus, which was later brought to Egypt. Taken as a whole, this is a fascinating work despite many errors, which can be explained because he took Cleitarchus as his source. However, sometimes Curtius corrects these mistakes, and what we are left with is a work that offers many interesting stories that we get from nowhere else.

Cleitarchus used most probably the work of Callisthenes as his main source, However, as already stated, this work only went up to 329 BCE and so Cleitarchus used other sources. Among these were the memoirs of Onesicritus of Astypalaea and Nearchus, Alexander's helmsman and his fleet commander. Other sources of information would have come from the numerous Macedonian and Greek veterans living in Alexandria. His book was extremely popular, perhaps the most entertaining history on Alexander's conquests. It offered vivid descriptions and eye witness accounts, many from a soldier's point of view. One such anecdote as recounted by Curtius quoting Cleitarchus as the source concerns Babylonian women:

> Alexander's stop in Babylon was longer than elsewhere, and here he undermined military discipline more than in any other place. The moral corruption there is unparalleled; its ability to stimulate and arouse unbridled passions is incomparable. Parents and husbands permit their children to have sex with strangers, as long as this infamy is addicted to wine and the excesses that go along with drunkenness. All over the Persian Empire kings and their courtiers are fond of parties, Babylonians are especially addicted to wine and the excesses that go along with drunkenness. Women attend dinner parties. At first they are decently dressed, then they remove their top clothing and by degrees disgrace their respectability until (I beg my reader's pardon for saying it) they finally throw off their most intimate garments. This disgusting conduct is characteristic not only of courtesans but also of married women and young girls, who regard such vile prostitution as 'being sociable'.
>
> (Section 5.1 36–8)

Such stories reflect eyewitness accounts; a man like the court historian Callisthenes would not write about the mass crucifixion at Tyre; and the *History* of Ptolemy which was written from a commander's point of view would not deal with the difficulties that the soldiers experienced in the Hindu Kush. The value of Cleitarchus (via Diodorus and Curtius) is the presence of such details which otherwise would remain unknown.

Cleitarchus also portrays the darker side of Alexander's character. He paints the picture of a young king corrupted by his constant successes and who became an alcoholic, tyrant and murderer. For example, according to Cleitarchus/Curtius,

Alexander's personality changed after the death of Darius III of Persia; from then on there was no check on Alexander's vices. But many incidents that should prove this psychological change are simply not there. Many modern historians would explain this change from the fact that Alexander had to behave as a Persian king if he wanted to be accepted by his new subjects. Cleitarchus' work provided a combination of vivid descriptions and eyewitness accounts. However, his desire to tell a good story led to many serious errors.

In order to study fully the life and campaigns of Alexander the student needs to study not only the sources written in Latin and Greek but also one primary source written in Babylonian. This is the *Astronomical Diaries* that was kept in Esagila in the temple of the supreme Babylonian god, Marduk. It contains a day-by-day account of celestial phenomena but also mentions other events, such as the level of the Euphrates, food prices, incidents concerning Babylon and its temple, and political events. It also contains interesting information on the prices of commodities when Alexander was in Babylon.

The most intriguing information from the *Diaries* relates to the Battle of Gaugamela which was fought on 1 October 331 BCE. It suggests that the Persian soldiers were demoralized and states that they left their king and fled during the battle. This is exactly opposite to what we read in the four tertiary sources; they write that Darius left his soldiers.

The *Astronomical Diaries* are a very important source, in fact the only contemporary, primary source on Alexander, and no doubt there are other similar sources awaiting discovery. Perhaps the student of Alexander should be prepared to learn Babylonian and Persian, as well as the Greek language. Finally there are the Zoroastrian texts, which tell stories of the religious persecution by 'the accused Alexander'. It is alleged that Alexander tried to destroy the Zoroastrian texts, and that might well be the case. However, that does not mean that oral traditions were also lost. While such texts can be extremely unreliable it is not wise to dismiss them entirely, as they can be useful to reconstruct the Persian side of the story, something about which the Greek sources are naturally silent.All the sources on Alexander should be handled with caution as there is a great deal of bias contained within them. Although we know a great deal about Alexander's campaigns we still know relatively little about the man himself, his thoughts and political agendas.

Chapter Twenty Nine

Concluding Remarks

There are many inadequacies and misinformation in the writings of the ancient historians; nevertheless there are many valid reasons for studying them. Despite all the deficiencies (from a modern perspective, that is) these works supply us with vital information about the ancient world and without them our knowledge of past times would indeed be meagre. As Grant says:

> Without awareness of this background we are blind-folded in our efforts to grapple with the future.
>
> (Grant, M., *A Short History of Classical Civilization* 1992 57)

Another point to make is that these historical works are brilliant pieces of literature, and worth reading if only from this perspective.

In order to obtain the most from these works we have to be aware of these inadequacies, and in order to do that we have to take into consideration the authors' lives, social status and motivation for writing. We also have to be aware that unlike today, when a variety of other material evidence presents itself to compliment written sources, i.e. archaeology, inscriptions, coins, etc., for the ancient historian little or no such evidence was available. Today a modern historian requires facts, with which to formulate an accurate or at least objective assessment of the social, political, economic and military conditions of the events under review. The ancient historian did not follow these criteria; often they used their sources in a way that we would find unacceptable. In the ancient works fact and fiction are merged and this would appear to diminish their value as records of past events. Yet, historians like Thucydides tried to be objective and realized that history was different from other forms of literary work. The pioneering spirit of such early historians to record and evaluate their historical periods is in itself a noteworthy accomplishment.

In fact the development of history writing had depended a great deal upon the epic, as well as tragic poetry, so it should come as no surprise that this material also provides a good deal of evidence that helps contribute to our knowledge of what was happening at the time. The Old Comedy of Aristophanes also provides the historian with some useful information.

> If a modern historian can grasp the reflection of reality in Attic comedy, he will be able to reconstruct the actuality of Athenian society and economy.
>
> (Gabba in Crawford, *Sources for Ancient History* 1983 58)

There is a considerable amount of information in other types of source material which the historian should also be prepared to consult, notably epigraphy and papyrology. Archaeology is of primary importance, and has yielded notable finds over the centuries, which offers a variety of private informal texts, letters, accounts, etc. The Egyptian town of Oxyrhynchus yielded in 1907 a valuable fragment of a lost Greek historian, known as the 'Oxyrhynchus Historian'.

> The writer dealt with events in the Greek world, 396–5 BCE, and was an authority of great importance. The papyrus indicates a strict chronological arrangement by summers and winters, competent criticism and analysis of motives, a first-hand knowledge of the topography of Asia Minor, and certain details found in no other work of the period.

> It was probably a continuation of Thucydides beginning with the autumn of 411 BCE, was written between 387 BCE and 346 BCE, and its elaborate scale suggests that it covered only a short period ... Three further fragments (90 lines) were published in 1949.
>
> (Barber *OCD* 766)

However, we must be wary of putting too much reliance upon archaeological, papyrological, and numismatic or inscription evidence. For example the *Res Gestae divi Augusti* (The Achievements of the Divine Augustus) was a huge inscription that Augustus had set up outside his mausoleum after his death recording all his achievements. There were copies made and erected, no doubt, throughout the Empire. If this was all the evidence we had of the reign of Augustus then what would we make of his boast of the 'restoration of the *republica*', and Mark Antony is hardly mentioned at all. These and many other examples of propaganda can be found in this inscription, none of them bearing any resemblance to the truth.

Most of the known inscriptions from the ancient world can be found in the Corpus Inscriptiones Latinum (*CIL*), Corpus Inscriptiones Graecae (*CIG*) and the Supplementum epigraphicum Graecum (*SEG*).

Although not a historical work the Old Oligarch is also a useful source of historical information. *The Constitution of Athens* was originally thought to have been composed by Xenophon because it was included among his works; now this work is seen as having been composed by an unknown author referred to as the Old Oligarch about whom Levi says:

He was the most bone headed kind of conservative, anti democratic, anti-Athenian, and violent against the slaves and the poor ...

He is hardly able to string a sentence together. His style is amusingly simple, but not genuinely archaic.

This buffoon is highly valued by scholars as a witness and rare example of the opposition of the Periclean party, and of a pristine, pre-sophistic prose ... My own view is that the author was some minor member of the circle of Four Hundred, writing between 413 and 411 BCE to promote sedition overseas.

(Levi, *A History of Greek Literature* 1985 307ff.)

It is therefore equally important to know how to handle literary source material to assess its respective value for historians. There is much historical information that can be gleaned by the historian from literary works, such as poetry, epic, plays, speeches, philosophical treatises and novels. For the most part these are products of a certain class of people, much like the histories, and they can reveal other aspects of the world they inhabited.

> It is a great mistake to suppose that historical experience is expressed in so-called historical records alone … Greek historical experience or mental history is better expressed in Greek literature than ours is in the literature of modern Europe … The surviving masterpieces of Greek literature give a better insight into the subjective side of Greek history … than any insight into the subjective history which we can obtain by studying it through modern literature.
>
> (Toynbee, *Legacy of Greece* 1921 300)

Bibliography

This bibliography is by no means exhaustive; there are many general works on Greek and Roman history that the student needs to consult when examining ancient source material. To slightly ease the burden of research all the major historians discussed and many of the minor authors are given here, in the order they appear in the main text. It is also advisable to consult the Encyclopedia's both for Classics and Early Church history.

GENERAL WORKS

Oxford Classical Dictionary (2nd Edition 1970), Oxford: Oxford University Press.

Bacon, Francis (1605), *The Advancement of Learning*. London: Oxford University Press.

Bagnall, Nigel (2006), *The Peloponnesian War: Athens, Sparta, and the Struggle for Greece*. NewYork: Thomas Dunne Books.

Bury, J. B. (1908), *Ancient Greek Historians*. New York: Dover, rep. 1958.

Cameron, A. and Hall, S. (1999), *Life of Constantine*. Oxford: Clarendon.

Crawford, M. ed. (1983), *Sources for Ancient History*. (Cambridge: Cambridge University Press).

Curtis Ford, M. (2002), *The 10,000*. (London: Orion).

De Montaigne, M (1993), *The Complete Essays* trans. M. A. Screech. London: Penguin.

Dorey, T. A. ed. (1966), *Latin Historians*. London: Routledge.

Finley, M. I. ed. (1959), *The Greek Historians*. London: Chatto & Windus.

Finley, M. I. ed. (1981), *The Legacy of Greece: A New Appraisal.* Oxford: Oxford University Press.

Fornara, C. W. (1983), *The Nature of History in Ancient Greece and Rome.* Berkeley: University of California Press.

Grant, M. (1952), *Ancient History.* London: Methuen.

Grant, M. (1970), *The Ancient Historians.* London: Weidenfeld & Nicolson.

Grant, M. (1991), *Short History of Classical Civilization.* London: Weidenfeld & Nicolson.

Grant, M. (1992), *Readings in the Classical Historians.* New York: Scribners.

Higden, Ranulphus (14th Century), *Polychronicon* in E. Rhys ed. (1920), *Growth of Political Liberation.* London: Dent.

Jenkins, K. (1991), *Re-thinking History.* London: Routledge.

Levi, P. (1985), *A History of Greek Literature.* Harmondsworth: Penguin.

Mellor, R. ed. (2004), *The Historians of Ancient Rome.* New York: Routledge.

Momigliano, A. (1966), *Studies in Historiography.* New York: Harper and Row.

Momigliano, A. (1971), *The Development of Greek Biography.* Harvard: Harvard University Press.

Raditsa, L. *Gallatin Review*, xii, 1, 1992–3, 19.

Rutter, N. (1996), *History of the Peloponnesian War.* Bristol: Bristol Classical Press.

Shotwell, J. (1922), *History of History.* New York: Columbia University Press.

Southgate, B. (1996), *History: What and Why?* London: Routledge.

Syme, R. (1988), 'The Date of Justin and the Discovery of Trogus' *Historia,* 37 358–371.

Toynbee, A. (1921), Essay in G. Murray & R.W. Livingstone (eds) *Legacy of Greece.* Oxford: Clarendon Press.

Woodman, A. J. (1983), *University of Leeds Journal.*

Usher, S. (2001), *The Historians of Greece and Rome.* Bristol: Duckworth.

GREEK HISTORIANS

Herodotus
Evans, J. A. S. (1991), *Herodotus: Explorer of the Past*. Princeton: Princeton University Press.
Gould, J. (1989), *Herodotus*. New York.
Hart, J. (1982), *Herodotus and Greek History*. London: Croom Helm.

Thucydides
Cawkwell, G. L. (1997), *Thucydides and the Peloponnesian War*. London: Routledge.
Connor, W. R. (1984), *Thucydides*. Princeton: Princeton University Press.
Hornblower, S. (1997), *Thucydides*. London: Duckworth.

Xenophon
Anderson, J. K. (1974), *Xenophon*. London: Duckworth.
Tuplin, (1993), *The Failings of Empire: A Reading of Xenophon Hellenica*.

Diodorus Siculus
Green, P. (2006), *Diodorus Siculus Books 11–12.37.1. Greek History, 480–431 BCE- the Alternative Version*. University of Texas Press.
Mommsen, T. CIL X p. 718 *Romanische Forschung* 2, 549 n 1.
Schwartz, E. (1901), Real Encylopädie 5, 682–684.
Sacks, K. (1990), *Diodorus Siculus and the First Century*. Princeton: Princeton University Press.

OTHER GREEK WRITERS

Hieronymus of Cardia
Hornblower, J. (1981), *Hieronymus of Cardia*. Oxford: Oxford University Press.
Roisman, J. (2010), "Hieronymus of Cardia: Causation and Bias from Alexander to his Successors" in Carney, E. and Ogden, D. (eds) *Phillip II and Alexander the Great: Father and Sons, Lives and Afterlives*. Oxford: Oxford University Press.

Timaeus

Brown, Truesdell, S. (1958), *Timaeus of Tauromenium*. Berkeley: University of California Press.

Ptolemy I Soter

Walter, M. Ellis. (1993), *Ptolemy of Egypt*. London.

Theopompus of Chios

Shrimpton, G. S. (1991), *Theopompus the Historian*. Montreal: McGill-Queens University Press.

Apollodorus

Hornblower, S. (1996), '*Apollodorus of Athens*', *The Oxford Classical Dictionary*. Oxford: Oxford University Press.

Posidanus

Irvine, W. B. (2008), *A Guide to the Good Life: the Ancient Art of Stoic Joy*. Oxford: Oxford University Press.

ROMAN HISTORIANS

Quintus Ennius

Skutsch, O. (1985), *The Annals of Q.Ennius*. Oxford: Oxford University Press

Cato

Badian, E. (1966), "The early historians" in Dorey, T. ed. *Latin Historians*. London: Routledge.

Cornell, T. J. (1972), *The Origines of Cato and the non-Roman historical tradition about ancient Italy* (Unpublished PhD thesis, London).

Polybius

Paton, W. R. (trans 1967) *Polybius. The Histories I*. Cambridge Mass: Harvard University Press.

Wallbank, F. W. (2002) *Polybius in the Roman and Hellenistic World*. Cambridge: Cambridge University Press.

Appian

Gowing, A. M. (1993), *The Triumviral Narratives of Arrian and Cassius Dio*. Ann Arbor.

Julius Caesar

Adcock, F. (1956), *Caesar as a Man of Letters*. Cambridge: Cambridge University Press.

Meier, C. (1982), *Caesar: A Biography*. New York.

Salllust

Earl, D. C. (1961), *The Political Thought of Sallust*. Cambridge: Cambridge University Press.

McGushin, P. (1995), *Sallust: Bellum Catilinae*. 3rd ed. London: Bristol Classical Press.

Syme, R. (2002), *Sallust*. Berkeley: University of California Press.

Livy

Dorey, T. (1970), *Livy*. London.

Luce, T. J. (1983), *Livy: The Composition of his History*. Princeton: University Press.

Walsh, P. J. *Livy: His Historical Aims and Methods*. Cambridge: Cambridge University Press.

Augustus

Brunt, P. & Moore, J. M (eds) (1967), *Res Gestae Divi Augusti*. Oxford: Oxford University Press.

Jones, A. H. M. (1970), *Augustus*. New York.

Southern, P. (1998), *Augustus*. London.

Josephus

Cohen, S. (2002), *Josephus in Galilee and Rome: His Vita and Development as a Historian*. Leiden.

Hadas-Lebel, M. (1993), trans. R. Millar *Flavius, Josephus: Eyewitness to Rome's First Century*. New York: Macmillan.

Meir, J. (1991), *A Marginal Jew*. New Haven: Yale University Press.

Rajak, T. (1983), *Josephus: The Historian and his Society*. London: Duckworth.

Tacitus
Martin, R. (1981), *Tacitus*. London: Batsford.
Syme, R. (1958), *Tacitus*. Oxford: Clarendon Press.
—(1970), *Ten Studies in Tacitus*. Oxford: Clarendon Press.

Arrian
Bosworth, R. B. (1980), *Arrian – A Critical Essay*. Oxford: Clarendon Press.
Cartledge, P., Romm, J. S., Robert, B. and Mensch, P. (2010), *The Landmark of Arrian: The Campaigns of Alexander*. New York: Pantheon.
Stadtler, P. A. (1980). *Arrian of Nicodemia*. Chapel Hill.
Syme, R. (1982), 'The Career of Arrian' *Harvard Studies in Classical Philology* Vol 86, 171–211.

Dio Cassius
Millar, F. (1964), *A Study of Cassius Dio*. Oxford: Oxford University Press.

Suetonius
Wallace-Hadrill, A. (1983), *Suetonius: The Scholar and His Caesars*. London: Duckworth.

Plutarch
Jones, C. P. (1971), *Plutarch and Rome*. Oxford: Clarendon Press.
Russell, D. A. (1973), *Plutarch*. London: Duckworth.
Stadter, P. A. ed. (1992), *Plutarch and the Historical Tradition*. London: Routledge.

Cicero
Fuhrmann, M. (1992), *Cicero and the Roman Republic*. Oxford: Blackwell.
Habricht, C. (1990), *Cicero the Politician*. Baltimore: John Hopkins.
Parenti, M. (2004), *The Assassination of Julius Caesar*. New York: The New Press.
Shackleton-Bailey, B. R. (1971), *Cicero*. London: Duckworth.

Pliny the Younger

Sherwin White, A. N. (1966), *The Letters of Pliny*. Oxford: Oxford University Press.

Ammianus Marcellinus

Barnes, T. J. (1998), *Ammianus Marcellinus and the Representation of Historical Reality*. Ithaca.

Seagar, R. (1986), *Ammianus Marcellinus; Seven Studies in his Language and Thought*. (Missouri: University of Missouri Press).

Tertullian

Barnes, T. D. (1971), *Tertullian: A Literary and Historical Study*. Oxford: Oxford University Press.

Eusebius of Caesarea

Louth, A. 'Eusebius and the Birth of Church History' Young, Ayres and Louth (eds) *The Cambridge History of early Christian literature*, 266–74. New York: Cambridge University Press.

Wallace-Hadrill, D. S. (1960), *Eusebius of Caesarea*. London: A. R. Mowbray.

OTHER ROMAN/CHRISTIAN WRITERS

Gnaeus Naevius

De Graff, T. B. (1931), *Naevian Studies*. New York.

Cornelius Nepos

Conte, G. B. (1994), *Latin Literature: A History*. Baltimore: John Hopkins University Press.

Quintus Curtius Rufus

Yardley, J. C. (2004), *History of Alexander: Quintus Curtius Rufus*. London: Penguin.

Velleius Paterculus

Shipley, F. W., trans. (1924), *Velleius Paterculus: Compendium of Roman History*. Loeb Classical Library: Harvard University Press.

Nicolaus of Damascus
Wacholder, B. Z. (1962), 'Nicolaus of Damascus' *University of California Studies in History, 75.*

Alexander Polyhistor
Schmitz, L (1867), 'Alexander Cornelius' in Smith, W. *Dictionary of Greek and Roman Biography and Mythology.* Boston: Little, Brown and Co, 115.

Pliny the Elder
Murphy, T. (2004), *Pliny the Elder's Natural History: the Empire in the Encyclopedia.* Oxford: Oxford University Press.

Appian
Gowing, A. (1992), *The Triumviral Narratives of Appian and Cassius Dio.* Ann Arbour.

Herodian
Muller, F. L. (1966), *Herodian. Geschichte des Kaisertums nach Marc Aurel: Greichisch und Deutsch.* Stuttgart.

Historia Augusta
Baynes, N. H. (1926), *The Historia Augusta: Its Dates and Purpose.* Oxford: Oxford University Press.
Syme, R. (1983), *The Historia Augusta Papers.* Oxford: Oxford University Press.

Marcus Terrentius Varro
Lindberg, D. (2007), *The Beginning of Western Science.* Chicago: Chicago University Press.

Dio Chrysostom
Jones, C. P. (1978), *The Roman World of Dio Chrysostom.* Harvard University Press.

Marcus Junianus Justus
Syme, R. (1988), 'The Date of Justin and the discovery of the Trogus' *Historia,* 37 358–71.

Sextus Julius Africanus

Habas, E. (1994), The Jewish Origin of Julius Africanus *JJS* 45, 86–9.

Zosimus

Ridley, R. T. (1982), *Zosimus: New History.* Australian Association of Byzantine Studies.

Sozomen

Leppin, H. (2003), 'The Church Historians I Soctares, Sozeomenus and Theodoretus' in Marasco, G *Greek and Roman Historiography in Late Antiquity.* Leiden: Brill, 219–254.

Index

ab urbe condita 63, 64, 105
Achaean League xiii, 76–7, 79
Achaeans 77
Achaemenid dynasty (of Persia) 217
Acropolis xi, xii, 18, 19, 46
Actium (battle of) xiii, xvi, 86, 113, 116
Adrianople (battle of) 174, 176, 181–2
aedile 58, 71, 74
    curule aedilship 58
Aegospotami 18
Africanus (Sextus Julius) 209, 213
    Chronographiai 209
Agesilaus I (king of Sparta) 38, 41
Agricola (Gnaeus Julius) 125–6, 131
Agrippa (Marcus Vipsanius) 137
Agrippa II (King of Judaea) 122
Agrippina (wife of Claudius) xvi, 88
Alcibiades 4, 16, 17, 18, 165
Alexander Polyhistor 196
Alexander the Great (king of
    Macedon) vii, viii,, xii, xiii, 19,
    53, 140, 192, 214–21
Alexandria xiii, xvii, 53, 55, 93, 94,
    119, 187, 199–8, 209, 210, 214, 219
Ammianus Marcellinus 176, 178–83,
    202, 205
    Roman History 178–83
Amphipolis 15, 29

Annals of the Pontifex Maximus
    (*Annales Maximi*) 63
annalists 47, 191
    annalistic 64, 65, 111, 138, 191
    'Gracchan' 64
    'Sullan' 65
Antioch 114, 178, 179, 181, 187, 201,
    209, 210
Antiochus III 72
Antoninus Pius (emperor) 89, 199,
    203
Apollo 12, 26, 37
Apollodorus 55
    Bibliotheca 55
    Chronicle 55
    On the Gods 55
apologetic 123, 142, 185, 189, 210
apologia 114
Appian of Alexandria 198–201, 202
    History of Rome 199
Archidamian war *see* Archidamus II
Archidamus II (king of Sparta) 15
archon 47, 54, 55, 142
Arian (Arianism) xx, 187, 210
Aristagoras 10
Aristophanes 19, 35, 223
Aristotle xii, 3, 4, 19, 51, 56, 149, 150
Armenia 89, 145, 181, 213
Arrian (Lucius Flavius Arrianus) 53,
    139–43, 192, 202, 214, 215, 216

Anabasis Alexandrou 140
Cynegeticus 142
Indica 142
Artaxerxes II (king of Persia) 37, 51
Artemisium (battle of) 11, 22
assembly
  Roman 58, 59, 145
  Spartan 14, 18, 33
Assyria 47, 195
Astronomical Diaries 214–5, 220
Athens 10, 11
  Delian league 12
  Melian debate 6
Atticus (Titus Pomponieus) 148–51,
  192
auctoritas 115
augur 74, 153
Augustus *see* Octavian xvi, 65, 87–8,
  90, 97, 106, 113–17, 126, 129–31,
  136–8, 153, 169, 171–6, 194–5,
  205, 208, 211, 224
  Res Gestae Divi Augusti 113–7, 224,
  230
Aventine Hill 58

Babylon 22, 37, 55, 214
  Alexander in 49, 220
  customs 219
  Diaries 215, 220
  History of 20
Berrosus 20
Betriacum (battle of) 167
Bibulus (Marcus Calpurnius) 84
biography 7, 41, 65, 130, 140, 142,
  159, 161–4, 170, 191, 195, 197
  bios 162
Bithynia 133, 139, 142, 153, 167, 207
Boeotia 13, 159, 161

Brasidas 15, 16, 29
brevaria 213
Britain xvi, xvii, xix, 48, 88, 95, 96, 97,
  125, 126, 176
Brutus (Marcus Junius) 86
Byzantium xx, 118
  Byzantine 177, 200, 211

Caesar (Gaius Julius) xv, 8, 38, 45, 62,
  84, 91–7, 99, 113, 146, 168, 194,
  206, 217
  Civil War, The 93–7
  Gallic War 48, 65, 93, 95–7
Caesarea (Palestine) 186, 187, 189,
  213
Caligula (Gaius, emperor) xvi, 87–8,
  128
Callisthenes of Olynthus 192, 214–9
Cambyses II 19
Cannae (battle of) xvii, 81, 191
Caracalla (emperor) xvii, 89, 134,
  136, 202
Carrhae (battle of) xv, 85, 92
Carthage *see* Punic Wars xiv, xvii,
  72–3, 77–8, 82, 100, 106–109, 184,
  190–1, 194, 200
Cassius Dio (Cassius Dio
  Coccianus) 133–9, 140, 172, 208
  Roman History 133–9
Catiline (Lucius Sergius) xv, 61–2, 84,
  98–9, 100–1, 103, 111, 145
  see Cicero, Sallust
Cato the Elder (Marcus Porcius) 64,
  67, 70–5, 84, 97, 145, 148, 151,
  192, 205
  De Agri Cultura 73
  Origines 73
censor 58–9, 70, 72, 74, 85–6, 98, 148

Christianity xix, 90, 117, 121, 175–6,
  184–5, 212–3
Christians xvii, xviii, xix, 184–5, 213
Cicero (Marcus Tullius) 2, 43, 45, 51,
  55, 56, 70, 91, 96, 99, 103, 113,
  127, 144–51, 153, 157, 165, 173,
  182, 191–2, 205, 206
  Catilene conspiracy 62
  in exile 84
  on history 105
  Philippics 147
  Works 144–51
Cinna, Lucius Cornelius 61, 91, 144–5
Cisalpine Gaul 106, 125, 191
Claudius (emperor) xvi, 88, 106, 128,
  169, 192
Cleitarchus 193, 214, 216–20
Cleon 15, 16, 33, 34
Cleopatra VII (Queen of Egypt) xiii,
  xv, xvi, 45, 86, 91, 92, 94, 113, 116,
  150, 166, 171, 195
cohort 87
Colosseum 88
Comitia Centuriata 58
commentarii 65
Commodus (emperor) xvii, 89, 201,
  204
Conon (Athenian general) 18
Constantine I (the Great,
  emperor) xix, 90
consul xv, 47–8, 57–9, 61–3, 71–2, 74,
  79, 81, 84–6, 92, 96, 99, 102, 115,
  126, 130, 133–34, 138, 140, 144–7,
  150, 153, 159, 194, 213
Corcyra *see* Corinth
Corinth xii, xiii-iv, 13, 14, 18, 27, 29,
  40, 44, 77, 78
Council of Nicaea 186

Crassus (Marcus Licinius) xv, 61,
  84–85, 92, 146–7
Croesus (king of Lydia) 23, 26
Ctesias of Cnidus 51
Cunaxa (battle of) 37, 51
  see Xenophon
Cyrus (son of Darius II) 18, 21, 37,
  38, 41, 42
Cyzicus (battle of) 17, 214

Dacia xvii, 89
Darius I (king of Persia) 10, 19, 21, 22
Darius II (king of Persia) 18
Darius III (king of Persia) 220
Decelea 17
  Decelean (Ionian) war 35
Delian League xii, 12, 14
Delos xii, 12
Delphi 23, 26, 37, 44, 160, 191, 207
demagogues 79, 165
Demetrius I (King of Syria) 77
Demosthenes 15, 16, 20, 165, 207
  Philippic attacks 20
Diadochi 49, 53
dictator xv, 59, 61, 86–7, 92–4, 102, 145
dictatorship xvii, 58, 61, 85, 91, 115,
  149
Dio Chrysostom 133, 179, 206–8
  Orations 207
Diocletian (emperor) xviii-ix, 90, 174,
  203, 211
Diodorus Siculus 45–49, 52–3, 55,
  141, 214, 218–9
  Library of World History 214
Dionysius of Halicarnassus 20, 32,
  47, 53, 54, 55, 191
Domitian (emperor) xvii, 89, 126–7,
  129, 152, 168, 198, 207

Edict of Milan xix, 90
Egypt xv, xvi, 11, 22–3, 26, 45, 46, 51,
    76, 92, 94, 159, 181, 189, 198, 214,
    218, 223
    customs 24, 25, 47, 210
    rulers of xiii, 53, 86, 113, 141, 150
Eleazar ben Yair 120
Elgin Marbles 35
Ennius (Quintus) 67–9, 71, 73
    Annals 67
Epaminondas (Theban leader) 40, 42
Ephesus 45, 210
ephors 54
Ephorus of Cyme 51–2
    Historia 51
epic 3, 19, 28, 67–8, 190, 223, 225
epitomes 82, 134
Equites 167
    Equestrian order 37
eulogia 63, 116
Eusebius (of Caesarea) 118, 123, 184,
    186–9, 196, 213
    Ecclesiastical History 184, 186–7

Fabius (Quintus) 63, 73, 108, 191
Flavian dynasty 88, 119, 127, 139, 164
forensic 147

Galba (emperor) xvi, 88, 164, 167, 171
Gallic wars 38, 45
    see also Julius Caesar
Gaugamela (battle of) xiii, 220
Gaul xiii, xiv, xv, xvi, xviii, 84, 92,
    95–7, 99, 102, 106, 108–9, 125,
    146, 174, 176, 180, 182, 191
Gnostic 185
Gracchi 56, 59, 64, 192, 200
    Gaius Gracchus xv, 65

Tiberius Gracchus xv, 59
Gylippus (Spartan general) 16

Hadrian (emperor) xvii, 89, 130, 140,
    161, 168, 203
Halicarnassus 19, 20–1, 32, 47, 53,
    55, 191
Hamilcar (king of Carthage) 107–8
Hannibal (king of Carthage) xiv, 107,
    108–11
Hasdrubal (general of Carthage) 82,
    108
Hecataeus of Abdera 50
    Genealogies 50
    Periegesis 50
Hecataeus of Miletus 24
hegemony 16, 41
Hellanicus of Lesbos 20, 50–1
    History of Athens 51
Hellenistic period 20, 56, 63, 82, 117,
    164
Hellespont 18, 39, 141
Herod the Great (King of
    Judaea) 121, 195
Herodian 201–2
    History of the Roman Empire 201
Herodotus 2, 5, 19, 20, 21–8, 30–2,
    35–6, 50–1, 76, 142, 160, 188
    Histories 21–28, 30, 50, 76
Hieronymus of Cardia 53–4
Higden (Ranulphus) 3
Hippias of Elis 20
Hispania Citerior 72
Historia Augusta 183, 202, 203–5
Historiography ix
    in antiquity 1, 2, 10
    Greek historiography 19, 20, 40,
    214

historia 22, 159
  modern 8
  Roman historiography 63–6, 100,
    159,170
Homer xi, 3, 5, 19, 23–5, 31, 55, 68,
    190, 215
  Iliad 3, 19, 24, 190, 215
  Odyssey 19, 68
hoplites 13, 15, 17
Horace 106, 157, 168, 182, 206
Hortensian law 59
hubris 6

Imperial period 1, 21, 57, 138
imperium 86, 116
Isocrates 38, 52, 54

Jerusalem xv, xvi, 88, 117–24, 178,
    186, 188, 198, 209
Jewish Revolt 88, 119
Jews xx, 7, 117, 119, 121, 123–4, 178,
    188, 198
Josephus (Flavius) 7, 117–24, 195
  Against Apion 122–3
  Antiquities 120–3
  Jewish War 7, 117, 119
  Life 122–3
Jotapata 118
Judaea xvii, 117, 119, 195
  Judaism 118, 121, 123–4
Jugurtha of Numidia xv, 60, 100, 101,
    102
  Jugurthine war 99, 100
Julio/Claudian dynasty 87
Justin (Marcus Junianus Justinus 188,
    208
  Historiarum Philippcarum libri 208
Juvenal 158

legate 60, 71, 92, 126, 134, 153, 205
Leonidas (Spartan king) 11, 24
Lepidus, Marcus xv, 86, 113, 147, 195
Leuctra (battle of) xii, 18, 44
Lex Oppia (Oppian Law) 71
Livia (wife of Augustus) 87, 130, 169,
    172
Livy (Titus Livius) 2, 5, 47, 64, 66,
    71–2, 75, 98, 105–12, 124, 182,
    191, 193, 206
  Ab Urbe Condita 105
  History 105–12
Locri 71
logographer 50
Longinus (Gaius Cassius) 86, 93
Luca 84
Lydia (Asia Minor) 10, 11, 195
  King Croesus of 23, 26
Lysander (Spartan general) 18

Maccabees 117, 121
Macedonian War
  First xiii
  Second xiii
  Third xiii, xiv, 76, 78
Maecenas (Gaius Cilnius) 137–8
Magistrate (Roman) 49, 58, 59, 72, 85,
    86, 185
  Aetolian 81
  Corinthian 14
Marathon (battle of) xi, 11, 26
Marcus Antonius (Mark Antony) xiii,
    xv, 86, 91, 93, 113, 116, 147, 151,
    195, 206, 224
Marcus Aurelius (emperor) xvii, 89,
    135, 142, 166, 198, 201
Marius, Gaius xv, 56, 60–1, 65, 91–2,
    100–2, 144–5, 167, 204

Martial 158
Masada 120
Matinea (battle of) 16
Mediolanum (Milan) 174–5, 181
Megalopolis 41, 76, 79, 82
Megara 13
Melos xii, 8, 34
  Melian debate 6, 34
Mesopotamia xvii, 11, 20, 46, 89, 179, 216
Messalina (wife of Claudius) 88
Miletus *see* Aristagoras 24, 39, 45
Miltiades *see* Marathon 11
Mithridates VI of Pontus 56, 61, 94, 102, 144, 145
'*monographic*' tradition 64, 65, 159
Monumentum Ancyranum 114
mythlogos 27
Mytilenian debate 33

Naevius (Gaius) 68, 73, 190
  Bellum Punicum 190
Narbonese Gaul 125
Naupactus 13, 15
nemesis 6
Nepos (Cornelius) 71, 74, 164, 191–2
  De Viris Illustribus 191
Nero (emperor) xvi, 88, 118, 125, 127–8, 131, 170–1, 197
Nerva (emperor) xvii, 89, 126, 153, 181, 204, 207
'*new regime*' 93, 127, 137, 194
Nicias 34
  Peace of xii, 16
Nicolaus of Damascus 121, 195–6
  Universal History 195
Nineveh 46

Octavian, Gaius *see* Augustus xiii, xv, xvi, 45, 86–7, 113, 147, 195
Octavius, Marcus 60
Old Oligarch 224
oligarchy
  Greek 17
  Roman 61, 91
Olympic
  games 20, 80
  years (Olympiads) 54, 63, 80–1
optimates 61, 91
oratory 1, 48, 96, 127, 144, 147–8, 155, 205
ornatus 105
Otho (emperor) xvi, 88, 164, 167
Ovinian law 58

panegyric 38, 188
Parthenon xii, 18, 35
Parthia xv, xvi, xvii, 85, 89, 92, 134, 142, 208, 216
  Parthian war 134
Pater Patriae 115
patricians 57–9, 110
Pausanias 12
pax romana 89
Peloponnesian War ix, xii, 6, 10, 29, 76
  battle of Matinea 16
  First War 13
  Herodotus on 21
  Peloponnesian League 14
  Second War 17
  Thucydides on 20, 30, 31–2,–36
  Xenophon on 37–40
Pentecontaetia 12, 31, 49
Pericles xii, 12, 15, 18, 21, 32, 33, 34, 35, 162, 163, 165

Funeral Oration 32, 34
Persian Wars ix, xii, xiii-xviii, 2, 5,
    10–18, 26, 27, 36
    campaigns under Alexander 143,
        180, 215, 219, 220
    control of ancient world 11
    Herodotus on 19, 21, 22–6
    history of 195, 211, 214
Pharnabazus (Persian satrap) 38
Pharsalus (Pharsalia battle of) xv, 92,
    94, 146, 205
Pheidias 35
Philip II (king of Macedon) xii, 18,
    20, 76
Philippi (battle of) 86, 113
Pictor (Quintus Fabius) 47, 63, 73,
    191–2
Plataea (battle of) xi, 12, 22, 27, 76
Plato xii, 19, 41–2, 149, 162
    Platonic school 148, 207
plebeians 57–9
Pliny the Elder (Gaius Plinius
    Secundus) 65, 75, 152, 168, 196–8
    History of the German Wars 197
    Naturalis Historia 152
Pliny the Younger (C. Plinius
    Caecilius) 112, 152–7, 167, 172,
    196
    Letters 152–7
Plutarch (L. Mestrius Plutarchus) 2,
    6, 7, 27, 35, 53, 55, 70, 71, 93, 128,
    130, 159–66, 168, 183, 191, 197,
    214, 217, 218
    Decline of the Oracles, The 159
    Moralia 160
    on Herodotus 27
    Parallel Lives 161–4
    Shakespeare's use of 166

polemic 185, 186
Pollio (Gaius Asinius) 97, 203, 206
Pompeii xvi, 152, 196
Polybius 33, 50, 52–4, 66, 76–83,
    105–7, 111, 191, 200, 211
    Histories 77–83
Pontifex Maximus 63, 92
Posidonius 55, 56
Potidaea 14, 29
praetor 58, 71–2, 125–6, 130, 133, 145,
    152, 155, 175, 193
Praetorian Guard xvi, xvii, xviii, xix,
    87–8, 134, 168, 197
Praxitelis 19
prefect 130, 152–31, 93, 202, 204
    Praetorian prefect 168, 175
    prefecture 153, 174–5
Principate 57, 116, 130
princeps 87, 132
prose 2, 28, 50, 63, 70, 73, 153, 205,
    224
proto-history 19
Psamtik III (Pharaoh) 19
Ptolemy I (Soter, Pharaoh) 20, 53, 216
Ptolemy XII (Pharaoh) 94
Pulcher (Publius Clodius) 84, 98
Punic War 190
    First xiv, 54, 68, 78, 107, 190
    Second 63, 68, 71, 78, 106–7, 110, 191
    Third 72, 77, 200
Pylos 15

quaestors 61, 125
    quaestorship 125
Quintilian 96, 103, 111, 152

reign of terror
    in Athens 40

under Commodus xvii
under Domitian 152
under Nero xvi
under Tiberius xvi, 87
rhetoric 1, 2, 56, 81, 125, 146, 148,
    152, 160, 179
Roman Republic xiii, xiv, 5, 57–8,
    62–3, 84, 86, 88, 93, 95, 110–11, 113,
    115–16, 127, 130–1, 135, 137, 144–9,
    151, 172–3, 195, 201, 217, 224
Rubicon xv, 85, 93
Rufus (Quintus Curtius) 192–3, 214,
    218
    *History of Alexander the Great of
        Macedon, The* 214
    Life of Atticus 193

Salamis (battle of) xi, 12, 22, 76
Sallust, Gaius Sallustius Crispus 2,
    8, 33, 64, 65, 66, 98–104, 111, 128,
    182, 194, 206
    Conspiracy of Catilene, The 98–101
    Historiae 99, 102
    Jugurthine War 99–100
Samos xi, 13
Sardis *see* Lydia 10, 11, 37
Scipio Africanus Mj, Publius
    Cornelius xiv, 67, 71, 77, 108, 109
Scythia 26, 47
senator 57–9, 62, 84, 85–6, 89, 102,
    106, 113, 130–3, 136–7, 145, 191
senatus consultum ultimum 60, 85
Septimius Severus (emperor) xvii, 89,
    133, 136
Septuagint 120
Seuthes (king of Thrace) 37
Sextus Pompeius (Pompey the
    Great) 46, 61–2, 116, 144

Sicily 6, 17, 34, 45, 49, 54, 71, 145,
    190, 214, 218
    ally of Athens 16
    history of 54
    slave revolt (Servile War) xiv, xv
Simonides 12
Socrates xii, 19, 35, 37–8, 42–3
Solon of Athens xi, 23, 164–5
Sozomen (Saminius Hermias
    Sozomenus) 212–3
Spacteria 15, 30
Spartacus xv, 61
Strabo 52, 55, 144
strategos (general) 18
Stoic 55, 79, 139, 148–9, 207
Suetonius (Gaius Suetonius
    Tranquillus) 114, 120, 128, 130,
    138, 167–73, 183, 197, 203–4
    Lives of the Caesars 168–73
Sulla, Lucius Cornelius xiii, xv,
    61–22, 65, 91–2, 99, 101–2, 144–5,
    149, 195
Sybota (battle of) 14

Tabulae Albatae (white tablets) 63
Tacitus (Publius Cornelius) 3, 8, 33,
    64–6, 98, 103, 120, 125–32, 138,
    156–8, 168, 172, 182, 195–7, 206
    Agricola 126
    Annals 125–31, 197
    Germania 126
    Histories 127, 130, 182
Tegea 16
Tempe (defence of) 11
Tertullian (Quintus Septimius
    Florens) 184–5
Tertullianus
    Apology 184

Testimonium Flavianum 122
Tetrachy xviii, 90
Thebes xii, 18, 41, 47
Themistocles 11
Theodoret 209–11, 223
   Church History 210
   Epistles, The 210
   Religious History 210
Theopompus of Chios 52–3
   Hellenica 52
   Philippica 52
Thermopylae (battle of 480 BCE) xi,
   11, 22, 24
   battle of 190 BCE 72
Thirty Tyrants xii, 18
Thirty Years Peace 13, 14
Thrace 29, 30, 35, 39, 53, 55, 182, 193
Thrasybulus 18
Thucydides 2–3, 6–7, 12, 15, 29–51, 52,
   76, 78, 103, 104, 119, 200, 222–3
   History of the Peloponnesian War,
     The 29–51
   on Herodotus 21
   on Megarian decree 14
   on style 20
Tiberias (Palestine) 123
   Justus of 123
Tiberius (emperor) xv, xvi, 87,
   128–31, 169, 171, 193–5, 197
Timaeus 54–55, 63, 80
   Histories 54
Titus (emperor) xvi, xvii, 72, 88, 119
Trajan (emperor) xvii, 89, 126, 130,
   153, 161, 167–8, 173, 175, 198,
   204, 207
Trapezus 37
tribune xvi, 58–61, 71–2, 86, 93, 98,
   125, 146, 190, 193

Triumvirate 84
   First xv, 48, 84, 92, 146
   Second xv, 86, 113, 147
Trojan wars 5, 24
tyche 8, 79
Tyre xii, 22, 187, 207, 219

Varro (Marcus Terentius) 94, 164,
   191, 205
   Imagines 205
   De Vita Populi Romani 205
Velleius Paterculus 193–5
   Historiae Romanae 194–5
Vercingetorix xv, 95
Vergil 106, 168, 206
Vespasian xvi, 87–8, 118–20, 128,
   196–7, 207
Vitellius (emperor) xvi, 88

Xenophon 20, 37–44, 143
   Agesilaus 41, 42
   Anabasis 7, 37–44, 139
   Constitution of the
     Lacedaemonians 41, 44
   Cyropaedia 41
   Essays 41, 43
   Hellenica 18, 40, 44
   Memorabilia 42, 43
Xerxes (king of Persia) xi, 6, 11, 21,
   22, 26

Year of the Four Emperors 132, 197

Zoroastrian texts 220
Zosimus 211–12
   Historia Nova 211